Encyclopedia
Cthulhiana

Encyclopedia Cthulhiana

by DANIEL HARMS

Chaosium, Inc.
1994

Please address questions and comments concerning this book, as well as requests for free notices of Chaosium publications, by mail to: Chaosium, Inc., 950-A 56th Street, Oakland, CA 94608-3129, U.S.A.

ISBN 1-56882-039-9.

FIRST EDITION

1 2 3 4 5 6 7 8 9 10

Chaosium Publication 6007. Published in December 1994.

Printed in the United States of America.

Foreword

The book you now hold in your hands is the first major attempt to provide a guide to Lovecraft's Cthulhu Mythos in many years. Since the publication of Lin Carter's articles "The Gods" and "The Books" in 1956, the Mythos has grown tremendously, and the time has come for someone to sit back, look at what has been accomplished, and make a chronicle before the cycle continues. If I had known when I started that I was going to be that chronicler, I probably would have quit then and there. Fortunately, I didn't understand what an undertaking this was going to be at the time, and was therefore able to see this project through to its completion. Thus, I present to you the *Encyclopedia Cthulhiana*, a resource book for readers of Cthulhu Mythos stories.

For those of you who are just starting your Mythos readings or who only picked up this book because you know me, a brief explanation is in order. The Cthulhu Mythos was invented or compiled by H. P. Lovecraft (1890-1937), a Providence author considered by many to be the finest horror story writer of the twentieth century. During his lifetime, though, he was virtually unheard of among the literary community. Lovecraft's tales, which only rarely appeared outside pulp magazines such as *Weird Tales*, were a blend of fantasy, science fiction, and horror, with the latter being especially prominent. While other authors in the pulp-horror tradition wrote stories about ghosts and vampires, Lovecraft looked for new sources of inspiration. Thus, his tales describe a pantheon of powerful beings, sometimes appearing as demons and at other times as aliens, known as the Great Old Ones. The Great Old Ones once ruled the earth, but had been incapacitated in some way long ago. Through their telepathic influence they had spoken to susceptible humans who then started cults which used manuals of sorcery to call back their masters. It's a good deal more complicated than this, since Lovecraft never developed a systematized pantheon of his deities, but this should do for a start.

Lovecraft also corresponded with other writers in his genre, and often borrowed elements from their stories to use in his own. Thus, he took Robert E. Howard's *Nameless Cults*, turned its title into German, and included *Unaussprechlichen Kulten* in his own works. The other authors would then return the favor; Howard later would mention Lovecraft's most famous creation, the *Necronomicon*, in his own stories. These additions, along with others borrowed from earlier authors such as Bierce and Machen, swelled Lovecraft's pantheon even further, and at the time of his death it had attained an impressive size. Later authors read these works and decided to try their own hands at writing tales like them. This list includes such notables as Ramsey Campbell, Robert Bloch, Brian Lumley, and Stephen King, but the most important one would have to be a man whose name has been almost forgotten by the general public — August Derleth.

Derleth, along with Donald Wandrei, founded Arkham House, a small Wisconsin publishing house which was dedicated to printing the works of Lovecraft and other authors of his time. It was Derleth who named Lovecraft's pantheon the "Cthulhu Mythos" after his friend's death. All this was well and good, but Derleth then proceeded to systematize the Mythos, turning Lovecraft's alien Great Old Ones into demons, setting a group of beings known as the "Elder Gods" against them, and assigning each member of the pantheon to one of the four elements. While opinions about Derleth's interpretations are mixed, it is certain that without Derleth's efforts, Lovecraft's work would have been forgotten.

There has been an effort in recent years to return the Mythos to a structure closer to Lovecraft's. As a part of this, some have proposed renaming the Cthulhu Mythos the "Lovecraft Mythos," to give its "inventor" his due. I can't help but be curious about this; does this label cover all of Lovecraft's works, many of which are not included in the Cthulhu Mythos? And what significance do the works of other authors have? The pantheons of the world's cultures are usually named after the people who kept their traditions alive, but I doubt the "Lovecraft-and-in-spired-writers'-Mythos" will become standard any time soon. Thus, while others debate the terminology, I'll continue to use the name by which these stories are known to most devotees — the Cthulhu Mythos.

As the Mythos has grown, though, some sort of guide has become more and more important. Why? Well, since Lovecraft's time the Cthulhu Mythos has grown exponentially, until it has become increasingly difficult to keep track of, even for the most devout fans. Often, Mythos writers have forgotten just where this book or that monstrosity originated, and when their works deviate from the originals, everyone else takes them to task for confusing the matter. The damage has already been done, though, and later readers often ask themselves, "So, which one of these versions is correct?" Hopefully, this book will eliminate most of this confusion, or at least insure that I'm to blame for any new problems that crop up.

A few notes on this glossary before you begin. This book is not intended for "experts" on the Mythos. If you feel that you could have written this book yourself, given sufficient time and resources, it may not do you much good. On the other hand, it should be handy if you're just starting to read Lovecraft, or if you've read some Mythos fiction but still feel as if you're missing the significance of a few references.

Also, the question could be asked: "What is in the Mythos?" This question is impossible to answer; if you asked twenty readers what material should be included, you'd receive twenty radically different replies. In most cases, I looked for the common threads running between various stories to determine whether they were Mythos tales. Sometimes I included stories which earlier scholars had designated as parts of the Mythos; in other cases, I used my gut reaction to the tale. If you think that something here doesn't belong, just ignore it. This book is by no means "the Mythos Gospel" (and I doubt many will accept it as such); instead of defining the Mythos, it attempts to provide a partial map for the casual reader.

I haven't covered every Mythos story available; such a task would take years for even the most dedicated researcher, and the amount of new material that continues to be published would make it even more bewildering. I have tried to concentrate on what seems important and not worry about the rest. While this may result in a few items being left out, I feel that most of the important material has been covered.

Some of the material within has been taken from scenarios and other resources for the game *Call of Cthulhu*. I realize many readers are gasping and crying, "Sacrilege!" at this point, but I believe this inclusion is justified. This game has provided an introduction to Mythos fiction for many people, including myself, and including these sources may help to bridge the gap between the gaming and literary aspects of the Mythos. In addition, the game has provided source information available nowhere else, such as the dates on which Lovecraft's imaginary towns were founded, which added greater detail to this book. In my opinion, nothing in the game is antithetical to the spirit of Lovecraft's work; if the Mythos can include the elaborations of Derleth, Carter, and Tierney, there is definitely room for *Call of Cthulhu* in this mix.

Finally, be warned that this book is in no way a substitute for reading the original stories from which this information is derived. I would encourage new readers to try to find these works; reading them will be more entertaining than looking over this book, and you may discover a new favorite author. These sources may be hard to find, but they are definitely worth the search.

I hope this book will in some small way encourage further interest in Lovecraft's pantheon and help to keep it alive in the years to come.

Nashville, Tennessee
November 2, 1994

How to Use This Book

Entries are arranged alphabetically. At the end of each entry is a paragraph with cross references ("See ..."). This is followed by a list of the stories used to compile the entry. The list of stories does not include every source detailing the subject, merely those considered to be the most important. Those sources relating to the game *Call of Cthulhu* are designated by the notation "(C)."

For those entries with multiple definitions, cross references and/or sources specific to an individual definition are listed at the end of the paragraph with the definition. Cross references and/or sources common to all of the definitions are listed in a separate paragraph at the end of the entry.

How to Use This Book in *Call of Cthulhu*

This book would make a handy general reference in a campaign, as it contains a broad overview of the Mythos. If you wish to have this volume available as a resource for investigators in your game, suggested values are Sanity loss 1d6/2d6, Cthulhu Mythos +8%, Occult +1%, spell multiplier x1, 6 weeks.

A

ABBITH. World of seven suns beyond which the binary star of Xoth may be found. The inhabitants of this planet are metallic minds which hold many of the universe's secrets. According to von Junzt, Nyarlathotep lives or is imprisoned on Abbith.

See Nyarlathotep, Xoth. ("Out of the Aeons", Carter; "Visions from Yaddith", Carter; "Zoth-Ommog", Carter.)

ABDUL ALHAZRED (also ABD AL-AZRAD; ?-738). Poet and mystic of Sanna in Yemen, and author of *Necronomicon*. This man's deeds are still matters of legend in Arabia. He spent ten years alone in the great Arabian wastes, studied under the mighty wizard Yakthoob, and visited both Irem and the Nameless City. Later in his life he wrote a treatise on magic titled *Kitab al-Azif*, which Theodorus Philetas retitled *Necronomicon* when he translated the volume into Greek. Alhazred was said to have worshiped both Cthulhu and Yog-Sothoth. Ibn Khallikan, Alhazred's 12th century biographer, tells of the "mad" poet being devoured in the market-place of Damascus in broad daylight by an invisible monster.

See *Al-Azif*, *Book of Thoth*, Great Old Ones, Ibn Schacabao, Irem, Kara-Shehr, Lamp of Alhazred, Leng, Nameless City, *Necronomicon* (Appendices), shoggoth, Yakthoob, *Yhe Rituals*. ("The Doom of Yakthoob", Carter; "History of the *Necronomicon*", Lovecraft; "The Nameless City", Lovecraft.)

ABHOTH. Being which signifies filth and disease within the Mythos. Abhoth lives beneath Mount Voormithadreth, and takes the form of a huge pool of grey slime. It continually spawns forth its children, beings whose anatomical diversity is infinite. Most of these are immediately devoured by Abhoth, but the rest may escape from their parent's cavern home.

In one recorded encounter with this being, Abhoth put out a pseudopod to feel the intruder, communicated with him telepathically, then allowed him to continue on his way. Others may not be so lucky.

Few instances of Abhoth's worship have been reported. The Hyperborean colony of Krannoria revered Abhoth, but in the end they were destroyed by their ungrateful deity. Abhoth the Dark is also mentioned in many Hittite inscriptions. Despite this worship, it is unlikely that Abhoth cares that such cults exist, and is unlikely to provide them with any benefits.

See Haon-Dor; Hyperborea; Outer Gods; Voormithadreth, Mount. (*Return to Dunwich*, Herber (C); "The Seven Geases", Smith; *The Mind Parasites*, C. Wilson.)

ADUMBRALI. Entities from another dimension which appear as globules of darkness. The most complete references to the adumbrali can be found in *Song of Yste*. These creatures are said to send messengers to other dimensions to attract prey for their own hunting pleasure. These messengers seem to be members of the alien culture, but have an unnatural grace and power about them; they are capable of great feats of hypnotism, which they use to ensnare their victims. The minds of these unfortunates are sent to the adumbrali's homeland, where they are tortured and devoured.

See *Song of Yste*. ("The Abyss", Lowndes.)

A'BYY. Site mentioned in both *G'harne Fragments* and *Pnakotic Manuscripts* as having some connection with the subterranean race of cthonians. Its exact location is unknown, but Sir Amery Wendy-Smith speculated that it was identical with Avebury, the site of a prehistoric "stone-circle" in England.

See *G'harne Fragments*; *Pnakotic Manuscripts*; Wendy-Smith, Amery. (*The Burrowers Beneath*, Lumley.)

AFRICA'S DARK SECRETS. Book written by Nigel Blackwell and published in the early 1920's. The authorities, horrified by its contents, burned every copy they could find. Only thirteen copies survived this destruction. Little is known of the book's contents, save that it describes the rituals of the Cult of the Bloody Tongue as well as the creation of zombies.

See Cult of the Bloody Tongue. ("New York", DiTillio and Willis (C).)

AHTU. See Nyarlathotep (Ahtu).

AHU-Y'HLOA. Deep one city located in the sea off Cornwall. This metropolis is still under construction by a group of deep ones who are aided by their brethren from Y'ha-nthlei.

See deep one, Y'ha-nthlei. ("The Return of the Deep Ones", Lumley.)

AJAR-ALAZWAT. Artifact which fell from the sky in the Hyborian Age. This object served as the focus for many dark cults in that time and the years following. Eventually it found its way to Ephesus, where it was worshiped as the embodiment of that city's goddess, Artemis. The Ajar-Alazwat has probably survived to the present day, but its location is a mystery.

Once every thousand years, the being Sakkuth comes to Earth to seek out the Ajar-Alazwat. With the aid of this powerful item, he attempts to summon Hastur and Shub-Niggurath to Earth so that their Thousand Young may populate the world. None of these summonings is believed to have been successful, but Sakkuth and his masters are patient.

See Hastur, Sakkuth, Shub-Niggurath. ("The Seed of the Star-God", Tierney.)

AKLO. Language used by certain esoteric cults throughout the ages. Aklo was originally the language of the Valusian serpent men, and it is still used in a modified form by the priests of the Great Old Ones.

E. A. Hitchcock's book, *Remarks on Alchemy*, makes reference to "the now unattainable secrets of the Aklo tablets", a set of writings which has never been discovered. However, Alonzo Typer, an occultist of some note, might have read these "Aklo writings" or others, and described rituals known as the Aklo formulae in his diary; the third of these formulae is useful in making the unseen visible.

See Aklo Sabaoth, Aklo Unveilings, *Ia*, N'gral Khul. (*Keeper's Companion*, Herber (C); "The Haunter of the Dark", Lovecraft; "The Diary of Alonzo Typer", Lovecraft and Lumley, W.; "The White People", Machen; "The Return of the Lloigor", C. Wilson.)

AKLO SABAOTH. Formula in the Aklo language used to invoke extradimensional beings. The Aklo Sabaoth may only be performed on clear nights when the moon is in its first phase. Two versions of this formula may be found, one which calls beings out of the hills, and another which calls them from the air. The second version is usually preferred, possibly because it may be performed everywhere, while the first is tied to a certain type of location.

See Aklo. ("The Tower on Yuggoth", Campbell; "The Dunwich Horror", Lovecraft.)

AKLO UNVEILINGS. Levels of initiation into the cult of Glaaki. A cult member may undergo up to forty-eight of these unveilings; the forty-ninth takes place when Glaaki calls his worshiper to him for the last time.
See Aklo, Glaaki. ("The Inhabitant of the Lake", Campbell.)

AL-AZIF (also *KITAB AL-AZIF*). Original Arabic title for Alhazred's *Necronomicon*. Al-Azif supposedly refers to the sounds made by insects at night, which the people of Alhazred's time took to be the calls of djinn.
See Abdul Alhazred; *Necronomicon* (Appendices); Philetas, Theodorus.

ALALA. Being alluded to in the infamous *Green Book*. Alala may be a native of the Gulf of S'lghuo.
See *Green Book*; S'lghuo, Gulf of. ("The Plain of Sound", Campbell; "The White People", Machen.)

ALAOZAR. Lost city located on the fabled Plateau of Sung. The city was built upon the Isle of Stars, where extraterrestrial beings landed thousands of years ago, within the Lake of Dread. No party of explorers has ever found this site, but it is a holy site for the Tcho-Tcho people. Beneath Alaozar lie the caverns in which Lloigor and Zhar dwell.
See Lloigor; Sung, Plateau of; Zhar. ("The Lair of the Star-Spawn", Derleth and Schorer.)

ALAR. 1) Character from the mysterious play *The King in Yellow*, in one account. 2) City which besieges the metropolis of Hastur in the same play, according to another account.
See Demhe, Hastur, King in Yellow, Yhtill. ("More Light", Blish; "The Repairer of Reputations", Chambers; "Tell Me, Have You Seen the Yellow Sign?", Ross (C).)

ALDEBARAN. Star located fifty light years from Earth in the constellation Taurus, near the Pleiades. Aldebaran is one of the brightest stars in the sky, and is said to be the dwelling place of the Great Old One Hastur.
See byakhee, Carcosa, Great Old Ones, Hali, Hastur, King in Yellow. ("The Festival", Lovecraft.)

ALDONES. 1) Character who seeks the throne of Yhtill in the play *The King in Yellow*. 2) The founder of the city of Hastur's ruling dynasty in the same play.

See King in Yellow, Last King. ("More Light", Blish; "The Repairer of Reputations", Chambers; "Tell Me, Have You Seen the Yellow Sign?", Ross (C).)

ALSOPHOCUS. Mighty wizard from the lost land of Erongill, and author of the mysterious *Black Tome of Alsophocus*.

See *Black Tome of Alsophocus*. ("The Black Tome of Alsophocus", Lovecraft and Warnes.)

ANCIENT ONES. Transmogrified beings of any race who have passed through the Ultimate Gate guarded by Tawil at'Umr. They appear in Tawil at'Umr's great temple as cloaked, sleeping figures bearing scepters and seated on pedestals. The Ancient Ones only awaken to aid those who desire to enter the Ultimate Gate and join their number.

See 'Umr at-Tawil, *Vatican Codex*. ("Through the Gates of the Silver Key", Lovecraft and Price.)

ANGELL, GEORGE GAMWELL. Professor Emeritus of Semitic Languages at Brown University, who succumbed to a heart attack during the winter of 1926-27. Angell pioneered research on the worldwide Cthulhu cult, and subsequent scholars have built their conclusions upon this man's work.

See Cthulhu, R'lyeh. ("The Call of Cthulhu", Lovecraft.)

ANGLES OF TAGH CLATUR. Set of incantations that may bring beings from the Other Side to this world. Only the reversed angles, which make beings partly corporeal, may be used at this time; some Egyptian high priests may have known these ceremonies and used them to bring Glaaki to Earth. The Reversed Angles may also be used to provide protection against such beings. It is likely that the non-reversed ceremony may not be used until the return of the Great Old Ones.

See Glaaki. ("The Inhabitant of the Lake", Campbell; "The Render of the Veils", Campbell, "Something in the Moonlight", Carter.)

ANKH (also CRUX ANSATA or IRISH CROSS). Occult symbol for life and fertility which originated in Egypt.

References to the ankh within the Mythos are quite varied. The ankh was used as a worship symbol in Providence's Starry Wisdom cult, and the symbol of Nyarlathotep's Cult of the Black Pharaoh is an inverted ankh.

The possession of an ankh will protect the wearer from the Great Old One Nyogtha, as well as the cthonians and other earth-dwellers to a lesser degree. *Book of Eibon* holds that such a symbol will provide protection against the ghouls of the underworld. The user of the ankh should be careful in these instances, as there are other methods of protection against Nyogtha, and the ghouls give only limited respect to the bearer of an ankh.

See ghoul, Nyogtha. ("Egypt", DiTillio and Willis (C); "Pickman's Student", Herber (C); "The Salem Horror", Kuttner; "The Haunter of the Dark", Lovecraft; *The Burrowers Beneath*, Lumley.)

ANTARKTOS, MOUNT. Mountain located near the South Pole, beneath which dwells the Great Old One Gol-Goroth.

See Gol-Goroth. ("The Fishers from Outside", Carter; "Antarktos", Lovecraft.)

THE ANTIQUITY OF THE EGYPTIAN RELIGION. Volume written by Dr. Karl von Petersdorf, a noted Egyptologist, representing the fruits of a lifetime of scholarship. Shortly after its publication, not only did the doctor have a fatal heart attack, but the warehouse where the publisher was holding the copies in preparation for shipment burned down. Only a few review copies still survive. In this rather curious book, von Petersdorf postulates that the rites of the Egyptian gods were derived from an earlier form of worship, involving deities with names such as "Kath-low" and others.

("Thoth's Dagger", Barton (C).)

APHOOM ZHAH. Flame-being spawned by Cthugha who came to Earth. At one time, Aphoom Zhah dwelt beneath Mount Yarak at the North Pole. According to *Pnakotic Manuscripts*, he was a being of cold flame, and was responsible for directing Rlim Shaikorth to destroy the land of Mhu Thulan. In the end, Aphoom Zhah himself created the cold which destroyed Hyperborea.

See Rlim Shaikorth. ("Zoth-Ommog", Carter; "The Light at the Pole", Carter and Smith.)

ARKAN TENGRI. Mysterious ruins found somewhere to the south of China's Kunlun Mountains.

(*The Transition of Titus Crow*, Lumley.)

ARKHAM. Town located on the Miskatonic River in Essex County, Massachusetts. Arkham was founded in the latter 17th century by free-thinkers who found the area's religious communities too strict. The town grew slowly at first, with agriculture being the primary source of revenue. Around the year 1692, the witchcraft fever which swept Salem also touched Arkham. At least one witch, Keziah Mason, was sent by the Arkham authorities for trial at Salem, and another, Hesper Payne, was burnt following her conviction by the Arkham town fathers.

During the middle of the 18th century, Arkham became a thriving seaport; it was one of the town's most influential captains, Jeremiah Orne, who imparted the books and funds which led to the founding of Miskatonic Liberal College. By the beginning of the 19th century the sea trade had failed, but many mills began to spring up upon the banks of the Miskatonic. In 1861 Miskatonic Liberal College, which already enjoyed the highest reputation, became Miskatonic University. The flood of 1888 and the cholera outbreak of 1905 led to a serious decline in the town's fortunes. Arkham recovered from these disasters after a while, and flourished until the disastrous storm and flood of 1980, which destroyed much of the town.

Today several factories still offer Arkham sources of employment, but the town's most important source of revenue is Miskatonic University, one of the nation's most renowned schools and the possessor of the largest known collection of occult lore in the western hemisphere. The town is a paradise for the scholar and antiquarian, but offers little for the casual traveller.

See Armitage, Henry; *Azathoth and Other Horrors*; Carter, Randolph; Derby, Edward Pickman; Kingsport; Mason, Keziah; Miskatonic River; Miskatonic University; Payne, Hesper; Shrewsbury, Laban; *Thaumaturgical Prodigies in the New-English Caanan*; Wilmarth, Albert. (*Arkham Unveiled*, Herber (C); "Season of the Witch", Launius (C); "The Dreams in the Witch-House", Lovecraft; "The Dunwich Horror", Lovecraft; "Herbert West—Reanimator", Lovecraft; *The Transition of Titus Crow*, Lumley.)

ARLYEH. See R'lyeh.

ARMITAGE, HENRY (1855-?). One-time head librarian at Miskatonic University, and a noted expert on the occult. Armitage attended Miskatonic University, later obtaining his doctorate at Princeton and his Doctor of Letters degree at Cambridge. The young man first became interested in uncanny subjects in 1882, when he heard of a mysterious meteor which had landed near Arkham. This occurrence led him to obtain the library's copy of *Necronomicon* and consult it for the first time. Later Armitage returned to this volume to solve the mysterious death of Wilbur Whateley, a longtime correspondent of his who lived in Dunwich. With the aid of Professors Rice and Morgan, he put an end to the horror which had ravaged Dunwich, though his health rapidly failed thereafter. Armitage was also the author of *Notes toward a Bibliography of World Occultism, Mysticism, and Magic* (Miskatonic University Press, 1927), as well as *Devils and Demons in the Miskatonic Valley*.

See Dunwich; Wilmarth, Albert. ("The Seven Cities of Gold", Burnham; "Zoth-Ommog", Carter; *Arkham Unveiled*, Herber (C); "The Terror from the Depths", Leiber; "The Dunwich Horror", Lovecraft.)

ARWASSA. Lesser Great Old One also known as the Silent Shouter. Arwassa is worshiped at monthly ceremonies, to which its cultists call it to partake of its sacrifices. There has only been one documented instance of Arwassa worship, but there may be other hidden cells.

("The Asylum", McCall (C).)

ATAL. High priest of the Elder Gods in Ulthar. Atal was born the son of an innkeeper, but was able to become apprenticed to the mighty Barzai, whom he accompanied on his climb of Mount Hatheg-Kla. He is now High Priest of the Temple of the Elder Gods, where he still presides over worship, though he is over three hundred years old.

See Barrier of Naach-Tith, Barzai, Ulthar. ("The Cats of Ulthar", Lovecraft; "The Dream-Quest of Unknown Kadath", Lovecraft; "The Other Gods", Lovecraft.)

ATLACH-NACHA. Great Old One which appears as a huge spider-like beast with an anthropoid head. Atlach-Nacha was said to have come to Earth from Saturn along with Tsathoggua. The spider god lives within a great chasm beneath Mount Voormithadreth in Hyperborea, or in Siberia or Peru. Atlach-Nacha spends all its time bridging a bottomless chasm with its web; when this web is completed, the end of the world will come.

Atlach-Nacha may be summoned from its chasm to possess one of its statues, though it hates to leave its spinning. A few cults devoted to Atlach-Nacha have existed at various times; the Phoenicians held this Great Old One in reverence, and small groups of worshipers are known to have existed in India and the Andaman Islands. This being deals mostly with sorcerers, however.

The Children of Atlach-Nacha are arachnid beings that lived during the early Mesozoic Era, and whose only traces are curious fossils found at only a few locations around the world. These remains may be returned to life by certain arcane procedures known only to Atlach-Nacha's most devoted shamans.

There has been one major attempt to find the dwelling place of Atlach-Nacha, the Barton-Doherty expedition. This brave band of explorers set out around 1985 for the Andes to attempt to locate the Great Old One, wearing fiberglass armor so that they might prove too difficult for Atlach-Nacha to devour them. Unfortunately, nothing has been heard of them since.

See Cykranosh, Tcho-Tcho, Tsathoggua. ("The Andaman Islands", Herber (C); *S. Petersen's Field Guide to the Creatures of the Dreamlands*, Petersen (C); "The Seven Geases", Smith; "Web of Memory", Szymanski (C); *The Philosopher's Stone*, C. Wilson.)

AVALOTH. Being referred to in the fifth Eltdown shard; known for its voracious appetite.

See *Eltdown Shards*. ("The Warder of Knowledge", Searight.)

AZATHI. Children of Azathoth formed from thermonuclear energy. Periodically in his mindless writhings, Azathoth disgorges one of these creatures. Most of these births result in the death of the child, as it is unable to control its body and explodes. Only a few are able to hold their internal energies in check and thus remain alive to leave the court of their father. Three Azathi, the beings titled Azatha, Azathe, and Azathu, still exist somewhere within the cosmos.

See Azathoth. (*Elysia*, Lumley.)

AZATHOTH (also AZAZOTH). Outer God known also as the Primal Chaos and the Daemon Sultan. Azathoth sits in his court at the center of the universe, mindlessly bubbling and blaspheming as he presides over the dance of the Other Gods. Azathoth may only leave his throne if summoned through incantation or through one of the special portals located in the insects from Shaggai's temples.

Very few humans worship Azathoth, but he has a large following among the insects from Shaggai. The insects' temples have an image within them of a hairy tentacled being within a shell much like that of an oyster. Possibly, this is intended to represent Azathoth's avatar Xada-Hgla. The rites the shan perform for Azathoth are wholly abominable.

Some modern thinkers have equated Azathoth with the Big Bang; this would seem to correlate with the Greek and Norse creation myths, which hold that the universe was created out of primal chaos. He may also be a personification of radioactivity; the formula in *De Vermis Mysteriis* for calling Azathoth requires a large quantity of fissionable material. Azathoth has also been given credit for the Tunguska explosion of 1908, though most scientists credit this destructive event to a regular asteroid impact instead.

Some assert that the Daemon Sultan was not always an Idiot Chaos; they say he lost his intellect and body in a great intercosmic battle, in which he may have been thrust entirely outside this dimension. This interpretation is found only within a few works, though.

The utterance of Azathoth's name gives one great power over beings from outside, and his unknown secret name gives even more influence. This respect has its limits, though, and not even *Necronomicon* contains Azathoth's secret name.

See Azathi, *Azathoth and Other Horrors*, *Book of Azathoth*, Cxaxukluth, Great Old Ones, L'gy'hx, *Massa di Requiem per Shuggay*, Mlandoth, Other Gods, Outer Gods, Outer Ones, Shaggai, shan, shantak, Shub-Niggurath, Sothoth, Thyoph, Tru'Nembra, Tulzscha, Ubbo-Sathla, Xada-Hgla, Yog-Sothoth. (*Strange Eons*, Bloch; "The Insects from Shaggai", Campbell; "The Mine on Yuggoth", Campbell; *Spawn of Azathoth*, Herber (C); *The Burrowers Beneath*, Lumley; *Elysia*, Lumley; *The Philosopher's Stone*, C. Wilson.)

AZATHOTH AND OTHER HORRORS. Book of poetry published in 1919 by Onyx Sphinx Press of Arkham, Massachusetts. The author of this volume was Edward Pickman Derby, at the age of eighteen a noted decadent and correspondent of the poet Justin Geoffrey. Unlike many other authors who have dealt with the Mythos, Derby survived for over twenty years following this book's publication. In the end, however, he was confined to Arkham Sanitarium following his divorce; just as his recovery seemed nearly complete, he was murdered by his lifelong friend Daniel Upton.

No specific poems have been cited from this volume, but *Azathoth and Other Horrors* is known to have influenced the work of Georg Fischer, collected in *The Tunneler Below*.

See Derby, Edward Pickman; *Tunneler Below, The*; Waite, Asenath. ("The Terror from the Depths", Leiber; "The Thing on the Doorstep", Lovecraft.)

B

BAALBO. Dead star, one of a binary pair about which the planet Tond revolves.

See Tond, Yifne. ("The Inhabitant of the Lake", Campbell.)

BAL-SAGOTH. Island in the Atlantic said to be the last surviving fragment of Atlantis. At the time of the Crusades, Norsemen landed upon this isle. They later reported the nature of its natives, their highly advanced civilization, and their worship of the god known as Gol-Goroth.

See Gol-Goroth, Groth-golka. ("The Fishers from Outside", Carter; "The Gods of Bal-Sagoth", Howard.)

BAOHT Z'UQQA-MOGG. Great Old One known as the Bringer of Pestilence. This being can be roughly described as a winged, spider-legged scorpion-like horror.

The shan revered Baoht Z'uqqa-Mogg centuries ago on their home world of Shaggai, and after that world's destruction the Great Old One followed his worshipers to Earth. Ghouls have also served Baoht; through their actions, they caused many of the plagues that have troubled the history of humanity.

See *Massa di Requiem per Shuggay*, shan. ("Fade to Grey", Aniolowski (C); "Mysterious Manuscripts", Aniolowski, *TUO3* (C).)

BARRIER OF NAACH-TITH (also WALL OF NAACH-TITH). Incantation that will "seal the souls" of the chanters when Yibb-Tstll is summoned, and that can also be used to provide a larger barrier against evil forces. This ritual is hinted at in *Cthaat Aquadingen*, but the complete version may only be found in the library of Celaeno, or possibly with the high priest Atal of Ulthar.

See Celaeno, *Cthaat Aquadingen*, *Fourth Book of D'harsis*, Sixth Sathlatta. ("Halls of Celaeno", Herber (C); *The Clock of Dreams*, Lumley; "The Horror at Oakdeene", Lumley.)

BARZAI. One-time high priest of Earth's gods in Ulthar. Barzai had read *Pnakotic Manuscripts* and *Seven Cryptical Books of Hsan*, and was very wise in the ways of Earth's gods. His desire for knowledge, however, proved to be his undoing, for he desired to gaze upon the gods themselves. He vanished from atop Mount Hatheg-Kla, where he had hoped to see the dancing of the gods.

See Atal; Hatheg-Kla, Mount; *Pnakotic Manuscripts*; Sign of Barzai. ("The Other Gods", Lovecraft.)

BAST. Egyptian goddess who took the form of a woman with the head of a cat. Bast was originally worshiped in Atlantis, and her worship was probably carried from that land to Egypt along with much of the sunken continent's lore. The center of Bast's cult in the land of the Nile was the city of Bubastis. The people of Bubastis revered felines, and many cats were mummified upon their deaths to please the goddess. Bast was also the goddess of pleasure, and was thus one of Egypt's most popular deities.

Prinn writes in *De Vermis Mysteriis* that the city of Bubastis was destroyed by the other religious factions of the Nile valley, due to the repulsive nature of some of Bast's rites. Most of the cult was put to the sword, but rumor has it that some escaped to Britain.

See Luveh-Keraphf, Nephren-Ka, "Saracenic Rituals". ("The Brood of Bubastis", Bloch; "The Mannikin", Bloch.)

BEAST, THE. See Nyarlathotep (The Beast).

BELED EL-DJINN. See Kara-Shehr.

BETHMOORA. City located somewhere beyond the hills of Hap, within the Dreamlands. Bethmoora was a thriving city, the most striking feature of which was its green copper gates. One day, when a festival was held in Bethmoora, three men on mules came from the desert, bringing a message whose exact nature and origin remains unknown. Some say it came from the desert itself, which desired to overrun the fair city; others assert that the messengers brought a decree from the emperor Thuba Mleen or from the gods, or even a warning of the plague. Upon hearing the words of these men, the entire population of Bethmoora deserted their city in one day, leaving it empty and shunned by all travellers.

("Bethmoora", Dunsany; "The Whisperer in Darkness", Lovecraft.)

BHOLE. See dhole.

BIG DIPPER. Constellation that has unusual significance in the mythology of some cultures. According to Pennacook myths, it was the home of the mysterious fungi from Yuggoth. The Aztecs called it "the footprint of Tezcatlipoca", their god of evil, who is linked by some with the Dark Demon form of Nyarlathotep. Across the Atlantic, the ancient Egyptians equated these stars with their own deity of darkness, Set. The Greek cult of Zeus Lycaeus revered the same constellation, and practiced human sacrifice on top of Mount Lycaeus to their god's glory. All of these cults seem to be connected to Nyarlathotep in one way or another, and thus the Big Dipper may explain the reference to the "World of the Seven Suns" mentioned by Wilmarth.

("The Whisperer in Darkness", Lovecraft; "The Cthulhu Mythos in Mesoamerican Religion", Tierney.)

BILLINGTON, ALIJAH. Descendant of Richard Billington who dwelt on his family's estate during the first years of the 19th century. He is said to have taken exception to certain things written about his forebear in Reverend Phillips' *Thaumaturgical Prodigies in the New-English Caanan*, and a lively debate ensued in which Phillips and his allies charged that Alijah was carrying on the dark practices of his ancestor in secret. After a few months of this controversy, John Druven, one of the Reverend's fellow advocates, disappeared following an inspection of the Billington estate. Shortly thereafter Alijah left with his son Laban and an Indian servant, Quamis, for England.

See Billington, Richard; *Thaumaturgical Prodigies in the New-English Caanan*. ("The Lurker at the Threshold", Derleth and Lovecraft.)

BILLINGTON, RICHARD. Wealthy landowner said to have dwelt in the area of New Dunnich, later known as Dunwich, in colonial times. This man was reputed to be a wizard who worshiped Satan in an old stone circle near his house. After several disappearances in the area, Billington himself dropped out of sight and was not heard from thereafter.

See Billington, Alijah; *Of Evill Sorceries Done in New-England of Daemons in No Human Shape*; *Thaumaturgical Prodigies in the New-English Caanan*. ("The Lurker at the Threshold", Derleth and Lovecraft.)

B'KAL. Ceremony performed once every thousand years in the city of N'gah-Kthun to summon the Elder God Ulthar.
(*The Sussex Manuscript*, Pelton.)

BLACK BOOK OF THE SKULL. Volume written at an unknown date by J'Cak Igguratian, a scholar from the city or land of Quy. The first known edition of *Black Book of the Skull* was in Greek, but almost all of these were burnt during the Inquisition. Later, *Black Book of the Skull* was translated into Latin; the translators refused to transcribe certain passages, though, so this particular edition is incomplete. Currently the only known surviving Greek copy is kept at Dwayne University in Amoston, Kansas, and a Latin edition may be found in the Special Collections of Miskatonic University.

This book gives an account of the occult delvings of its author, and his warnings against the dangers inherent in dealing with the Great Old Ones. The being Othuyeg and the Seven Cities of Cibola are also discussed.

See Othuyeg. ("The Seven Cities of Gold", Burnham.)

BLACK BROTHERHOOD. International terrorist organization devoted to the cause of the Old Ones. The members of the Black Brotherhood, who come from all backgrounds and ethnicities, carry out covert assassination attempts against various government officials, choosing their targets in no discernible pattern. The perpetrators of these attacks usually die shortly thereafter, so very few interrogations of its members have taken place. Those of the Brotherhood believe that the Great Old Ones will awaken soon, and that their actions will make Earth ready for their masters.
(*Strange Eons*, Robert Bloch.)

BLACK GOAT OF THE WOODS WITH A THOUSAND YOUNG. See Shub-Niggurath.

BLACK GOD OF MADNESS. Novel by Amadaeus Carson, a writer of popular romances whose work took a morbid turn following an occurrence at his rented home in Salem. None of Carson's regular publishers would agree to publish this book, and the original manuscript has since dropped out of sight. From what little is known of

Carson's experiences, it is likely that this novel deals with the Great
Old One Nyogtha.

("The Winfield Inheritance", Carter; "The Salem Horror", Kuttner.)

BLACK LITANIES OF NUG AND YEB. Ritual of worship for the
twin entities Nug and Yeb which deals with something known as the
Black Fire. The only complete rendering of Yeb's Litany was found on a
wall in ancient Irem.

See Nug and Yeb. ("To Clear the Earth", Murray; "Lovecraft's
'Artificial Mythology'", Price.)

BLACK LOTUS. Flower from the jungles of Khitai, an eastern
country of the Hyborian Age, where only the priests of the mysterious
god Yun dwelt. It was used to induce slumber in even the most ferocious
beast. The black lotus is still used by present-day cults to distill a drug
which opens up the mind to dreams of other dimensions.

("The Black Lotus", Carter; "The Tower of the Elephant", Howard.)

BLACK PHARAOH. See Nephren-Ka, Nyarlathotep (Black Pharaoh).

BLACK RITES. Book written by the Atlantean high priest Luveh-
Keraphf, and passed down by the Egyptians to the present day.

See Luveh-Keraphf. ("The Suicide in the Study", Bloch; "Zoth-
Ommog", Carter.)

BLACK STONE. Monument located near the town of Stregoicavar, Hungary. The Black Stone is shaped like an obelisk, and is
carved from a strange translucent stone. This monument is engraved
with indecipherable carvings, but most of these have been chipped
or weathered away. No one knows what civilization erected the Black
Stone. Some say that it was left by the Huns, but others, including
Friedrich von Junzt, insist that it is a remnant of an even earlier time.

For hundreds of years the Black Stone was the site of rituals
conducted by the primitive hill people who lived in the area. In 1526
a Muslim army under Suleiman marched into the area. When a
division commander, the scribe Selim Bahadur, discovered the locals'
worship practices, he had all the tribesmen killed and destroyed their
village, ending the cult's reign of terror over the surrounding region.

Even though over four centuries have passed since the land's
purging, the Black Stone is shunned by those who live nearby. Gazing
at the stone for any length of time causes insanity, and those who have
slept nearby are haunted in their dreams for the rest of their lives. At

one time the natives set out to destroy the Stone, but all who participated were cursed and they allowed it to stand. This monument might have inspired Justin Geoffrey's poem "People of the Monolith", as the poet is known to have visited this area.

See *Remnants of Lost Empires*, Stregoicavar, *Unaussprechlichen Kulten*, Xuthltan. ("The Black Stone", Howard.)

BLACK SUTRA. Volume written by U Pao, one of Burma's earliest scholars. We know nothing else of him, but his *Black Sutra* shows great insight into the nature of life on Earth, including passages suggesting the theory of evolution. In addition, *Black Sutra* deals with the being known as Yidhra.

("Where Yidhra Walks", DeBill.)

BLACK, THE. Dark, flaky substance which serves as blood for the entity Yibb-Tstll. The Black may be called by sorcerers to assault their foes. To do so, the caster must first inscribe the Sixth Sathlatta in its original Ptetholite characters (shown in *Cthaat Aquadingen*) on a wafer of flour and water. This wafer then must be given to the intended victim; although some say that the victim must touch the wafer for the spell to take effect, evidence would seem to suggest otherwise. Then, when the target can hear the caster, the wizard must recite the Hoy-Dhin Chant from *Necronomicon*. As the sorcerer chants, the Black will manifest itself, falling upon and adhering to the spell's target. Soon the victim will be completely covered and suffocate. The Black will then return to Yibb-Tstll with the person's soul, leaving behind no trace. If a person afflicted by the Black is able to reach running water, the spell will cease and return to its caster, taking full effect upon the would-be murderer.

See Hoy-Dhin Chant, Sixth Sathlatta, Yibb-Tstll. ("The Black Recalled", Lumley; "The Caller of the Black", Lumley; "The Horror at Oakdeene", Lumley.)

BLACK TOME OF ALSOPHOCUS (also THE BLACK TOME). Volume written by the great wizard Alsophocus of Erongill. It held such powerful information as the citing of Boromir, the secrets of the Shining Trapezohedron, and the calling of Cthulhu from his tomb.

See Alsophocus, Shining Trapezohedron. ("The Black Tome of Alsophocus", Lovecraft and Warnes.)

BLAKE, ROBERT HARRISON (?-1935). Milwaukee painter and weird fiction author. Due to difficulties in finding work, Blake turned to writing as a source of income. Though his works met with little commercial success at first, over time they began to gather acclaim. Later Blake took up painting as well, mostly depicting scenes of alien landscapes.

In search of greater thrills for use in his fiction, Blake searched for forbidden books, in the end discovering a copy of *De Vermis Mysteriis*. He made a journey to Providence so that a friend might translate the archaic Latin in which the book was written. During this visit his friend's house burnt to the ground, with its tenant supposedly trapped inside. Blake left Providence rather hastily following this incident.

During the winter of 1935, Blake returned to Providence and took up residence in an apartment on College Street. It was here that he completed many of his most famous stories. That spring and summer, however, Blake became increasingly obsessed with a deserted church on French Hill. He disclosed to friends that a series of strange events connected with this structure had befallen him; many consider these assertions to be part of a tremendous hoax engineered at least partially by Blake himself. On August 8, 1935, Blake was found dead from electrical shock in his rooms following a thunderstorm.

("The Shadow from the Steeple", Bloch; "The Shambler from the Stars", Bloch; "The Haunter of the Dark", Lovecraft.)

BLIND APE OF TRUTH. Embodiment of Destiny in the doctrines of Nephren-Ka's cult of Nyarlathotep. To the cultists, the Blind Ape of Truth represented the way Fate smashes the lives and hopes of humanity. Statues of the Ape are sometimes found in the cult's temples. It is possible that the Blind Ape of Truth is yet another of Nyarlathotep's manifestations.

See Nyarlathotep. ("Fane of the Black Pharaoh", Howard.)

BLOATED WOMAN. See Nyarlathotep (Bloated Woman).

B'MOTH (also BEHEMOTH or PHEMAUT). Oceanic deity worshiped in many parts of the world. B'moth desires to return all of humanity to the savage state which it once held, and can control weather and animals to accomplish this purpose. This creature may be another name for Cthulhu, or may be associated with the Great Old One in some way.

See *Magic and the Black Arts*. ("The Scourge of B'Moth", Russell.)

BOKRUG. God who took the shape of a water lizard, and who was worshiped by the amphibian people of Ib. He is especially noted for his vengeance upon those who offend him; his revenge may take hundreds of years to visit itself upon his foes, but when it comes, it is swift and devastating. The entire city of Sarnath blasphemed against this deity for many centuries, but in the end Bokrug's wrath visited itself upon the metropolis. Bokrug is worshiped today in the city of Ilarnek in the Dreamlands, and possibly in the lost prehuman city of Lh-Yib.

Some evidence suggests that Bokrug may not actually be a god, but is in fact one of a race of humanoid beings who have set themselves up as gods of the Thuum'ha, as the people of Ib are known.

See Ib, Sarnath, Thuum'ha. ("The Doom that Came to Sarnath", Lovecraft; *Beneath the Moors*, Lumley.)

BOOK OF AZATHOTH. Volume which anyone who enters the service of the Outer Gods must sign with his blood. It may possibly be the book spoken of by the victims of the witchcraft trials; if so, it would explain why only a few of these volumes were ever found. *Book of Azathoth* also contains some material in parody of Scripture, praising the Outer Gods and denigrating Christianity.

See Azathoth, Nyarlathotep (Black Man). (*Devil's Children*, Conyers, Godley, and Witteveen (C); "The Dreams in the Witch-House", Lovecraft.)

BOOK OF DAGON. Set of stone cones given by the deep ones to Captain Obed Marsh after he had founded the Esoteric Order of Dagon in Innsmouth. Through help from his inhuman visitors, Marsh was able to translate the R'lyehian glyphs on the cones into English. The book was never published, and only a few handwritten copies exist.

This book, which serves as the scripture for the deep one cults, tells the history of the deep ones, and of the proper ways in which various religious ceremonies are to be carried out by the faithful.

See deep one; Marsh, Obed. (*Escape from Innsmouth*, Ross (C).)

BOOK OF DZYAN (also *STANZAS OF DZYAN*). Libram supposedly transcribed by Madame Blavatsky. In her book *The Secret Doctrine*, Blavatsky told how her spirit guide had shown her the volume in a vision. (The word "Dzyan" used in the book's title is derived from "dhyan", the Sanskrit term for mystical meditation.) *Book of Dzyan* is the first of fifteen esoteric commentaries on the thirty-five books of Kiu-te. This volume was written on palm leaves in the Atlantean language of Senzar, which Blavatsky's spirit guide translated for her. Even if Ms. Blavatsky invented this description of the volume, it is true that other editions of the book have been rumored to exist.

According to tradition, the first six chapters of this book antedate humanity. Little else is known about this volume. Madame Blavatsky's translation, included in *The Secret Doctrine*, seems to have little to do with the Mythos, but it is possible that she misread certain portions of the document, or heard rumors upon which she based her own rendering of the volume.

See Feery, Joachim; *Study of the* Book of Dzyan, A. (*The Secret Doctrine*, Blavatsky; "The Diary of Alonzo Typer", Lovecraft and W. Lumley.)

BOOK OF EIBON. Tome originally penned by the great Hyperborean wizard Eibon, found amid the ruins of his blasted tower. After the destruction of Hyperborea by the Ice Ages, copies of the book made their way to Atlantis by way of a secretive cult, from whence they travelled to Egypt and to the rest of the world. *Book of Eibon* was translated from the original Hyperborean into Egyptian hieroglyphics, Punic, and Greek; the earliest copy to survive, however, is the 9th century Latin translation by Philippus Faber. Rumors of a Greek copy occasionally are heard, and the original Hyperborean edition was said to have existed up until the 14th century.

A French translation from the Greek was made by Gaspard du Nord of Averoigne in the 13th century. This Gaspard was a sorcerer of some note, who saved his home city of Vyones from the designs of an evil magician. In their gratitude, the authorities allowed him to continue in his occult studies, which presumably allowed him to translate *Book of Eibon* free from all popular censure. Several copies of this edition still survive. During the 15th century, *Book of Eibon* was translated into English by an unknown scribe; a few of these may still be found by the dedicated scholar. A Latin copy may be found at Miskatonic University, and Harvard also possesses the volume. A "complete" edition is held at the British Museum.

Though the knowledge in *Book of Eibon* is great, only a fraction of the original work survives. For instance, certain rituals intended to call down dholes to serve the summoner have survived in no known translation, and an encoded one-page appendix regarding the Antarctic Old Ones is found in only a few volumes. The book contains information on the rites of Tsathoggua, the artist Rhydagand, and tales of the great Rlim Shaikorth, as well as Eibon's journeys to Shaggai and the Vale of Pnath. Incantations for calling forth the emanation of Yoth and the Green Decay are also held within, along with the formula for a powder which will destroy certain star-spawned monstrosities.

See ankh; dark young of Shub-Niggurath; dhole; du Nord, Gaspard; emanation of Yoth; *Ghorl Nigral*; Green Decay; Hyperborea; *Liber Ivonis*; *Livre d'Ivon*; "Papyrus of the Dark Wisdom"; Rhydagand; Rlim Shaikorth; *Selections de* Livre d'Ivon; Zon Mezzamalech. ("The Horror from the Bridge", Campbell; "The Book of Eibon", Carter; "In the Vale of Pnath", Carter; "Shaggai", Carter; "The Man of Stone", Heald and Lovecraft; "By the Bay Part I", Herber (C); *Keeper's Compendium*, Herber (C); "Pickman's Student", Herber (C); *Dreams and Fancies*, Lovecraft; *Selected Letters V*, Lovecraft; "The Thing at the Threshold", McConnell and Sutton (C); "The Beast of Averoigne", Smith; "The Colossus of Ylourgne", Smith; "The Coming of the White Worm", Smith; "The Holiness of Azedarac", Smith; "Ubbo-Sathla", Smith.)

BOOK OF ELDERS. Volume supposedly written by a man named Alorri-Zrokros and featured in the works of the horror author H. Kenneth Allard. Only one fragment of this volume's writings is known: the partial ritual, "*Yogth-Yugth-Sut-Hyrath-Yogng ...*"
("Sticks", Wagner.)

BOOK OF HIDDEN THINGS. Volume mentioned in a manuscript discovered by Alonzo Typer. Nothing else is known of this book, though it may have to do with the lost city of Yian-ho.
("The Diary of Alonzo Typer", Lovecraft and Lumley, W.)

BOOK OF IOD. Book of unknown origin. Only one copy of the volume in the original "Ancient Tongue" is known to exist, but Johann Negus later published an expurgated translation, a copy of which is kept at the Huntington Library. The book discusses Iod the Shining Hunter and Zuchequon.
("Bells of Horror", Kuttner.)

BOOK OF KARNAK. Tome of evidently Egyptian origin, which may contain information regarding Iod the Hunter of Souls.
("The Hunt", Kuttner.)

BOOK OF SKELOS. Grimoire likely to have been written by the serpent mages of Valusia. In the Hyborian Age only three copies were known to exist; since that period, no mention has been made of it. Its contents remain a mystery, but we do know that the book was coveted by all of the Hyborian world's mages.
(*Conan the Buccaneer*, Carter and de Camp.)

BOOK OF THOTH. Volume supposedly written by Hermes Trismegistus in ancient Egypt, and said by some occultists to be the inspiration for the Tarot deck's design. According to other sources, *Book of Thoth* was originally written by Thoth-Amon, a priest of Set and the mightiest wizard of the land of Hyboria. After the destruction of that continent, *Book of Thoth* was preserved by the high priests of Egypt. Abdul Alhazred is known to have perused this volume, but no one has seen this book in present times.

Book of Thoth discusses the being known as Tawil at'Umr, as well as the Great Old Ones and the history of Hyboria.

See 'Umr at-Tawil. ("Through the Gate of the Silver Key", Lovecraft and Price; *The Winds of Zarr*, Tierney.)

BOREA. World in a parallel universe upon which Ithaqua was at one time imprisoned. The world has three moons, Dromos, Numinos, and another unnamed satellite, as well as a sun. Due to the physics of this particular dimension, however, none of these bodies turns around another. Thus, parts of Borea are left in perpetual cold, while others enjoy an eternal tropical summer.

Legend has it that Ithaqua was confined in a plateau near Borea's southern pole by the Elder Gods following the revolt of the Great Old Ones. After many years the Wendigo was able to obtain his freedom and travel to other worlds and dimensions, yet he still returns to Borea from time to time. Over the years Ithaqua has brought many sorts of life to this world and its moons, including various sorts of plants, bats, wolves, bears, whales, and even humans.

Ithaqua's habit of taking away with him those who have stirred his displeasure is well known. Though these victims are usually dropped from the sky by Ithaqua after a space of weeks or months, others are taken by him to Borea. These unfortunates are altered so that not even the most bitter cold may affect them; this trait, however, also makes them somewhat vulnerable to the same forces which repel the Great Old Ones themselves. Upon their arrival most of these are inducted into the Children of the Winds, Ithaqua's cult on Borea, which boasts hundreds of thousands of members. Some, however, rebel against the Wind-Walker; colonies of these outcasts may be found in the plateau in which Ithaqua was imprisoned, as well as upon the Isle of Mountains on Numinos. These colonies are a consistent irritation for Ithaqua, but his many forays against them have never been completely successful in eradicating them.

See Children of the Winds, Dromos, Ithaqua, Khrissa, Numinos. (*In the Moons of Borea*, Lumley; *Spawn of the Winds*, Lumley.)

BRAN MAK MORN. King of the Pictish peoples of Caledonia at the time of the Roman occupation of Britain. Before Bran's arrival, the Picts of this region had been split into many small, feuding tribes for over five hundred years. Under the rule of Bran, these people were once again united under one king. Bran was known to his people as a brave and just ruler. One of his most famous deeds was the summoning of the Worms of the Earth to take revenge against the Roman legions, though in doing so he called down doom upon himself.

Over time, Bran's memory has become distorted, and many legends about his legendary prowess have been invented. In his *Unaussprechlichen Kulten*, von Junzt mentions a statue of the king into which the spirit of Bran journeyed after his death. This effigy was hidden in a cave, which remains the focus for a religion centering around Bran to this day. Members of this cult, made up of the descendants of the Picts, are expected to make a pilgrimage to this statue once in their lifetimes. According to the group's teachings, one day the statue of Bran will return to life, and he and his people will come forth to rule the world.

See Worms of the Earth. ("The Children of the Night", Howard; "The Dark Man", Howard; "The Worms of the Earth", Howard; "The Whisperer in Darkness", Lovecraft.)

BRETHREN OF THE NEW LIGHT. 18th century religious group based in New York and founded by Shadrach Ireland. Its members believed that the time when the monstrous Primal Ones would return was quite near. Upon the return of their gods, all the cultists would become immortal. To bring this about, the Brethren held ceremonies near certain stone monoliths and laid their dead upon tablets of stone so that they too could receive the blessing of the gods. In 1781, when the promised resurrection still had not occurred, the Brethren were absorbed by the Shakers, and most of their dead were buried in a traditional manner.

("Sticks", Wagner.)

BRICHESTER. Commercial hub of England's Severn River Valley. The town may be split into three parts: Mercy Hill to the north, Brichester proper, and Lower Brichester. Brichester is home to Brichester University, one of the area's most respected institutions of learning.

This town has been the site of many strange happenings. At one time, Brichester University held a copy of *Revelations of Glaaki*, but this has since disappeared. A congregation of Brichester University students worshiping the Great Old Ones was broken up in the 1920's;

many of the professors at that institution also possess knowledge of the paranormal events in the surrounding countryside. It was in Brichester that the eccentric cult leader Roland Franklyn lived and published his book on reincarnation, *We Pass from View*. Finally, a man living on Mercy Hill was induced through dream communications to write the twelfth volume of *Revelations of Glaaki*.

See Devil's Steps; Eihort; Franklyn, Roland; Glaaki; Goatswood; Mercy Hill; *Revelations of Glaaki*; Severnford; Temphill; *We Pass from View*. ("Cold Print", Campbell; "The Franklyn Paragraphs", Campbell; "The Horror from the Bridge", Campbell; "The Mine on Yuggoth", Campbell; "Behold, I Stand at the Door and Knock", Price.)

BRICK CYLINDERS OF KADATHERON. Seven artifacts brought out of the Middle East by an expedition led by a Mr. Angstrom. They were translated by the use of the late Professor Gordon Walmsley's work, and are currently being kept at the British Museum. They are believed to deal with the history of the land of Mnar, especially as it relates to the prehuman city of Ib.

See Ib, Lh-yib. ("The Doom that Came to Sarnath", Lovecraft; *Beneath the Moors*, Lumley.)

BROKEN COLUMNS OF GEPH. Monuments located within the coastal jungles of Liberia. No one knows how old the Columns of Geph are, but they are mentioned in the writings of Teh Atht, a great wizard from the primal land of Theem'hdra. Upon these pillars the elders of the Ptetholites carved a warning against those who would use black magic against their foes, as well as the images of the Great Old Ones. Though the Great Old Ones have attempted to destroy the Columns, these monuments have survived to this day, and are thought to be the center of worship for the natives of that region. With the help of Professor Walmsley of Goole, the characters upon these monuments were deciphered several years ago.

See *Geph Transcriptions*; Ptetholite; Walmsley, Gordon. ("The Caller of the Black", Lumley; "The Return of the Deep Ones", Lumley; "Rising with Surtsey", Lumley; "The Sorcerer's Dream", Lumley; *The Transition of Titus Crow*, Lumley.)

BROTHERHOOD OF THE BEAST. Organization founded in the 12th century by a Chinese sage and a Romanian noble, so that the prophecy of Nophru-Ka, an Egyptian priest of the Fourteenth Dynasty, might be fulfilled. The followers of Nophru-Ka were led from their exile in G'harne by the Brotherhood's founders, and were brought to Europe to intermarry with other groups of people. As this assimilation of Egyptian blood into the European population progressed, the Brotherhood kept detailed genealogical records of these matings. They hoped that one day a child would be born who would fulfill the high priest's prophecy and aid Nyarlathotep in returning to Earth.

Over the centuries, the Brotherhood has gained a great deal of power and has greatly expanded its membership as it continues to strive toward its goals. It has failed in several of its schemes, however. Its attempts to form its own East European state were unsuccessful, and one chosen child was killed by a summoned being. More recently, the Brotherhood, having realized that the time of the Great Dying is approaching, has begun preparations for a great globe-spanning operation calculated to destroy much of human civilization. The success of this plan remains to be seen, however.

See Nophru-Ka, Nyarlathotep (The Beast). ("The Brotherhood of the Beast", Herber (C).)

BROTHERS OF CHAUGNAR FAUGN. Creatures which look like smaller versions of Chaugnar Faugn. When Chaugnar was taken to the East by the Miri Nigri, the Brothers remained beneath the Pyrenees. They have been known to come forth when Chaugnar Faugn himself is active. When Chaugnar awakens and devours the world, his brothers will be called out of their sleep to join him and become part of their great master.

See Chaugnar Faugn. ("The Horror from the Hills", Long.)

BROTHERS OF THE YELLOW SIGN. Cult of worshipers of Hastur which has connections to the King in Yellow. The Brothers congregate to destroy the outposts of the fungi from Yuggoth, as well as to torture members of the Great Race of Yith for information about other times and places.

See Hastur, Yellow Sign. (*Keeper's Compendium*, Herber (C); "The Shadow Out of Time", Lovecraft; "The Whisperer in Darkness", Lovecraft.)

BUGG-SHASH. Great Old One who takes the form of an inky blackness interspersed with many eyes, and many mouths which emit a chittering sound. Bugg-Shash manifests itself when called by wizards into this dimension. Bugg-Shash can only exist in darkness, but bringing the Great Old One into the light will not banish it permanently: Bugg-Shash must remain in this dimension until it has found and feasted upon a victim, after which it will return to its home. Bugg-Shash is known to be one of the servants of Yog-Sothoth.

See *Cthaat Aquadingen*, *Necronomicon* (Appendices). (*Elysia*, Lumley; "The Kiss of Bugg-Shash", Lumley; *The Transition of Titus Crow*, Lumley.)

BYAGOONA. Being known only as "the Faceless One", to whom a "Secret Parable" is attributed. Byagoona may be identical to Nyarlathotep, who was worshiped in the form of the Faceless God in ancient Egypt.

See Nyarlathotep. ("The Faceless God", Bloch; "The Grinning Ghoul", Bloch.)

BYAKHEE. Creatures resembling bats, birds, and humans to some degree. The byakhee are servitors of the Great Old One Hastur, and are sometimes involved in his rituals. The byakhee are also used as mounts that may carry a rider between the stars, provided that he has drunk the magical space mead.

To summon a byakhee, the wizard waits until a night when Aldebaran is above the horizon. Then he blows a special whistle and chants the following words:

> *Ia! Ia! Hastur! Hastur cf'ayak 'vulgtmm, vulgtmm, vulgtmm! Ai! Ai! Hastur!*

After this is done, the byakhee will fly down from space to the caster. See Hastur, *Legends of the Olden Runes*. (*The Trail of Cthulhu*, Derleth.)

BYATIS (a.k.a. "The Berkeley Toad"). Great Old One known as "serpent-bearded Byatis." As implied by its epithets, it appears much like a multi-colored, one-eyed shimmering toad; it has a proboscis, claws like those of a crab, and a row of tentacles below its mouth. Byatis is capable of hypnotizing those it chooses to prey upon, and with each victim devoured by Byatis, the Great Old One grows larger.

According to Prinn's *De Vermis Mysteriis*, Byatis was called to Earth by obeisances made to its image, which was carried to this world by the deep ones. Byatis was later worshiped by the serpent men of Valusia, and also by the people of the lost continent of Mu.

Many years later, Roman legionnaires occupying Britain's Severn River Valley discovered Byatis behind a stone door in an ancient camp. Horrified by what they saw, they imprisoned it with a five-pointed star before continuing on their way. From time to time, Byatis broke free of its prison to stalk and feast upon its victims, creating the legend of the "Berkeley Toad", a monster whose activities were centered around that town. During the 18th century, the Norman castle upon which Byatis had been chained was purchased by Sir Gilbert Morley, a wizard of some note. He made contact with Byatis, and in return for sacrifices the Great Old One allowed him to communicate with the rest of its kindred. One day, after Morley had closed the prison of Byatis, he vanished and was never seen again.

Some sources label Byatis as the son of Yig, but the two beings bear little resemblance to each other.

See Camside, *De Vermis Mysteriis*, deep one, serpent people. ("The Shambler from the Stars", Bloch; "The Room in the Castle", Campbell; "Zoth-Ommog", Carter.)

C

CABALA OF SABOTH. Book of unknown significance which may or may not have ties to the Mythos. A Greek translation of *Cabala* was made in 1686.

("The Mannikin", Bloch; "The Secret in the Tomb", Bloch.)

CAMILLA. Character from *The King in Yellow*.

See King in Yellow. ("The Repairer of Reputations", Chambers; "Tell Me, Have You Seen the Yellow Sign?", Ross (C).)

CAMSIDE. Village located between Severnford and Berkeley in the Severn River Valley. Byatis (the Berkeley Toad) often prowled near this town during its brief freedom. Beneath a house in this town exists an entrance to Eihort's labyrinth.

See Eihort. ("The Room in the Castle", Campbell.)

CARCOSA. Alien city in the Hyades on the shore of the Lake of Hali (though it may also lie in the Gobi Desert, or even near the Lake of Galilee). Carcosa is a metropolis of tall, black buildings, mysterious events, and inexplicable sounds and sights. Overhead are the planet's two moons, as well as Aldebaran and the Hyades. Very few have visited Carcosa and returned to tell the tale. It may be here that the play *The King in Yellow* takes place.

See Hali, Hastur, King in Yellow, Naotalba, Uoht, Yellow Sign. ("An Inhabitant of Carcosa", Bierce; "The Yellow Sign", Chambers; "Tatterdemalion", Love, Ross, and Watts (C); "Tell Me, Have You Seen the Yellow Sign?", Ross (C); *The Illuminatus! Trilogy*, Shea and R. Wilson; *House of the Toad*, Tierney.)

CARTER, RANDOLPH (1873-1928?). Boston author and mystic. Carter's family was one of the oldest in New England; in fact, Randolph's ancestor Edmund Carter had nearly been hung during the Salem witch-trials. Beginning at the age of ten, Carter began to show a gift for prophesying the future which never quite departed from him.

In his early years, Carter became known as one of the Dreamlands' greatest travellers. His most famous task, the quest to discover Kadath in the Cold Waste and the sunset city of his dreams, is still remembered among the people of those lands. As Carter grew older, however, his dream voyages became less and less frequent, until at the age of thirty they ceased entirely. It was at this time that Carter began a search for personal meaning that would last the rest of his life.

During World War I, Carter served in the French Foreign Legion. It was here that he made the acquaintance of Etienne-Laurent de Marigny, a fellow dreamer with whom he travelled into the crypts below the town of Bayonne and forged a friendship that would last for years.

After his discharge, Carter returned to the United States. Shortly thereafter he became the pupil of Harley Warren, a scholar who had delved deeply into the occult. One night Carter accompanied Warren to a cemetery in Florida for an unknown purpose. During the course of their investigation Warren vanished. Carter was questioned by the police, but was proved innocent of any wrongdoing and was released.

Carter was a writer of great ability, though he was not well known during his lifetime. His book *A War Come Near*, published in 1919, detailed his wartime experiences, and his horror story "The Attic Window", printed in the magazine *Whispers* in 1922, was so disturbing that many newsstands kept the issue off their shelves. Carter is best known, though, for his fantasy novels. His earlier ones, written during his years of dreaming, met with little success; the later, more sophisticated ones garnered him some attention. By the time of his disappearance, however, Carter had burnt all of his manuscripts, having found his career as an author unsatisfying.

On October 7, 1928 Carter made a trip to the ruins of his ancestral mansion outside Arkham. Searchers discovered his car and a handkerchief which might have belonged to him, but no other trace of Randolph Carter was ever found. A few of his friends asserted that he had gone back to the land of dreams to become the king of Ilek-Vad, but this speculation was not taken seriously.

See Chandraputra, Swami; de Marigny, Etienne-Laurent; Dreamlands; Ilek-Vad; Klarkash-Ton; Leng; Silver Key; time-clock; Warren, Harley. ("The Dream-Quest of Unknown Kadath", Lovecraft; "The Silver Key", Lovecraft; "The Statement of Randolph

Carter", Lovecraft; "Through the Gates of the Silver Key", Lovecraft; "The Unnameable", Lovecraft.)

CASSILDA. Character from *The King in Yellow*.

See King in Yellow. ("The Repairer of Reputations", Chambers; "Tell Me, Have You Seen the Yellow Sign?", Ross (C).)

CASTRO. Ancient sailor captured during a raid upon a sacrificial ritual in Louisiana on November 1, 1907. Of all the prisoners taken during that night, Castro proved to be the best informant on the nature of the cult. He said that he was a worshiper of Cthulhu, and had seen its immortal leaders who dwelt in China. Castro's confession to his captors later formed a cornerstone of George Angell's work on the Cthulhu cult.

See Cthulhu; Kuen-Yuin; Legrasse, John Raymond; Zuchequon. ("The Call of Cthulhu", Lovecraft.)

CASTRO MANUSCRIPT. Transcript of the ravings of Castro, a man who was executed by the Spanish Inquisition because his mental illness was misinterpreted as demonic possession. The Castro Manuscript includes information regarding the Elder Sign. No one knows where Castro picked up his knowledge of the Mythos, or why the monk who took down his speech felt it important enough to record.

("The Sanatorium", Herber (C).)

CATECHISM OF THE KNIGHTS OF THE OUTER VOID. Manual used for the instruction of its members who have reached the level of the Silver Twilight named in the title.

("The Hermetic Order of the Silver Twilight", Hutchinson (C).)

CATHURIA. Land of the Dreamlands which once lay beyond the Basalt Pillars of the West, and is held to be the land where all ideals are true. Cathuria has many golden cities built of marble and porphyry with roofs of gold. The land is ruled by King Dorieb, whom many hold to be a god. Unfortunately, the gods took Cathuria away from the land of dream, and no one knows where it now lies. The great dreamer Basil Elton failed in his quest to attain this land; his grandson Nathaniel was said to have found it, but was cast out soon thereafter.

("The Return of the White Ship", Breach; "The White Ship", Lovecraft.)

CELAENO. One of the seven stars in the Pleiades. The Great Library of Celaeno may be found on Celaeno's fourth planet, where the lore stolen by the Great Old Ones from the Elder Gods is kept. Just how the information is stored is unclear; some references indicate that it is held on books and tablets, but others assert that the elder lore rests in living organisms designed for that purpose. Visitors to the library should bear the sign of the Elder Ones and not remove any written knowledge, lest the Sleeper of the Lake prevent their escape. The noted scholar Laban Shrewsbury may have deciphered *Celaeno Fragments* from stone tablets he found in this place.

See Barrier of Naach-Tith, *Celaeno Fragments*, Naotalba. (*The Trail of Cthulhu*, Derleth; "Halls of Celaeno", Herber (C); *House of the Toad*, Tierney.)

CELAENO FRAGMENTS. Transcript deposited at Miskatonic University Library in 1915 by Professor Laban Shrewsbury, who disappeared shortly thereafter. Shrewsbury had seen the original broken stone tablets from the Great Library of Celaeno, and left behind notes which he claimed were a translation of the tablets. Translations of the tablets have turned up elsewhere; this could mean that the book was brought back to Earth by cultists before Shrewsbury, or that the *Fragments* were transcribed from Shrewsbury's notes and later published.

See Celaeno; Shrewsbury, Laban; *Necronomicon* (Appendices). ("The Gods", Carter; *The Trail of Cthulhu*, Derleth; "The Gable Window", Derleth and Lovecraft.)

CELEPHAIS. City of the Dreamlands found in the Valley of Ooth-Nargai near Mount Aran, beyond the Tanarian Hills. In Celephais, time seems not to pass at all, and a visitor may return many years later to find things almost as they were when he left.

Celephais was built in the dreams of Kuranes, a London dreamer of some note. When he passed away, he went to dwell in Celephais forever as its ruler.

See Dreamlands, Ooth-Nargai, Tanarian Hills. ("Celephais", Lovecraft.)

CELESTIAL PROVIDENCE. Chicago-based cult which was founded in 1865. Some say this group emerged from the East Coast; others suggest that it was brought to Chicago by newly-freed slaves. Whatever its origin, Celestial Providence may have been responsible for a string of disappearances from 1865-71 in this area. The cult is believed to have been completely destroyed by the Great Chicago Fire in 1871.

("King of Chicago", Sumpter (C).)

CHALMERS, HALPIN (?-1928). Noted mystic who served as the Curator of Archaeology at the Manhattan Museum of Fine Arts for some time. He was the author of a large number of occult volumes, including his famous *The Secret Watcher*, published by London's Charnel House Press. Chalmers was found dead in his apartment in Partridgeville, New Jersey on July 3, 1928, and his apparent murder has never been solved.

See *Secret Watcher, The*. ("The Winfield Inheritance", Carter; *The Horror from the Hills*, Long; "The Hounds of Tindalos", Long.)

CHANDRAPUTRA, SWAMI. East Indian individual of whom little is known. Swami Chandraputra first appeared in 1930, taking up residence in Boston's West End. He is known to have sent letters of inquiry to many occultists, and even frequented the Cabot Museum once to view an ancient mummy housed there. The Swami impressed all who met him as an intelligent, learned individual who possessed a prodigious knowledge of uncanny subjects.

In 1932, the Swami left Boston for the New Orleans home of Etienne-Laurent de Marigny, so that he might provide evidence at the reading of Randolph Carter's will. During that conference, however, the Carter family's lawyer died of apoplexy, and the Swami, who is believed to have been responsible, disappeared.

See de Marigny, Etienne-Laurent; time-clock. ("Out of the Aeons", Heald and Lovecraft; "Through the Gates of the Silver Key", Lovecraft and Price.)

CHATEAU DES FAUSSESFLAMES. Ruined manor located in the woods of Averoigne, near the abbey of Perigon. In medieval times, the chateau was the home of Sieur du Malinbous and his wife, who were suspected of practicing witchcraft. Even after the death of the pair the site's ill repute remained. Many who have visited the ruins of the chateau have not returned, and even centuries later most curiosity-seekers shun its ruined walls.

("Out of the Aeons", Heald and Lovecraft; "The End of the Story", Smith; "A Rendezvous in Averoigne", Smith.)

CHAUGNAR FAUGN. Hyperdimensional creature slightly resembling an elephant-headed human. He spends most of his time immobile in a cavern within the Plateau of Tsang, only shifting his bulk when feeding upon a sacrificial victim.

When Chaugnar came to Earth, the most advanced life forms on this planet were amphibians. Desiring to have a race of servitors, he used amphibian tissue to create the Miri Nigri. Over the long eons these beings continued to worship Chaugnar. The Miri Nigri consorted with the first humans to create a hybrid race, which eventually gave rise to the abominable Tcho-Tcho people.

In the times of the Roman Empire, Chaugnar and his "brothers", beings who bore a likeness to him but were lesser in power, dwelt beneath the Pyrenees in northern Spain, near the town of Pompelo. The Miri Nigri who lived in the nearby hills would kidnap villagers to be sacrificed to their gods each year before Hallowe'en. Eventually these kidnapings came to the attention of the Roman governors, who sent out an expedition to put an end to the hill-dwellers' depredations. Though this force was destroyed by the Miri Nigri, Chaugnar knew that this would not put an end to the Roman threat. He might be able to destroy his foes himself, but his time had not yet come. Rather, he decided to journey to the East, to await the time of his greatness. When his Brothers balked at making the journey, Chaugnar cursed them and promised to devour them after his resurgence.

Currently Chaugnar Faugn is worshiped in a cavern on the Plateau of Tsang. Though he rarely awakens, his one-time high priest, Mu Sang, prophesied that one day the White Acolyte would come from the west and bear Chaugnar away to a new land. In this land the elephant god would feed until he devoured the entire universe, as well as his Brothers.

See Brothers of Chaugnar Faugn; Magnum Innominandum; *Pnakotic Manuscripts*; Tcho-Tcho; Tsang, Plateau of; White Acolyte. ("The Curse of Chaugnar Faugn", Barton (C); *The Horror from the Hills*, Long.)

CHIAN. Language mentioned in the *Green Book*. Chian was originally a drink composed of garlic, leeks, cheese, oil, vinegar and dried herbs imbibed at the mysteries of Artemis at Ephesus, so it seems likely that the "Ephesian letters of good omen" mentioned by Athaenus are actually the Chian language. These letters were supposed to form words representing the words for darkness, light, the Earth, the sun, the year, and truth, as well as other concepts. They were found on the feet, girdle, and crown of the Ephesian statue of Artemis.

Much has been said of the letters' powers. The possession of these letters made their possessor invincible at sports, but their use was illegal in such contests; one wrestler won three hundred bouts before the nature of his victories became known. King Croesus was said to have escaped being burned to death by saying the words over his pyre, and King Solomon himself was said to have used the Chian letters to exorcise demons. Certain cults may have passed down the mystical traditions of Chian down to present times.

See *Green Book*. ("The White People", Machen.)

CHIG. Entity worshiped on the world of Tond. The ritual of Chig's priests lasts one puslt, or three and a quarter years, and none care to disturb them during it.

See puslt. ("The Inhabitant of the Lake", Campbell.)

CHILDREN OF THE WINDS. Title given to the physiologically-altered worshipers of Ithaqua who dwell on the world of Borea. This may be a generic name given to all of the Wind-Walker's followers.

See Borea, Ithaqua. (*Spawn of the Winds*, Lumley.)

CHIME OF TEZCHAPTL. Magical item which *Turner Codex* describes. Using the Chime, one may protect oneself against any spell involving song, and may reflect the energy within the spell back upon its caster.

See *Turner Codex*. ("The Evil Stars", Herber (C).)

CHORAZIN. 1) Cthulhu's will, or id. This is Cthulhu's most psychically accessible part, and is responsible for most of his dream sendings. See Cthulhu. ("Dreams Dark and Deadly", Szymanski (C).)

2) Town in upstate New York near both Attica and the ancestral van der Heyl mansion visited by Alonzo Typer. Most of the people here belong to a loathsome cult, which meets on a hill near the old mansion. ("The Diary of Alonzo Typer", Lovecraft and W. Lumley.)

3) Ruined city in Israel. This city was condemned by Jesus in the Bible (Matthew 11:21, Luke 10:13). It should be noted that Ludvig Prinn, author of *De Vermis Mysteriis*, is said to have spent a great deal of time in this place. ("Lord of the Worms", Lumley.)

CHORAZOS CULT. Cult of Yog-Sothoth worshipers. It was established in the mountains of Romania in the late 16th century by a man named Chorazos, who was supposedly of gypsy extraction. The members of the cult came from such diverse places as Hungary, Africa, Arabia, and China. The cult was exiled from its former continental site to England, where a temple was established in London. In turn, the cult was hounded out of London due to an investigation by the queen (who had been advised about the matter by Dr. John Dee) and then moved their base of operations to a house known as the Oaks.

Though the Chorazos Cult spent only a year in the Oaks, it became well known throughout the area as an evil group. When Parson Goodly of the local church asked Chorazos of the type of worship the cult practiced, Chorazos cursed the whole surrounding land, which to this day remains poor and deserted. Finally, the countrymen banded together and burned down the Oaks. Chorazos and a few other members escaped to Scotland.

Chorazos established the cult's final chapter in the Pentland Hills, but King James VI of Scotland was extremely opposed to witchcraft. The people living nearby rose up following a series of disappearances, destroying the sect once and for all.

See Yog-Sothoth. ("The Running Man", Lumley.)

CHRONICLES OF NATH (originally *Chronike von Nath*). Volume written by Rudolf Yergler, a German mystic who finished it in 1653, shortly before he became completely blind. When the first edition was published, the authorities in Berlin reacted by sending Yergler to a madhouse, where he died under mysterious circumstances. In 1781, James Sheffield translated *Chronike* into English, expurgating the volume to some degree.

The tome deals somewhat with the history of Nath, Land of the Three Suns. In addition, it contains certain musical compositions said to bring star-spawned monstrosities into our dimension, and may deal with the mystical traditions of Hermes Trismegistus.

See Nath. ("The Tree on the Hill", Lovecraft and Rimel; "Music of the Stars", Rimel.)

CHRONICLES OF THRANG. Volume written before the beginning of accepted human history, and amended in the land of Ngarathoe before the rise of Sumeria. *Chronicles* deals in some detail with the nature of Yidhra.

("Where Yidhra Walks", DeBill.)

CHTHONIAN. See cthonian.

CHTHONIOI. Beings of the underworld which, according to Roman myths, existed before even the Olympians came into power. The Chthonioi were usually connected with the Greek Titans and with the Jotuns of Norse mythology. Some sorcerers made pacts with the Chthonioi, but such arrangements were fraught with peril and required great personal sacrifice.

The Chthonioi are probably the same beings as the Great Old Ones, and indeed, distorted variants of Cthulhu and Shub-Niggurath numbered among them. Why the Lord of R'lyeh is included among the subterranean deities is unknown.

(*Heir of Darkness*, Rahman.)

CIMMERIA. Land of northwestern Hyboria from which the famous warrior Conan originally came. Today most of Hyboria lies beneath the ocean, with only the portion which is now northeastern England lying above the waters. This Cimmeria is probably not the same as that of the Cimmerians, a race which dwelt at one time in Anatolia and died out around 500 B.C.

See Hyboria, Lh-Yib, *Testament of Carnamagos*. ("The Hyborian Age", Howard; *Beneath the Moors*, Lumley.)

CIRCLES OF THAOL. Diagram consisting of three concentric circles. When used in conjunction with the star-stones of Mnar, the Circles can be used to imprison a summoned creature.

See star-stone of Mnar. ("Andalous and the Chimera", Hjort.)

CLITHANUS. See *Confessions of the Mad Monk Clithanus*.

CLOTTON. Village located on the Ton River, a tributary of the Severn. Clotton has declined greatly since its heyday, and now cannot be found on most maps. Following events in 1931 of which the townspeople are disinclined to speak, the people of Clotton tore down many of the riverfront buildings and erected a huge concrete pillar on the Ton's bank.

("The Horror from the Bridge", Campbell.)

COLD WASTE. Region to the north of the Dreamlands in which the mountain of Kadath may be found.

See Carter, Randolph; Dreamlands; Kadath in the Cold Waste; Leng; Yr-Nhhngr. ("The Dream-Quest of Unknown Kadath", Lovecraft; "The Dunwich Horror", Lovecraft.)

COMMORIOM. One-time capital city of the land of Hyperborea. Legend has it that the White Sybil of Polarion foretold that Commoriom would be destroyed. Upon hearing these words, the entire population of the doomed city left, leaving Commoriom to the jungle and setting up the new capital in Uzuldaroum, a day's journey away. However, other accounts have it that the city was deserted due to the depredations of an accomplished criminal.

Klarkash-Ton of Atlantis preserved the myth-cycle of fabled Commoriom, which includes tales of Tsathoggua and other entities.

See Hyperborea, Klarkash-Ton, Uzuldaroum. ("The Whisperer in Darkness", Lovecraft; "The Tale of Satampra Zeiros", Smith; "The Testament of Athammaus", Smith.)

CONFESSIONS OF THE MAD MONK CLITHANUS. Volume written by Clithanus circa A.D. 400, and printed in Latin in 1675. Copies are held at the British Museum, as well as the Field Museum in Chicago.

Clithanus had read a great deal of *Necronomicon*, and used this information to free a "follower of mad Cthulhu" which was imprisoned within the tunnels beneath an abbey at Lynwold, on England's northeastern coast. After seeing what he had done, Clithanus became afraid and went to St. Augustine, the Bishop of Hippo, for assistance. Through the use of a star-shaped symbol, Augustine returned the monster to its prison, and sent Clithanus, who had been driven out of his mind, to Rome.

This book contains the formulae for calling a lesser being much like Cthulhu, another for sending the creature back on its original summoner, and the signs of protection needed to avert its wrath. Clithanus also tells of a time when a large number of Cthulhu-spawn were called out of the deeps, ravaged the land, and were imprisoned once again in a faraway land by priests from Central Europe.

("The Passing of Eric Holm", Derleth; "Something from Out There", Derleth; "The Horror from the Depths", Derleth and Schorer; "Fischbuchs", Ross, *TU02* (C).)

COPELAND, HAROLD HADLEY (?-1926). One-time leading anthropological authority on Pacific cultures, as well as co-founder and president of the Pacific Area Archaeological Association. Copeland's first book, *Prehistory in the Pacific: A Preliminary Investigation with References to the Myth-Patterns of Southeast Asia*, established his reputation in the field when it was published in 1902. In 1906 Copeland completed his second volume, *Polynesian Mythology, with a Note on the Cthulhu Legend-Cycle*; even here, Copeland's material remains on solid scientific ground, but this book also shows the first signs of what was to become a lifelong obsession for the distinguished scientist.

Copeland's preoccupation with lost civilizations came to the fore in his 1911 work, *The Prehistoric Pacific in Light of the "Ponape Scripture."* In this book, Copeland asserted that the continent of Mu, which various occultists believe to lie sunken beneath the Pacific, had actually existed. To support his hypothesis Copeland cited the colossal stone ruins found on many Pacific islands, the similar myth patterns of the widely scattered peoples of the region, and the *Ponape Scripture*, a work discovered on the isle of Ponape in 1734 by Captain Abner Ezekiel Hoag. *The Prehistoric Pacific* was derided in the scientific community, and Copeland was forced to step down from the presidency of the Pacific Area Archaeological Association.

In 1913 Copeland, accompanied by a colleague named Ellington, set off for the mountains beyond the Plateau of Tsang in central Asia. The Copeland-Ellington expedition met with disaster; Ellington died in the first few days, most of the group's bearers perished or deserted, and Copeland was not heard from until three months later, when he was discovered in Mongolia, raving about the things he had seen and carrying ten stone tablets which, he vowed, had been inscribed with the words of the Muvian high priest Zanthu. Three years later *The Zanthu Tablets: A Conjectural Translation* was released to the public. The book was decried in all quarters, and shortly after its release Copeland was confined to a San Francisco sanitarium, where he died in 1926. Copeland left his estate, including all his notes and a sizable collection of Polynesian artifacts, to the Sanbourne Institute of Pacific Antiquities.

See Lesser Old Ones; *Ponape Scripture*; Sanbourne Institute of Pacific Antituiqies; Tsang, Plateau of; *Yuggya Chants*; Zanthu Tablets. ("The Dweller in the Tomb", Carter; "Out of the Ages", Carter; "Zoth-Ommog", Carter.)

CRAWLING CHAOS. See Nyarlathotep.

CROTH. Great underground city discovered by the Great Northern Expedition in 1933. Croth can be found in the caverns which lead to the Great White Space. Nothing is known about the former inhabitants of this city except that they had a huge building like a library, where movie-like "books" were projected onto a large screen so that many could read them at once. Other features of note are the non-Euclidean patterns of the cobblestones and the stupendous arched metal bridges.

See Great Northern Expedition, Great White Space. (*The Great White Space*, Copper.)

CROW, TITUS (1916-1969?). British occultist and psychic who dedicated his life to the study of the paranormal, especially the Cthulhu Mythos. Titus Crow was born December 2, 1916 into a well-to-do

London family. He inherited his love of learning from his father, an archaeologist of some note. During World War II, Crow used his talents in the War Department as an adviser on the occult and the Third Reich, as well as to help break the German military's codes. Later Crow purchased a country estate, Blowne Manor, and began his probing into the occult in earnest along with his close friend Henri-Laurent de Marigny. He became one of the country's greatest occultists, as well as the possessor of a noteworthy library on uncanny subjects.

In his last years, Crow joined Miskatonic University's Wilmarth Foundation in their assault upon the Great Old Ones, and for a brief while became the head of the Foundation's British operations. Crow's life probably came to an end, however, when Blowne Manor was destroyed by occult forces on October 4, 1969.

See *Cthaat Aquadingen*; *Cultes des Goules*; Davies, Chandler; de Marigny, Henri-Laurent; *Geph Transcriptions*; *G'harne Fragments*; Ibigib; *Legends of Liqualia*; time-clock; Yian-Ho. ("Billy's Oak", Lumley; *The Burrowers Beneath*, Lumley; "Inception", Lumley; "The Lord of the Worms", Lumley.)

CRYSTALLIZER OF DREAMS. Yellow egg-shaped item which periodically emits a whistling noise. *Revelations of Glaaki* mentions the Crystallizer, which can be used to view far-off places (such as the world of Tond) in dreams, as well as to perceive higher dimensions. According to some, the Crystallizer can also allow its user to bring items or creatures back from the Dreamlands to the waking world for a brief while. However, the Crystallizer is said to have a guardian whose nature is to be feared. This guardian, which is sometimes said to be Hypnos, is very difficult to elude.

See Hypnos, Tond. ("The Inhabitant of the Lake", Campbell; "The Render of the Veils", Campbell; "Entering the Dreamlands", Petersen and Willis (C).)

CTHAAT AQUADINGEN. Mythos tome by an unknown early medieval author. This book is in English, though it was probably originally written in German; one Hindi copy has been found, however. Only five copies of *Cthaat Aquadingen* are known to exist. One version, bound in human skin, was rumored to be held in the library of Titus Crow, but if Crow did own it, it was probably destroyed when his home was demolished by occult forces in 1969. The British Museum has repeatedly denied possessing any copy of this work, though it has been suggested that the copy is kept in its restricted collection. One copied manuscript and partial translation is kept at Oakdeene Sanitarium in

England, and the Great Library of the Dreamlands possesses this book as well.

Cthaat Aquadingen holds information about the Small Crawler aspect of Nyarlathotep, as well as Yibb-Tstll. It also contains certain Tsathogguan rituals, the Sixth Sathlatta, a spell to dismiss Bugg-Shash, and information on the Barrier of Naach-Tith. As its title implies, though, it is mainly focused on rituals related to Cthulhu and the other ocean-dwelling members of the Mythos.

See Barrier of Naach-Tith; Black, the; Feery, Joachim; Hoy-Dhin Chant; *Notes on the* Cthaat Aquadingen; Nyarlathotep (Small Crawler); Nyhargo Dirge; Sathlattae; Sixth Sathlatta. (*Keeper's Compendium*, Herber (C); "Ulthar and Beyond", Herber (C); "Billy's Oak", Lumley; *The Burrowers Beneath*, Lumley; "The Horror at Oakdeene", Lumley; "The Kiss of Bugg-Shash", Lumley; "The Return of the Deep Ones", Lumley; "Kenya", DiTillio and Willis (C).)

CTHONIAN. One of a race of subterranean burrowers resembling short-tentacled, eyeless squids. They are led by a gigantic member of their species named Shudde-M'ell. These beings were originally imprisoned near the African city of G'harne, but escaped their bondage and spread throughout the world by tunneling through the Earth's crust. The cthonians move by burrowing through rock, using a process that seems to melt the stone through which they travel. By use of a similar ability, the cthonians may create earthquakes and subsidences whenever they desire. In fact, the San Francisco earthquake of 1906 has been accredited to this species.

The cthonians possess amazing telepathic powers. Not only are they able to communicate with each other (and psychically sensitive members of other species) via mental waves, they can also keep a human mentally chained to one place, or confuse a person so he stumbles into an ambush, by mentally overpowering the victim's will. Fortunately, the cthonians only use the latter ability when they or their young are threatened, or sometimes against those who have made themselves nuisances.

The life cycle of cthonians is quite lengthy. A female only lays a few eggs at a time. As a consequence of this, cthonians are quite protective of their eggs (which appear to be spherical mineral formations) and young, and will go to great lengths to rescue them if they are removed from their nests.

Cthonians are vulnerable to very few substances. They are not seriously hurt by highly-powered explosives, and, as evidenced by their tunneling activities, are unaffected by extremes of temperature.

On the other hand, the Tikkoun Elixir and Vach-Viraj Incantation, and possibly the Elder Sign, can be of some use against them. Radiation or immersion in water can also cause serious damage to cthonians. It should be noted, though, that the cthonians are quite intelligent and are unlikely to put themselves in a position where they might be in danger.

See A'byy; ankh; de Marigny, Henri-Laurent; Elder Sign; G'harne; Kagwamon K'thaat; Lesser Old Ones; Shudde-M'ell; Tikkoun Elixir; Vach-Viraj Incantation; Wilmarth Foundation. ("The Statue of the Sorcerer", Edwards and Eliot (C); *The Burrowers Beneath*, Lumley.)

CTHONIC REVELATIONS. Volume by Thanang Phram which deals with Yidhra.

("Where Yidhra Walks", DeBill.)

CTHUGHA. Great Old One who takes the form of a huge airborne conflagration. Cthugha dwells somewhere near the star Fomalhaut, and is served by the fire vampires. He has sometimes been classified as a fire elemental.

Some say Cthugha participated in a war between the Great Old Ones and Elder Gods; during the battle, he was irradiated and became permanently insane. Some sort of enmity also exists between Cthugha and Nyarlathotep.

If a person wishes to summon Cthugha, the following chant must be repeated three times when Fomalhaut is over the horizon:

> *Ph'nglui mglw'nafh Cthugha Fomalhaut n'gha-ghaa naf'l thagn! Ia! Cthugha!*

The only known cult to Cthugha was that of Nestar Mobedan Mobed, a Zoroastrian prophet who lived during the 6th century A.D. Except for some studies linking Cthugha with the Aztec fire god Xiuhtecuhtli, no other instance of worship has been documented.

See Aphoom Zhah, elemental theory, fire vampire, Fthaggua, Gn'icht' Tyaacht, *Letters of Nestar*, Nestar Mobedan Mobed, T'gaorl. ("This Fire Shall Kill", Bishop (C); "The Dweller in Darkness", Derleth; *Elysia*, Lumley; "The Cthulhu Mythos in Mesoamerican Religion", Tierney.)

CTHULHI (also STAR-SPAWN OF CTHULHU). Beings that came to Earth with Cthulhu, that dream with their master in the corpse-city of R'lyeh. Despite their ability to mold their form at will, they always resemble their master to some degree; indeed, they may all be descended from him.

The Cthulhu-spawn arrived on Earth many eons ago, building a great city on the newly-risen continent of R'lyeh. This incursion was resisted by the Elder Things of the Antarctic, but the Cthulhi beat them back into the ocean. Peace was finally declared, and both races settled back into their cities. In the end, however, R'lyeh sank beneath the waves, trapping Cthulhu and all of his spawn. Presumably the Cthulhi will awaken with their master when R'lyeh rises above the ocean.

See Cthulhu. ("At the Mountains of Madness", Lovecraft; *The Transition of Titus Crow*, Lumley.)

CTHULHU. Great Old One resembling a clawed, octopus-headed humanoid with great bat-like wings. Cthulhu sleeps beneath the Pacific Ocean, but according to legend, he will one day awaken to rule the world.

Records of Cthulhu's origins are fragmentary, but it seems that he originated on the world of Vhoorl in the twenty-third nebula. He later travelled to the green double star of Xoth, where he mated with a creature named Idh-yaa to produce the Great Old Ones Ghatanothoa, Ythogtha, and Zoth-Ommog. From here Cthulhu, his children and a race of beings known as the Cthulhi flew to Saturn, and from there descended to Earth.

Upon their arrival, Cthulhu and his retinue took up residence on a continent in the Pacific Ocean, where they built the great stone city of R'lyeh. At first Cthulhu's spawn encountered resistance from the Elder Things, who had dwelt on Earth for millions of years before Cthulhu's coming. Following a war in which Cthulhu's spawn destroyed all of the Elder Things' land cities, the two species declared peace and agreed not to harass each other.

Following this arrangement, Cthulhu enjoyed many years of freedom on this world. During these millions of years humanity slowly evolved. Cthulhu spoke to these new beings telepathically and in their dreams, telling them where to find the statues in his image he had brought down from the stars and instructing them in the proper worship of the lord of R'lyeh. In this way the cult of Cthulhu began.

One day disaster struck black R'lyeh. It may have been the vengeance of unknown deities, changes in the stars, or the moon being ripped from the Earth (though evidence suggests that Cthulhu's followers might have had a hand in this). No matter the cause, the city of R'lyeh sank beneath the Pacific Ocean, trapping

Cthulhu and all of his spawn. The water blocked most of their telepathic signals, making them able to communicate with their worshipers only through dreams. They fell asleep, but they could not die. They were helpless to do anything but wait until the stars came right and they would be freed from their prisons.

Since then, Cthulhu's tomb has emerged from the water from time to time, freeing him for brief durations. These have only been short respites for the Great Old One, for each time R'lyeh has sunk back beneath the sea after a few days or weeks. A day will come, however, when the black city will not return to the sea floor. Cthulhu will then kill and destroy across the world, ushering in a new age.

Cthulhu's cults are quite widespread; traces of his worship have appeared in Haiti, Louisiana, the South Pacific, Mexico, Arabia, Siberia, K'n-yan, and Greenland. The deathless priests who lead the cult live somewhere in the mountains of China, but the cult's true center is or was located somewhere in the Arabian desert. For the most part this cult has remained secret, but the Hawaiian islanders still tell legends of Kana-loa, the evil squid god who was imprisoned in the underworld, and the pioneering work of Professor Angell and his successors has given us much information about this secretive organization.

Rumor has it that Cthulhu himself is merely the high priest of Yog-Sothoth. Some enmity exists between Cthulhu and his "half-brother" Hastur the Unspeakable. Still, no one knows just how Cthulhu and Hastur are related, and why this conflict between them exists.

In some texts, Cthulhu is called a water elemental. This information is probably erroneous, however, as it is the ocean that blocks his telepathic signals to humanity.

See Abdul Alhazred; Angell, George Gamwell; *Black Tome of Alsophocus*; B'moth; Castro; Chorazin; Chthonioi; *Confessions of the Mad Monk Clithanus*; Copeland, Harold Hadley; *Cthaat Aquadingen*; Cthulhi; *Cthulhu Among the Victorians*; *Cthulhu in the Necronomicon*; Cthylla; deep one; Dreamlands; *Dwellers in the Depths*; Elder Sign; Elder Things; elemental theory; Esoteric Order of Dagon; Fishers from Outside; Ghatanothoa; Great Old Ones; Hastur; Idh-yaa; *Investigation into the Myth-Patterns of Latter-Day Primitives with Especial Reference to the R'lyeh Text, An*; K'n-yan; Kthanid; Kuen-Yuin; *Legends of the Olden Runes*; Legrasse, John Raymond; Mark of Cthulhu; Masters of the Silver Twilight; Mylakhrion; Nug and Yeb; Othuum; *Ph'nglui mglw'nafh Cthulhu R'lyeh wgah'nagl fhtagn*; R'lyeh; *R'lyeh Text*; Seal of R'lyeh; shoggoth; *Unaussprechlichen Kulten*; Vhoorl; Xoth; Yian; Yog-Sothoth; Ythogtha. (*Strange Eons*, Bloch; "The Tugging", Campbell; "The Mound", Heald and Lovecraft; "Castle Dark", Herber (C); "At the Mountains of Madness", Lovecraft; "The Call of Cthulhu", Lovecraft.)

CTHULHU AMONG THE VICTORIANS. Volume by Laban Shrewsbury published by Miskatonic University Press in 1929. Since the book was issued during Shrewsbury's twenty-year absence, it was likely assembled from the professor's notes and published in memory of the vanished anthropologist.

This book seems to be a collection of Cthulhoid events which happened during the last few decades of the 19th century. Shrewsbury asserts that this age was one of the critical times in our planet's history, when the Mythos made great strides in retaking the world.

See Shrewsbury, Laban. (*Cthulhu by Gaslight*, Barton (C); *The Trail of Cthulhu*, Derleth.)

CTHULHU IN THE NECRONOMICON. Manuscript by Professor Laban Shrewsbury, intended to be a sequel to his *An Investigation into the Myth-Patterns of Latter-Day Primitives.* The first part of Shrewsbury's unfinished book arrived at the publishers in 1938, shortly before his supposed death in a mysterious fire at his home. This portion was probably published even though the rest of the manuscript no longer exists, as the book has turned up in several places since then.

In this book Shrewsbury correlates the Cthulhu Mythos with the myths of cultures around the world, and speculates on pitting the Great Old Ones, especially Cthulhu and Hastur, against each other.

See *Necronomicon* (Appendices); Shrewsbury, Laban. (*Dreams from R'lyeh*, Carter; *The Trail of Cthulhu*, Derleth.)

CTHYLLA. Cthulhu's daughter, mothered by Idh-yaa, a creature from the black star of Xoth. She is rarely alluded to within the books of the Mythos, for her destiny was so hideous even the authors of these volumes feared to speak of her. If ever Cthulhu is destroyed, his spirit will depart and be reincarnated in the womb of Cthylla. Thus Cthulhu might return to the world, even in the event of his complete destruction.

(*The Transition of Titus Crow*, Lumley.)

CULT OF THE BLOODY TONGUE. Religion based in the Kenyan bush which has taken a form of Nyarlathotep as its god. The cult's power in this area is great, and few can be induced to speak of its rites. It has a few branches elsewhere in the world, but these are quite weak in comparison to the main organization. The Cult was possibly responsible for the Mau Mau reign of terror in the 1950's.

See *Africa's Dark Secrets*, Nyarlathotep (Black Wind, God of the Bloody Tongue). (*Masks of Nyarlathotep*, DiTillio and Willis (C).)

CULTES DES GOULES. Book by François-Honoré Balfour, Comte d'Erlette, published in 1703. In this book the Comte, a French nobleman and noted occultist, spoke of his membership in a Parisian ghoul cult. Upon its release it was widely condemned by the church, and the Comte went into seclusion until his death in 1724. Later an expurgated version of the original text was published, but there is no information as to location or time. Fourteen copies of this book are known to exist, one in the Miskatonic University library and another in the destroyed personal library of Titus Crow. Despite the number of times this book has been mentioned, little is known about it.

During the French Revolution the d'Erlettes were forced to flee to Bavaria. Upon their arrival there they changed their names to Derleth. In fact, the Comte is an ancestor of August Derleth, co-founder of Arkham House.

("Darkness, My Name Is", Bertin; "The Grinning Ghoul", Bloch; *Keeper's Companion*, Herber (C); "Books of the Cthulhu Mythos", Herber and Ross (C); *Spawn of Azathoth*, Herber (C); "The Caller of the Black", Lumley.)

CULTUS MALEFICARUM (also *THE SUSSEX MANUSCRIPT*). Partial translation of the Latin *Necronomicon*, made by a Baron Frederic of Sussex and published in 1597 in an octavo edition.

See *Necronomicon* (Appendices). (*The Sussex Manuscript*, Pelton.)

CURWEN, JOSEPH (1662?-1771). Wealthy trader and reputed sorcerer from Providence, Rhode Island. Born in Danvers, Massachusetts, Curwen went to sea at an early age. Having returned to Salem after several years, he was forced to leave at the beginning of the great witchcraft panic. He then took up residence in Providence, where he lived for the rest of his life.

Curwen quickly became one of Providence's most powerful merchants, bringing the colony great wealth from his overseas trade. Despite this, he was not highly thought of by his fellow townspeople, who spread rumors about disappearances seemingly connected with him, as well as the mysterious cargo brought to his house and a Pawtuxet farm in which he had set up a laboratory. Others whispered about the advanced age which Curwen had reached without any physical signs of deterioration.

Curwen married Eliza Tillinghast in 1763, and the couple had a daughter, Ann, two years later. While at first his alliance to one of Providence's most influential families brought Curwen some public acceptance, the old rumors began again soon thereafter. By 1770, it was clear that Curwen was indeed performing some sort of illegal acts, and a committee of Providence's most powerful men met to decide what action should be taken. On April 12, 1771, a party of raiders led by this committee marched on Curwen's Pawtuxet farm. What exactly happened during the raid is unclear, but following this action Joseph Curwen was seen no more.

See *Liber Damnatus Damnationum, Necronomicon* (Appendices), *Reflections*. ("The Case of Charles Dexter Ward", Lovecraft.)

CXAXUKLUTH. Androgynous spawn of Azathoth who was the progenitor of both Hziulquoigmnzhah and Ghisguth, who was in turn Tsathoggua's father. He and his children dwelt on Yuggoth for a while, but his companions soon left him on account of his cannibalistic tendencies.

See Ghisguth, Hziulquoigmnzhah, Yuggoth. ("Some Observations on the Carter Glossary", Cockcroft.)

CYAEGHA. Great Old One appearing as a great black mass with one red eye at the center. Cyaegha is a god of the caverns and darkness. He sleeps for centuries on end, but when he is awakened his wrath is terrible.

Beginning in the 17th century, Cyaegha was worshiped in the small German town of Freihausgarten. According to the cult Cyaegha dwelt beneath the Dark Hill near the town, where all the townspeople journeyed to worship him. Cyaegha seemed to exert some sort of hypnotic control over the people; they came unfailingly to his rites, but afterward could remember nothing of what had happened. Around the year 1860, however, a young priest came to Freihausgarten and broke up the cult.

Although Cyaegha's cult ostensibly serves the Great Old One, in fact its members are dedicated to keeping their god imprisoned so that they might draw upon his power and vitality in their rites. To help in keeping Cyaegha immobile, the people use five guardian spirits known as vaeyen, who not only protect Cyaegha but act as his jailers as well.

See elemental theory, nagaae, Othuyeg, Vach-Viraj Incantation, vaeyen. ("Darkness, My Name Is", Bertin.)

CYKRANOSH. The planet Saturn, as it was known in Mhu Thulan. Tsathoggua and Atlach-Nacha came to Earth from Cykranosh, and Tsathoggua's paternal uncle Hziulquoigmnzhah still resides there. When the priests of Yhoundeh came to capture Eibon, that wizard made his escape through a magical portal to Cykranosh.

("The Door to Saturn", Smith; *The Philosopher's Stone*, C. Wilson.)

CYNOTHOGLYS. 1) Deity which appears as a formless mound topped with an arm-like appendage. Cynothoglys is the god of transformation and death. If properly supplicated, Cynothoglys may provide his supplicant with whatever death he may desire. This death will not necessarily take place immediately, but its eventual coming is certain. ("The Prodigy of Dreams", Ligotti.)

2) Book which may contain prayers or information on the Mortician God. ("Vastarien", Ligotti.)

47

D

DAEMONIGRAPHIA. Slim volume published in colonial times containing a New England churchman's account of demons which walk in disguise among humanity. This volume provides useful information on detecting and unmasking these spirits for the good of the community.

("With Malice Afterthought", Anderson and Lehmann (C).)

DAGON. Fish god worshiped by the Canaanites and adopted by the Philistines. Dagon has been connected with both agriculture and marine life, and may have been revered in order to bring fruitful harvests for both the farmer and the fisherman. It was the temple of Dagon, according to the Bible, which Samson brought down upon his tormentors (Judges 16:23). Later, when the Ark of the Covenant was left in the temple of Dagon, the statue of that deity was mutilated (1 Samuel 5:2). Legend has it that the Phoenicians came to power through the influence of Dagon and his minions, and that the end of their supremacy came when they turned away from him to other gods.

Dagon plays a minor yet important role in the Cthulhu Mythos. In these texts he appears as a deep one of tremendous proportions, and is worshiped by deep ones and some coastal dwellers alongside his mate, Mother Hydra. One of his cults, the Esoteric Order of Dagon in Innsmouth, Massachusetts, was raided by government agents in 1927 due to reports of strange disappearances and illegal activities in that town.

See *Book of Dagon*, deep one, elemental theory, Esoteric Order of Dagon, Hydra, *Invocations to Dagon*, Lesser Old Ones, Oaths of Dagon, *Ponape Scripture*, Yhe. ("Dagon", Lovecraft; "The Shadow Over Innsmouth", Lovecraft; "The Return of the Deep Ones", Lumley.)

DAOLOTH. Being also known as the Render of the Veils. Daoloth appears as a shapeless mass of color surrounded by plastic-like rods, between which eyes seem to peer at the viewer.

The seers of Atlantis held Daoloth in especial esteem, and the Render of the Veils is still worshiped by the inhabitants of Yuggoth and Tond. Daoloth may bestow the ability to view the past and future upon his worshipers, as well as allowing them to perceive higher dimensions.

A person who desires to call Daoloth must wait until a cosmically significant time, and should also hold an image of Daoloth, an object which exists nowhere on this planet. When Daoloth is summoned, the Render of the Veils should be contained within the Pentacle of Planes and allowed to taste a small amount of the caster's blood. Daoloth will then perform one service for the wizard before returning to his home. Daoloth can give the summoner insight into the nature of the universe, though this often drives the receiver mad.

See Outer Gods, Pentacle of Planes, *Revelations of Glaaki*, Saaamaaa Ritual, *We Pass from View*. ("The Render of the Veils", Campbell.)

DARK ANGEL'S KISS. Book of poems by an unknown author which alludes to Cthulhu and his kindred.

("The Secret of Castronegro", Petersen and Pettigrew (C).)

DARK HAN. See Han.

DARK YOUNG OF SHUB-NIGGURATH. Creatures said to be the spawn of the Outer God. They have tremendous black bodies with many thick tentacles sprouting from their tops, and hoofed feet supporting their masses. Shub-Niggurath's children normally dwell only in forests where cults of that deity meet.

Dark young may be summoned by a ceremony in *Book of Eibon*. According to that tome, the caller must wait until the dark of the moon, and then make a blood sacrifice on a stone altar deep within the woods. Only then will the dark young come forth to accept the offering.

See Shub-Niggurath. ("Notebook Found in a Deserted House", Bloch; "Mr. Skin", Milan; *Call of Cthulhu* rulebook, Petersen *et al.* (C).)

DAVENPORT, ELI. Folklorist who was responsible for an 1839 monograph detailing some of the legends of Vermont. The monograph focused on certain legends of the mountain people of the region, which suggested that a race of crustacean-like beings dwelt beneath the mountains of the region.

("The Whisperer in Darkness", Lovecraft.)

DAVIES, CHANDLER. Noted British weird painter, connoisseur of horror fiction, and friend of Titus Crow. Davies' work in the field of horrific art remains unparalleled, with his most famous work being "Stars and Faces", printed in *Grotesque* magazine and now considered a collector's item. Nevertheless, Davies is best remembered for the events which took place in the last days of his life. In May of 1962 the artist, working in a feverish trance-state, completed an arrangement in black and grey which he entitled "G'harne Landscape." His mistress set fire to the painting immediately thereafter, sending Davies into a frenzy of rage. He was committed to Woodholme Sanitorium, where he died several days later.

(*The Burrowers Beneath*, Lumley; "The Fairground Horror", Lumley; "An Item of Supporting Evidence", Lumley; "Rising with Surtsey", Lumley.)

DE MARIGNY, ETIENNE-LAURENT. New Orleans mystic and expert on Eastern antiques, known for his work *The Tarot: A Treatise* and his translation of *Seven Cryptical Books of Hsan*. (The de Marigny family name goes back for centuries in French history; in fact, a court official named Enguerrand de Marigny was executed on trumped-up charges of sorcery in 1315.) He served in the French Foreign Legion during World War I, where he made the acquaintance of Randolph Carter. An expedition into the tunnels beneath the town of Bayonne brought them even closer together, and they maintained their friendship up until Carter's disappearance in 1928. De Marigny was appointed the executor of his estate, and during the settlement of the estate became involved in a scandal when, at the meeting held to apportion Carter's property, the Carter family's lawyer died and a Hindu mystic who had been asked to attend vanished. The exact facts behind this case are still unknown.

Later de Marigny became involved in the Coffin Club, a group of magical adepts based in New Orleans which was dissolved shortly after the death of its founder, Henricus Vanning. In 1940 de Marigny's translation of *Seven Cryptical Books of Hsan* was published by Silver Key Press of Boston. The exact date of his death is unknown, but some dreamers say that de Marigny rejoined his friend Randolph Carter in the city of Ilek-Vad following his demise.

See Carter, Randolph; Chandraputra, Swami; Dreamlands; Hiamaldi, Yogi; *Seven Cryptical Books of Hsan*; time-clock; Yian-Ho. ("The Secret of Sebek", Bloch; "Through the Gates of the Silver Key", Lovecraft and Price; *Clock of Dreams*, Lumley; "Lord of the Worms", Lumley; "Typo", Winkle.)

DE MARIGNY, HENRI-LAURENT (1923-1980?). Son of Etienne-Laurent de Marigny and a famous occultist in his own right. During the late 1930's, when only a boy, Henri was sent by his father to England, where he made the acquaintance of Titus Crow, a mystic who would later enjoy worldwide acclaim and notoriety. The two were virtually inseparable, and de Marigny often accompanied Crow on his forays into occult investigation.

In the 1960's de Marigny and Crow became embroiled in the ongoing investigation of Britain's Mythos horrors by the Wilmarth Foundation. The two took an active part in the battle against the cthonians and their kin, and served for a time as the heads of the Foundation's English branch. Their actions were taken note of by the opposition, and on October 4, 1969, de Marigny was present at Blowne Manor, Crow's residence on Leonard's-Walk Heath, when a freak windstorm destroyed that place.

Though neither his nor Crow's remains were found in the ruins, de Marigny was pronounced dead. Then on September 4, 1979, a boater discovered Henri clinging desperately to a buoy in the Thames, with all of his limbs broken and no recollection of how he had spent the last ten years. On March 11, 1980, de Marigny vanished again, leaving behind a letter to Wingate Peaslee, the director of the Wilmarth Foundation, the contents of which are known only to the members of the Foundation.

See Crow, Titus; time-clock. (*The Burrowers Beneath*, Lumley; "Name and Number", Lumley; *The Transition of Titus Crow*, Lumley.)

DE VERMIS MYSTERIIS (also *MYSTERIES OF THE WORM*). Book written by Ludvig Prinn circa 1542. Just before the author's death at the hands of the Inquisition, this volume was smuggled out of his cell; the persons responsible for this remain unknown.

One year following its author's death, a Latin edition of *De Vermis Mysteriis* was published in Cologne. This is considered to be the sole truly reliable printing of this manuscript. Much of the original volume was written not in Latin, but in characters which resemble the runic alphabets of the Celts. It may be that Prinn came upon a copy of the druidic rituals which were preserved by the Roman scribes, or possibly the "runes" are part of a cipher used by Prinn to disguise certain portions of his manuscript.

At a later date a black-letter German translation was also published; this edition, however, is of less use to the scholar, as much of the material contained in the Latin edition was expurgated. During the 19th century a certain "Clergyman X" published a heavily expurgated English pamphlet delineating the contents of the book's most famous chapter,

"Saracenic Rituals", but due to certain omissions it is almost useless to the serious scholar. A Mr. Charles Leggett translated the book into English and published it in 1821, in a very limited edition illustrated by woodcuts from the original Latin. However, this book is not considered as valuable as the Latin edition.

Copies of *De Vermis Mysteriis* may be found at the Huntington Library in California and in the vaults of Miskatonic University. The British Museum possesses a complete German edition as well as half of the original Latin, though the latter is in very poor condition. A Latin copy was kept at one time in the now-deserted town of Jerusalem's Lot, Massachusetts, but it probably disappeared with that town's inhabitants in 1789.

De Vermis Mysteriis is divided into sixteen chapters, each dealing with a different topic such as divination, familiars, necromancy, elementals, and vampires. Probably the most famous chapter, though, deals with the rituals of the Saracens, from whom Prinn had learned during his imprisonment after the Crusades. Spells to call down invisible monsters from the skies are also held within this volume, along with tales of Byatis and the worm-wizards of Irem, the true nature of the Egyptian crocodile god Sebek, the formula of the drug known as Liao, and a series of operations intended to speed the transformation of a human-deep one hybrid.

See Azathoth; Bast; Blake, Robert Harrison; Byatis; Chorazin; Feery, Joachim; Han; Jerusalem's Lot; Magnum Innominandum; Nephren-Ka; Nyarlathotep; Prinn, Ludvig; "Saracenic Rituals". ("The Secret of Sebek", Bloch; "The Shambler from the Stars", Bloch; "The Survivor", Derleth and Lovecraft; "Jerusalem's Lot", King; "The Invaders", Kuttner; "Lord of the Worms", Lumley; "Signs Writ in Scarlet", Ross (C.).)

DEATH-WALKER. See Ithaqua.

DEEP DENDO. Place where "wicked voorish domes" may be found, and whose people may help a wizard who appeals to them properly. This place might be part of the fabled land of Voor.

("Something in the Moonlight", Carter; "The White People", Machen.)

DEEP ONE. Fish-like humanoid being that worships Dagon, Hydra, and Cthulhu, though this name may also be applied to other aquatic creatures which worship the Great Old Ones. Some believe that the deep ones came to Earth at the same time Cthulhu and his kin arrived, but others in direct contact with these amphibious creatures believe that they evolved upon this planet. Most deep ones look much like bipedal frogs, with scaly skin, bulging eyes, gills, and webbed hands and feet. Communication between deep ones seems to be telepathic in nature, though they may also convey meaning to their human agents through croaking noises.

These creatures are immortal, never dying except from acts of violence. Because of these great life spans, the deep ones have become scientists and priests of great ability. Over the course of its life, a deep one continues to grow; Father Dagon and Mother Hydra, the leaders of the race, may only be the two largest and oldest of the race. Prolonged starvation may cause the deep one to shrink until it is only a tiny fraction of its former size, but the famished creature will never die from its condition.

Deep ones dwell beneath the world's oceans in cities built of stone and decorated with mother-of-pearl coating. These metropoli, which may be found in all major seas of the world, include Y'ha-nthlei off the coast of Massachusetts, Ahu-Y'hloa near Cornwall, and G'll-Hoo in the North Sea. Activity within these cities is quite coordinated; each deep one carries out what is necessary for the community without question. Though this race is highly individualistic, dissent among deep ones is virtually unknown. The deep ones worship Great Cthulhu as well as Dagon and Hydra; some also revere Byatis and others of the Great Old Ones, but Cthulhu's cult is definitely the most popular among them.

For the most part, the deep ones remain apart from humanity. Chance meetings do occur, however. Some of these encounters have given rise to sailors' tales of "mermaids" and other people of the ocean, such as the adaro sea-spirits feared by the Solomon Islanders. Sometimes deep ones establish cults among coast dwellers that have contacted them through accident or by dropping specially inscribed tablets into the ocean. The most famous of these sects was the Esoteric Order of Dagon, which was destroyed in the government raid on Innsmouth, Massachusetts in 1928. Other outbreaks have occurred throughout the world, though Polynesia is the major center of the deep ones' worship.

A major part of the rites of the human-deep one cults is the mating between the two races. The children who result from these unions appear to be normal humans, but after many years they undergo a metamorphosis into deep ones, diving down into the ocean to join their kindred. The effects of this change vary widely between individuals; the length of time the transformation takes is different for every sufferer. Some never complete the transition between human and deep one; others, affected in their mother's wombs by Cthulhu's dreams, become monstrosities resembling neither of their parent races. The transformation may possibly be accelerated by proximity to the ocean or other deep ones; drugs and certain surgical procedures given in Prinn's *De Vermis Mysteriis* have also been used. A transformation into a deep one may also take place in dolphins as well as humans, but the evidence for this is scanty.

See Ahu-Y'hloa, *Book of Dagon*, Byatis, Dagon, *De Vermis Mysteriis*, *Dwellers in the Depths*, *Fischbuch*, Ghadamon, G'll-hoo, Hydra, Lesser Old Ones, mapulo, Nameless City, Oaths of Dagon, Shining Trapezohedron, shoggoth, shoggoth-tshwa, *Unter Zee Kulten*, Yatta-Uc, Y'ha-nthlei. ("The Room in the Castle", Campbell; "The Shuttered Room", Derleth and Lovecraft; "The Survivor", Derleth and Lovecraft; "The Songs of Fantari", Detwiler and Isinwyll (C); "The Shadow Over Innsmouth", Lovecraft; *The Burrowers Beneath*, Lumley; "The Return of the Deep Ones", Lumley; *S. Petersen's Field Guide to Cthulhu Monsters*, Petersen (C); *Escape from Innsmouth*, Ross (C); "The City in the Sea", Thomas and Willis (C); "The Deep Ones", Wade.)

DEMHE. Region whose "cloudy depths" are mentioned in references to Hastur and the King in Yellow. The city of Alar may stand on this shore.

("More Light", Blish; "The Repairer of Reputations", Chambers.)

DERBY, EDWARD PICKMAN (1890?-1932?). Poet whose best-known work is *Azathoth and Other Horrors*. Derby grew up in Arkham, and was admitted to Miskatonic University at the age of sixteen. When he was eighteen he published *Azathoth and Other Horrors*, a book of poetry which earned him some acclaim.

Following the death of his mother, the poet joined the Bohemian circles of the university, where he may have participated in black magic rituals. It was at one of these gatherings that he met Asenath Waite, a woman from Kingsport and the daughter of the reputed wizard Ephraim Waite. The pair were married a few months after their first encounter, afterward moving into the Crowninshield mansion on the outskirts of Arkham. At first Derby was highly satisfied with the union, but after three years of increasing tension between the two, Asenath disappeared and Edward applied for a divorce. The strain proved too much for him, and Derby was committed to Arkham Sanitarium. After a few months at the institution, he seemed to have almost recovered from his ordeal. Before he could be discharged, though, Daniel Upton, a close friend of the poet, shot his friend in an apparent fit of madness.

See *Azathoth and Other Horrors*; *People of the Monolith*; *Tunneler Below, The*; Waite, Asenath. ("The Thing on the Doorstep", Lovecraft.)

DEVIL'S REEF. Low outcropping just outside the harbor of Innsmouth, Massachusetts. The reef was given this name by Captain John Smith, who landed here during an exploration of the New England coast. Around the middle of the 19th century this place was a favorite location of Captain Obed Marsh, whom the locals said was looking for pirate treasure hidden within the many caverns which dot the top of the reef. Later, Devil's Reef was often visited by Marsh's Esoteric Order of Dagon, until that cult was closed down by Federal agents in 1928. Despite this, most of the local fishermen still refuse to sail anywhere near Devil's Reef.

See Innsmouth, Wilmarth Foundation, Y'ha-nthlei. ("The Shadow over Innsmouth", Lovecraft; *Escape from Innsmouth*, Ross (C).)

DEVIL'S STEPS. Rock formation located to the northeast of Brichester. Erosion has carved this tremendous outcropping into what appears to be a staircase leading up into the sky. No one in memory has climbed this formation, and the place is shunned by the local people.

("The Mine on Yuggoth", Campbell.)

DHO-HNA FORMULA. Formula which allows the user to view the inner city at the two magnetic poles and the ultimate gulf beyond space and time, and possibly other locations. The Dho part of the formula gives the caster a view of the desired location, and the Hna portion gives the caster the power to travel to the location visualized. Sometimes the Hna portion of the formula does not perform correctly; it is possible that it will only work when the Great Old Ones return.

(*The* Necronomicon: *The Book of Dead Names*, Hay, ed.; "The Dunwich Horror", Lovecraft.)

DHOL CHANTS. Burmese book from the Plateau of Leng. Sometime before World War I, Heinrich Zimmerman wrote a volume in German of the same name. Zimmerman wrote his book on the similarities between the music of the Caribbean and that of West Africa. Zimmerman's volume may have incorporated material from the Plateau of Leng or the original *Dhol Chants*, whether the author credited his sources or not.

This book contains five hundred fifty-five different chants, which may be performed by a human voice or a nonfretted stringed instrument, such as a violin. Chants include one used in the worship of Ahtu, a form of Nyarlathotep, and others which are used to command spirits. The title of this book implies that it might also deal with those beings known as dholes.

See Leng, Nyarlathotep (Ahtu). ("The Horror in the Museum", Heald and Lovecraft; "Dead of Night", Herber (C); "Yohk the Necromancer", Myers.)

DHOLE (also DOEL or DHOL, possibly BHOLE). 1) A creature which resembles a huge white worm with an open cavity at one end that serves as a mouth. From this cavity, the dhole may spit a huge quantity of mucus that engulfs anything it touches.

Whenever dholes arrive upon a world (some suggest that dholes are the spawn of the Dreamland beings known as bholes, who send their children elsewhere through wormholes), they tunnel through the world until nothing else can inhabit that world. Not even the mighty sorceries of the people of Yaddith could save their world from these mighty beasts. Luckily for Earth, there have been no reported sightings of an active dhole on this planet.

In the earlier copies of *Book of Eibon*, there was a formula for the calling of dholes to Earth. Fortunately, the last edition to contain this ritual was the Egyptian, of which all copies have been lost.

It has been said that dholes have the ability to follow those who escape them through their dreams and various incarnations, but no one knows how these beasts may use this power. The dholes might also be the servitors of Shub-Niggurath. See *Book of Eibon, Dhol Chants, Ghorl Nigral*, Nug-Soth, Shub-Niggurath, Yaddith, Zkauba. ("Dreams in the House of Weir", Carter; "The Lambton Worm", Hatherly, *TUO5* (C); "Sands of Time", Herber (C); "Through the Gate of the Silver Key", Lovecraft and Price; "The White People", Machen; *S. Petersen's Field Guide to Cthulhu Monsters*, Petersen (C).)

2) Another type of being known as a "dhol" exists. This creature looks like a black quadrupedal animal which is able to secrete poison from its body. Usually, however, a dhol possesses a living creature, such as a farm animal or even a human, to perform its mission. A dhol-possessed being becomes extremely hostile, may attack or kill other creatures for no apparent reason, and may even have a poisoned claw or bite. Whenever it desires, the dhol may move from one body to another, leaving its former host dead. This sort of dhol may be connected with the Little People of Welsh legend, and is believed to play a role in their most important ceremonies. See *Green Book*. (*The Ceremonies*, Klein; "The White People", Machen.)

DHORIC SHRINE. Temple of Ghatanothoa at which the king of Kn'aa in the land of Mu worshiped.

See Ghatanothoa, Kn'aa. ("Out of the Aeons," Heald and Lovecraft.)

DIRKA. Family of magical adepts whose history dates back to the dawn of humanity. They are said to have translated the mystical book *Song of Yste*.

See *Song of Yste*. ("The Abyss", Lowndes.)

DREAMLANDS. Alternate dimension accessible through a person's dreams. Early in life most people can enter the Dreamlands at will, but as adulthood approaches, this gateway closes for the majority of dreamers. Only a few adults have been able to enter this land again, through the use of certain narcotics or simply by dedicated dreaming. Some physical portals between the Dreamlands and the waking world do exist, but these gateways are few and are often found in dangerous locales in both realms.

A journey to the Dreamlands typically begins with the dreamer descending the Seventy Steps of Light Slumber to the Cavern of Flame, where he will meet the high priests Nasht and Kaman-Tha. If the two priests find the dreamer worthy, he may then continue down the Seven Hundred Steps of Deeper Slumber to the Enchanted Wood. After avoiding the dangers of this wood, the dreamer is free to roam the lands of dream.

Waking-worlders are the Dreamlands' greatest heroes. These individuals may create entire cities in their dreams, and many have taken up residence in the Dreamlands following their deaths in the waking world. This dimension's most famous individuals include King Kuranes, who dreamt of the timeless city of Celephais; Etienne-Laurent de Marigny, the New Orleans mystic; and Randolph Carter, whose quest to the home of the gods on unknown Kadath is one of the Dreamlands' greatest legends.

Usually, the name "Dreamlands" is only applied to that dimension visited by humans, but other dreamlands do exist. Such worlds as Saturn, Jupiter, and Pluto have their dream-reflections as well, which are visited by the respective denizens of those bodies. These lands can be reached from Earth's Dreamlands by persistent dreamers, but such visits may prove quite dangerous to the unprepared traveller.

The influence of Cthulhu and the other Great Old Ones in the Dreamlands is minimal, though these beings do possess some power over this realm. Out of all the Mythos, Nyarlathotep holds the most power in this land. The main deities of the Dreamlands are the Great Ones, or the gods of Earth, weak beings easily overcome or outwitted by mortals, yet who do take part in mortal affairs fairly often. These gods used to dance on the highest peaks of the Dreamlands, but as humans began to climb their beloved mountains, they withdrew to their home in Kadath in the Cold Waste, to be ruled by Nyarlathotep. Only Randolph Carter ever ascended Kadath, and his journey was fraught with the greatest perils.

See Atal; Barzai; Bokrug; Bethmoora; Carter, Randolph; Cathuria; Celephais; Cold Waste; Crystallizer of Dreams; *Cthaat Aquadingen*; de Marigny, Etienne-Laurent; dhole; Dylath-Leen; Elder Gods; Enchanted Wood; Fly-the-Light; *Fourth Book of D'harsis*; Ghadamon; ghast; ghoul; Great Ones; gug; Haon-Dor; Hatheg-Kla; Ilek-Vad; Inganok; Kadath in the Cold Waste; Koth; Leng; Lomar; Nasht and Kaman-tha; Nodens; Nyarlathotep; Oorn; Ooth-Nargai; Other Gods; Pickman, Richard Upton; Pnath; Sansu; shantak; Sign of Koth; Skai; *Synarchobiblaron*; Tanarian Hills; Ulthar; Yibb-Tstll. ("Celephais", Lovecraft; "The Dream-Quest of Unknown Kadath", Lovecraft; *The Clock of Dreams*, Lumley; "The House of the Worm", Myers; "The Three Enchantments", Myers.)

DREAMS OF THE CIRCLE. Volume written by Hassan ibn Abbas, a student of the famous mathematician al Kashi, in 1456. He describes a trip across the Arabian desert in which he encountered bandits and lost all his water. In his delirium, he stumbled upon the city of Irem. While there he heard voices emanating from the tallest tower of the City of a Thousand Pillars. *Dreams of the Circle* is an account of what was revealed to him by the voices, as well as their pertinence to his own mathematical researches. The book concludes with a listing of pi to one thousand decimal places, the calculation of which was accomplished by the incantations contained within the book.

See Irem. ("What Goes Around, Comes Around", Moeller, *TU08/9* (C).)

DROMOS. One of the moons of Borea. At one time Dromos had a high level of volcanic activity, but Ithaqua used his command of the winds and temperature to snuff the fires of these peaks. To aid him in this endeavor he enlisted the ice priests of Khrissa millions of years ago. These mighty wizards, possibly the only living creatures on this satellite, still dwell within the cone of Dromos' largest volcano.

See Borea, Khrissa. (*In the Moons of Borea*, Lumley.)

DU NORD, GASPARD. Wizard who dwelt in Averoigne, a part of modern-day France, during the 13th century. Born of a fairly well-to-do family, du Nord earned his father's displeasure through his study of the magical arts. For a year he studied under the sorcerer Nathaire, but he eventually left his master due to the repugnant acts Nathaire was committing. He then took up residence in the cathedral town of Vyones, where he continued his experiments. In 1232 du Nord rendered Vyones a great service by dispelling one of Nathaire's mightiest works of sorcery. By doing so he earned himself immunity from any persecution by the church, and was able to live peacefully in Vyones until his death.

Du Nord is best remembered for translating *Book of Eibon* from Greek to French. No one knows where he obtained the Greek volume or why he decided to translate it, however.

See *Book of Eibon, Selections de* Livre d'Ivon. ("The Colossus of Ylourgne", Smith; "Ubbo-Sathla", Smith.)

DUNWICH. 1) (Originally NEW DUNNICH) Town located in north central Massachusetts, a few miles west of Aylesbury. Dunwich was founded in 1692 by a group of settlers who left Salem just before the infamous witch trials. Members of the Whateley family later built a large number of mills in the area, and Dunwich prospered until a tragedy in 1806 caused the mental collapse of George Whateley, the owner of these industries. From that time onward the Dunwich economy spiralled downward as more and more people left the area to look for jobs outside the town.

Today Dunwich is mostly deserted. Over the years the remaining population has become so inbred and degenerate that during World War I the township was unable to meet its quota for the draft. Crimes of the most hideous nature have been known to occur on a regular basis, though the townspeople attempt to keep outsiders out of their affairs as much as possible. Some branches of the Whateleys and Bishops have remained above the town's degradation, but for the most part the people of Dunwich are uneducated and depraved.

During the late summer of 1928, a strange calamity occurred in Dunwich. On August 3 a Dunwich resident named Wilbur Whateley, noted by his neighbors for his magical delvings and preternatural size, was killed while trying to obtain *Necronomicon* from the Miskatonic University library. A month later the horror began in Dunwich; Wilbur Whateley's unoccupied house was destroyed by a mysterious blast, and tales of the disappearances of cattle and people began to filter out of the township. When Henry Armitage, Miskatonic University's librarian and a long-time correspondent of Whateley, heard of what was occurring in Dunwich, he journeyed to the town, along with Professors Rice and Morgan, to perform an exorcism of sorts. They performed this ceremony on September 15, bringing the horror to an end. Following these events all of the signs to Dunwich were torn down, and the town was nearly forgotten by the outside world.

Although the scenery in the surrounding countryside is breathtaking, there is little else to attract the casual visitor to Dunwich. The village is known to scholarly types for the stone circles which top many of the nearby hills, as well as the mysterious noises heard around Walpurgis and Hallowe'en. See Armitage, Henry; Billington, Richard; Miskatonic River. ("The Lurker at the Threshold", Derleth and Lovecraft; *Return to Dunwich*, Herber (C); "The Dunwich Horror", Lovecraft.)

2) Town in the Flint Hills of Kansas. Dunwich was founded in 1833 by settlers from the original Dunwich. They were led by the Reverend Ezekiel O'Sullivan, who had received a vision of a golden city to the west. The townspeople of Dunwich avoided most of the nearby communities, and the town took a neutral stance during the Civil War. In 1893, the entire population of Dunwich vanished over the space of a few days. ("The Seven Cities of Gold", Burnham.)

DWELLER IN DARKNESS. See Nyarlathotep (Dweller in Darkness).

DWELLERS IN THE DEPTHS. Book on Cthulhu and his minions written by Gaston Le Fe who, according to the book's introduction, died insane. It was later published in both French and English editions.

This book details the race of aquatic beings known as deep ones, and hints at the monstrous entities which they often worship.

See deep one. ("The Aquarium", Carl Jacobi.)

DYER, WILLIAM. Professor of geology at Miskatonic University. Dyer is especially remembered for his leadership of the University's 1930-31 Pabodie Expedition to Antarctica, as well as his role in the 1935 trip to the prehuman ruins in the deserts of Australia.

See Pabodie Expedition; Peaslee, Nathaniel; Starkweather-Moore Expedition. ("At the Mountains of Madness", Lovecraft; "The Shadow Out of Time", Lovecraft.)

DYLATH-LEEN. Basalt city located on the shore of the Dream-lands' Southern Sea. Dylath-Leen is unpopular with its neighbors due to the mysterious black galleys which dock there to sell their cargoes of rubies.

("The Dream-Quest of Unknown Kadath", Lovecraft.)

E

EIBON. Ancient prehuman sorcerer who wrote *Book of Eibon*. Eibon lived in Hyperborea on the peninsula of Mhu Thulan, where he cast many great magics. He derived much of this power from a pact with Tsathoggua, whom he worshiped in return for greater magical ability. The great wizard once penetrated the caverns beneath Mount Voormithadreth to see his master sleeping on his throne. Another Hyperborean tale tells how Eibon looked through a magical viewing portal to the future to see Earth being destroyed by some huge celestial body. His response was to construct two great webs across space in which to trap the entity. Then he planned to temporally freeze the entire planet of Earth, so that it would never know destruction. These accounts have possibly been exaggerated; even so, Eibon was one of the greatest sorcerers who ever walked this planet.

Two contradictory tales are associated with Eibon's end. According to the first, Eibon's tower exploded one star-lit night; *Book of Eibon* was found in the ruins, but the great magician's body was never recovered. The more commonly accepted account, though, relates that Eibon fled from the persecution of the priests of Yhoundeh through a door made of a mysterious metal, and emerged on the planet Saturn.

See *Book of Eibon*; Cykranosh; Haon-Dor; Hyperborea; *Life of Eibon*; Mhu Thulan; Pharol; Ring of Eibon; Rlim Shaikorth; Sign of Eibon; Sign of Koth; Voormithadreth, Mount; Yhoundeh. ("Tsathoggua", Carter; *Spawn of Azathoth*, Herber (C); "The Coming of the White Worm", Smith; "The Door to Saturn", Smith.)

EIHORT. Great Old One known as the God of the Labyrinth. Eihort is a huge white oval mass with innumerable legs and eyes. Eihort lives in a maze beneath an abandoned house in Camside, England, but can create gates that lead to other parts of the world.

When a person visits Eihort, it contacts him telepathically and asks if he wishes to be its servant. If the unfortunate answers no, Eihort crushes him. If the victim says yes, Eihort paralyzes him and channels immature members of its brood into him. Since this process includes a form of hypnosis, the person may not remember what happened upon waking. At first an infested person acts normally, but then begins to have visions of horrific alien events. After a while these visions increase in intensity and duration, until finally the Bargainer bursts open, with hundreds of Eihort's small spawn emerging and running away. For obvious reasons, few people now make the Bargain with Eihort.

A curious reference to Eihort may be found in the book *We Pass from View*, which served as the scripture for a small cult in Brichester led by its author, Roland Franklyn. According to this self-styled prophet, an initiate of his cult must be cremated so that the person's soul can escape. Otherwise, if the initiate is buried, the soul will remain in the body, and burrowing monsters will drag the believer's corpse down beneath the earth to Eihort's feast.

See Camside. ("Before the Storm", Campbell; "The Franklyn Paragraphs", Campbell; "The Pale God", Ross (C.).)

ELDER GODS. According to some scholars, a group of beings opposed to the Great Old Ones. The Elder Gods supposedly live somewhere near Betelgeuse, or in an alternate dimension known as Elysia. At some point in the past, the Great Old Ones "rebelled" against the Elder Gods, taking certain documents from the possession of their foes. In retribution for this affront, the Elder Gods came to Earth and battled with the Great Old Ones. This war concluded with the imprisonment of the Great Old Ones and the return of the Elder Gods to their homes. Many consider this to be merely speculation, but others hold that the Elder Gods, including Nodens, Kthanid, and Yag-Thaddag, will return to combat their ancient foes when the stars are right again.

One divergent theory should be noted here. Some say that the Elder Gods are in fact the Great Ones, the little gods of Earth which rule the Dreamlands. These beings came into existence during the sleep of the Great Old Ones. Finding the Old Ones in their tombs, the Elder Gods were terrified, sealed the tombs of the evil ones with the Elder Sign, and consigned their care to Nodens, Lord of the Great Abyss. When the time comes for Nodens to sleep, then the seals on the tombs may be broken and the Great Old Ones may emerge to rule the world.

See Atal, Borea, Celaeno, Cthugha, Elder Sign, Elysia, *Fourth Book of D'harsis*, Glyu-Uho, Great Old Ones, Great Ones, Kthanid, Nodens, Rigel, star-stone of Mnar, time-clock, Ubbo-Sathla, Ulthar, Ultharathotep, Yag-Thaddag, Zathog. (*The Lurker at the Threshold*, Derleth and Lovecraft; *The Trail of Cthulhu*, Derleth; *Elysia*, Lumley; "The House of the Worm", Myers.)

ELDER SIGN (also SARNATH-SIGIL, SIGN OF KISH, and STAR-STONE OF MNAR). Magical symbol which may have been created by the Elder Gods or possibly the Elder Things. The Elder Sign usually is drawn as a star with an eye in the center, with a pillar of flame where the pupil should be. Other versions, including one resembling an eye in a pentagon and a sign made with the hand, are lesser known variants which may or may not substitute for the more traditional design.

The Elder Sign protects its user from the minions of the Great Old Ones. Why this glyph has the effects it does can only be conjectured. As the Elder Gods thrust the Great Old Ones into their prisons, they might have inserted certain memory patterns into their foes' minds that rendered the Great Old Ones helpless against certain syllables and sigils, of which the Elder Sign was one. One of these signs is carved on the doorway of Cthulhu's tomb, and Shudde-M'ell and his cthonians were imprisoned in G'harne by large quantities of stones engraved with this symbol.

The degree to which the Elder Sign will protect a human wielder against a Mythos creature is debatable. Some say it will protect him from even human servants of the Mythos, others from the non-human followers of the Great Old Ones only, and still others hold that it provides no personal defense at all.

One reference cites the Elder Sign as setting free the imprisoned beings of darkness. The meaning of this is unclear, though, and may refer to another design entirely.

See Castro Manuscript, cthonian, Elder Gods, G'harne, Mnar, *Necronomicon* (Appendices), nightgaunt, R'lyeh, Shudde-M'ell, Sign of Kish, star-stone of Mnar, Wilmarth Foundation, Yog-Sothoth, Ythogtha. (*The Lurker at the Threshold*, Derleth and Lovecraft; "Spawn of the Maelstrom", Derleth and Schorer; *The Necronomicon: The Book of Dead Names*, Hay, ed.; "The Messenger", Lovecraft; *Selected letters Vol. 3*, Lovecraft; *The Burrowers Beneath*, Lumley.)

ELDER THINGS (also OLD ONES). Alien creatures whose features included elements of both the animal and the vegetable kingdoms. An

Elder Thing resembled a cylinder which tapered at either end. This cylinder was topped by a starfish-shaped head which bore five eyes at each corner, a set of cilia which enabled the Thing to sense its surroundings without light, and five tubes used for the intake of food. At its base, five muscular tentacles tipped with paddles sprouted. Five sets of tentacles protruded at regular intervals from the central mass, and the creature also possessed five wings, which could retract into the body when not needed. The Elder Things preferred to live beneath the water, but they could dwell on land or fly with equal ease.

The Elder Things came to our planet when it was still quite young, flying here through outer space. They built a great city near the South Pole, and migrated from there to settle the rest of the planet. While performing these feats of colonization they created Ubbo-Sathla, which later became the source of all earthly life, along with a servitor race, the shoggoths. During their heyday these beings fought wars with the mi-go and spawn of Cthulhu who were carving out their own earthly territory, and dealt with an insurrection of their shoggoth servants. Due to these defeats the Elder Things were eventually pushed back to their southern cities. Their science and art, however, remained as great as ever.

As the cold crept over their Antarctic home, the Elder Things decided that they wanted no more to do with the outer world. They removed themselves to a vast underground lake beneath their first and greatest city. No traces of them have been discovered since, except possibly the reports of the Pabodie and Starkweather-Moore expeditions.

See Cthulhi, Cthulhu, Elder Sign, *Eltdown Shards*, *G'harne Fragments*, mi-go, Nath, Nyogtha, R'lyeh, Shining Trapezohedron, shoggoth, Spheres of Nath, Ubbo-Sathla, Winged Ones. ("At the Mountains of Madness", Lovecraft.)

ELEMENTAL THEORY. Classification system, first used by the Comte d'Erlette, which links each Great Old One with one of the four elements. These classifications are as follows:

Air: Hastur, Ithaqua, Zhar, Lloigor

Earth: Nyarlathotep, Yog-Sothoth, Shub-Niggurath, Tsathoggua, Cyaegha, Nyogtha

Fire: Cthugha

Water: Cthulhu, Dagon, Hydra, Zoth-Ommog, Ghatanothoa

The whole theory is difficult to understand and apply. For example, if Cthulhu is indeed a water elemental, why is he currently imprisoned under the ocean, where his telepathic signals are blocked by the water?

And how can Yog-Sothoth, the Outer God who is everywhere and nowhere, be connected with any certainty to the element of earth? Also, in alchemy, it was thought that the forces of earth and air opposed each other, as did those of fire and water. In this cosmology, however, the fire beings oppose their counterparts of earth, as the air beings fight those of water. The elemental theory does appear to apply in some cases, but in others its interpretation easily leads to confusion.

("Darkness, My Name Is", Bertin; "Zoth-Ommog", Carter; *The Lurker at the Threshold*, Derleth and Lovecraft.)

ELTDOWN SHARDS. Dubious translation of pottery shards found near Eltdown in southern England. Psychic evidence from Professor Turkoff of Beloin College suggests that the Elder Things inscribed these ceramics and buried them when Great Britain was still part of Panagaea. The shards, which were discovered in a Triassic rock stratum, are inscribed with many strange markings of unknown meaning. The first two scholars to examine the shards, Drs. Woodford and Dalton, hastily pronounced them to be untranslatable. Since the discovery of the shards, however, several manuscripts purported to hold the true secrets of these artifacts have been circulated among certain occult groups. In 1912, the Sussex clergyman Reverend Arthur Brooke Winters-Hall published a thick pamphlet including the results of his own translation. Though the pamphlet was seen as being much too long to be a translation of the relatively small amount of writing found on the shards, it has been quoted in the works of many occult writers since its publication.

In addition to the commonly accepted version of the origin of the shards, there are two "alternate versions." Lin Carter speculates that the original authors of the work were the Great Race of Yith; this is unlikely, since the Great Race's range seems to have been limited to Australia, so that they could not conceivably leave the shards to be discovered in the British Isles. Another theory has it that the shards were discovered in 1903 in Greenland, but this too flies in the face of the evidence.

The libram contains references to such topics as the planet of Yith, from which the Great Race came to Earth, and the entity known as the Warder of Knowledge. It also tells of the colonization attempts made by the beings from Yekub.

See Avaloth, *Pnakotic Manuscripts*, Warder of Knowledge, Yekub. ("Zoth-Ommog", Carter; "The Shadow Out of Time", Lovecraft; "The Challenge from Beyond", Lovecraft *et al.*; "The Warder of Knowledge", Searight.)

ELYSIA. Mythical home of the Elder Gods. Elysia is a seemingly infinite land in which the chosen of the Elder Gods from many different worlds and dimensions may come together and live in harmony. Only those whom the Elder Gods deem worthy may enter Elysia, and the journey there is long and difficult, even with the help of Elysia's lords themselves.

See Elder Gods, lithard, n'hlathi. (*Elysia*, Lumley; *The Transition of Titus Crow*, Lumley.)

EMANATION OF YOTH. Entity probably from the underground cavern of Yoth. A ritual in *Book of Eibon* which requires the blood of a child may be used to call it forth.

See *Book of Eibon*. ("The Man of Stone", Heald and Lovecraft.)

ENCHANTED WOOD. Forest through which a dreamer first enters the Dreamlands. The Enchanted Wood is relatively safe, save for the furry zoogs which inhabit it.

See Dreamlands, zoog. ("The Dream-Quest of Unknown Kadath", Lovecraft.)

EPHIROTH. Land mentioned in connection with the Cthulhu myth cycle.

(*The Burrowers Beneath*, Lumley.)

ESOTERIC ORDER OF DAGON. Cult devoted to the worship of Dagon, Hydra, and Cthulhu. Captain Obed Marsh founded the Order around 1840 in Innsmouth, Massachusetts. Marsh had learned a great deal in Polynesia about Dagon, and the new religion he preached included elements of the native tales intermingled with Holy Scripture and the doctrines of Middle Eastern fertility cults. The Esoteric Order of Dagon drove out all other churches in Innsmouth and set itself up as the only religious center in the community. The Order was decimated in the government raid on Innsmouth in 1928, though other secret branches of this church still exist elsewhere.

See *Book of Dagon*; Dagon; deep one; Devil's Reef; Innsmouth; Marsh, Obed. ("The Shadow Over Innsmouth", Lovecraft; *Escape from Innsmouth*, Ross (C).)

ETHICS OF YGOR. Ancient book written in Latin by an unknown author. *Ethics* gives the meanings of such things as the Magnetic Ring and the Great White Space, and possibly provides a map of the route leading to the latter.

See Great White Space, Magnetic Ring. (*The Great White Space*, Copper.)

EXIOR K'MOOL. One-time apprentice of Mylakhrion and Theem'hdra's third most powerful mage, after his former master and Teh Atht. In his own search for eternal life, he made the same bargain Mylakhrion had made with the Great Old Ones, thinking he could escape his former master's fate. In the end, however, he was overwhelmed when Nyarlathotep came to deal with him personally, destroying the wizard's home and the city of Humquass in the process.

See Mylakhrion, Theem'hdra. (*Elysia*, Lumley; "The Sorcerer's Book", Lumley.)

EYE OF LIGHT AND DARKNESS. Egyptian sigil which may only be created on the night of the full moon. At moonrise, the pupil of the Eye must be filled with the blood of an innocent, and a chant must be maintained by a large group of people until the morning. When properly enchanted, the eye will protect all the land within ten miles from the forces of evil. This sigil may be removed by its makers' enemies, but it requires the discovery of another enchantment individual to each Eye created.

The formula for creating the Eye of Light and Darkness can be found in the fifth of the *Seven Cryptical Books of Hsan*, but a very complete edition of this tome is required.

See *Seven Cryptical Books of Hsan*. ("Shanghai", DiTillio and Willis (C).)

F

FABLE OF NYARLATHOTEP. The history of Nyarlathotep's rise to power, the forgetfulness of his worshipers, and the legend of his eventual return. The high priests of Egypt suppressed this fable, but it has survived until the present nevertheless.

("The Faceless God", Bloch; "The Grinning Ghoul", Bloch.)

FALCON POINT. Outcropping jutting into the Atlantic Ocean a few miles south of Innsmouth, named for the large number of raptors that may be seen there. This place was the home of Enoch Conger before his disappearance, and his ruined house may still be seen there.

("The Fisherman of Falcon Point", Derleth and Lovecraft.)

FANG OF YIG. Beings who have contacted Yig and hope for his favor. In exchange for personal power, they receive telepathic signals from Yig and do his bidding.

("Where a God Shall Tread", Aniolowski (C).)

FEASTER FROM AFAR. Manifestation of Hastur which flies through the air; it looks like a huge, dark, shimmering thing with claw-tipped tendrils. Unlike other avatars, this creature seems to take up long-term residence in a certain area, from which it drives all ordinary animal life. On certain nights, the Feaster comes forth to feed upon anyone brave enough to dwell within its domain.

See Hastur. ("The Feaster from Afar", Brennan.)

FEERY, JOACHIM (?-1934). Son of Baron Kant and noted researcher in matters occult. He published many limited-edition books containing quotes from such works as *Cthaat Aquadingen* and *De Vermis Mysteriis*. His most famous works were his *Notes on the* Necronomicon, *Notes on the* Cthaat Aquadingen, and *A Study of the* Book of Dzyan. Though the author said he had taken his quotes for his books from the original works, there are often many discrepancies between Feery's versions and the originals. When readers called these contradictions to his attention, Feery declared he had gained this "extra" occult knowledge through his dreams. Because of this, his books have been discredited by scholars.

See Kant, Ernst; *Necronomicon* (Appendices); *Notes on the* Cthaat Aquadingen, *Notes on the* Necronomicon, Original *Notes on the* Necronomicon, *Study of the* Book of Dzyan. (*Keeper's Compendium*, Herber (C); "Aunt Hester", Lumley; "The Fairground Horror", Lumley.)

FIRE VAMPIRE. Being resembling thousands of pinpoints of light, or sometimes red flashes of lightning, who serves the Great Old One Cthugha. They dwell with their lord Fthaggua on the planetoid Ktynga, upon which they travel through the cosmos, seeking out intelligent life from which they may draw energy. Fire vampires may also come to Earth when Cthugha is summoned, forming an escort for their ruler.

The attack of a fire vampire is heralded by a flash of crimson lightning; it leaves the victim destroyed by what appears to be spontaneous human combustion. Not only does this attack provide the fire vampire with the energy it requires to survive, it also bestows upon the victorious creature all of the target's memories. Fire vampires seem to possess a hive mentality, so that all other vampires, as well as Fthaggua, gain knowledge whenever someone is killed by the vampires. Using this information, Fthaggua and his minions plot their strategy for subjugating worlds to provide themselves with a ready source of energy.

See Cthugha, Fthaggua, Fthagguans, Ktynga, Lesser Old Ones, T'gaorl. ("Zoth-Ommog", Carter; "Dwellers in Darkness", Derleth; "The Fire-Vampires", Wandrei.)

FISCHBUCH. Book written by Konrad von Gerner and published in 1598. It deals mostly with mundane marine life, but von Gerner also expresses his belief in an aquatic race of beings known as the "deep ones."

See deep one. ("Name and Number", Lumley; "Fischbuchs", Ross, *TUO*1 (C).)

FISHERS FROM OUTSIDE. Creatures from outer space said by the explorer Slauenwite to have built the ruins of Zimbabwe and believed to have some connection to Tsathoggua and Cthulhu. These beings presumably at one time had a great interstellar empire, of which the Zimbabwe cities are only the merest outposts. The Fishers have been connected by some with shantaks, a race of horse-headed birds usually considered to be unintelligent and thought to be native only to the Dreamlands. Whatever the true nature of the Fishers, the natives realize the danger of such places, and shun them whenever possible.

See *Glossina palpalis*, Gol-Goroth, *Remnants of Lost Empires*, Winged Ones. ("The Fishers from Outside", Carter; "Winged Death", Heald and Lovecraft; "The Outpost", Lovecraft.)

FLY-THE-LIGHT. Being from Yuggoth which may be dismissed through prolonged exposure to sunlight, hence its title. On Yuggoth Fly-the-Light was imprisoned within a huge ruby which was taken to Earth's Dreamlands. There, it brought ruin and destruction upon all those who came near it. Fly-the-Light seems to be some sort of vampire, who feeds on the life forces of those around it.

The title "Fly-the-Light" is connected with the Haunter of the Dark, an avatar of Nyarlathotep. Since its powers and abilities are similar, this particular being may actually be the Crawling Chaos.

See Nyarlathotep (Haunter of the Dark). ("City in the Sands", DiTillio and Willis (C); "The Haunter of the Dark", Lovecraft; *Clock of Dreams*, Lumley.)

FLYING POLYP. Species which came to Earth and three other planets in our solar system around six hundred million years ago. Details of this race are sketchy, but they seem to be able to make themselves invisible at will, and are able to control winds in some way not fully understood.

While on this world the flying polyps built great basalt towers in which to live. After a few million years, however, the minds of the conical beings upon which the polyps preyed became inhabited by the Great Race of Yith. The Race struck back against the polyps, using their lightning guns to drive the creatures beneath the ground and afterward sealing off all but a few of the entrances into the caverns.

The flying polyps did not require light to sense their surroundings, so their imprisonment did not unduly affect them. They built their towers in the vast chambers beneath the ground, and awaited the time of their revenge. Fifty million years ago, the opportunity came. The polyps burst forth from the caverns, destroying the cities of the Great Race with their winds and killing every Yithian on this world. The Great Race, however, had already projected their minds forward into the future, so the flying polyps were ultimately unsuccessful in their endeavor.

Following their triumph the polyps returned to their caverns. Since their original defeat, this species had been in decline, and in our own time these creatures are few in number. By the time the Great Race takes up residence in the insectoid intelligences of Earth's future, the flying polyps will be extinct.

See Great Race of Yith. ("The Shadow Out of Time", Lovecraft.)

FOURTH BOOK OF D'HARSIS. Book written by D'harsis, one of the Dreamland's greatest mages. The only known copy is kept in the library of the Temple of the Elder Gods in Ulthar. The *Fourth Book* includes some information on the entity Fly-the-Light and the evil queen Yath-Lhi, and possibly the formula for the Barrier of Naach-Tith.

("A-mazed in Oriab", Lumley; *Clock of Dreams*, Lumley.)

FRANKLYN, ROLAND (?-1967). Leader of a Brichester cult in the late 1960's. Almost nothing is known of his past. It is believed that he attended Brichester Uiversity, but if this is true he was later expelled from that institution. In 1963 he became the head of a small sect of young men in the Brichester area. This cult advocated heavy drug use, and often made journeys to places of occult power in the Severn River Valley. This organization is also believed to have been responsible for the disappearance of Brichester University's copy of *Revelations of Glaaki* around this time.

In January of 1964, Franklyn published his cult's doctrine in the book *We Pass from View*. Most of the copies were stolen shortly after publication, however, so Franklyn's ideas did not receive as great a circulation as he had hoped. Franklyn died on July 3, 1967, and was buried in the Mercy Hill cemetery.

See Brichester, Eihort, Mercy Hill, *We Pass from View*. ("The Franklyn Paragraphs", Campbell; "Behold, I Stand at the Door and Knock", Price.)

FRONTIER GARRISON. Volume written by Lollius Urbicus, a Roman scholar living near present-day York, in 183 A.D. This tome documents many mysterious events that took place during the Roman occupation of Britain, including an explosion a few miles from Urbicus' home and the assault made upon the vicious Yegg-Ha near Hadrian's Wall.

See Yegg-Ha. ("An Item of Supporting Evidence", Lumley; *The Transition of Titus Crow*, Lumley.)

FTHAGGUA. Being which appears as a huge mass of blue-tinged lightning. Fthaggua has dominion over the fire vampires; these beings seem to have a hive mentality, and Fthaggua could be the nerve center of the vampires' mentality.

Fthaggua and his minions dwell upon a comet known as Ktynga, the trajectory and speed of which are controlled by him. The fire vampires travel between the stars on this comet, seeking out worlds inhabited by intelligent beings. Whenever they find such a planet they return at periodic intervals, demanding the sacrifice of thousands of the world's natives to appease their hunger.

The relationship between Fthaggua and Cthugha remains unclear. Cthugha seems to have some control over the fire vampires, but even though some have speculated that Cthugha and Fthaggua are the same, the two entities possess different appearances, and Cthugha is usually thought to be imprisoned somewhere near Fomalhaut. Fthaggua might serve the Great Old One, or could possibly be one of Cthugha's avatars.

See Cthugha, fire vampire, Fthagguans, Ktynga. ("Zoth-Ommog", Carter; "The Fire-Vampires", Wandrei.)

FTHAGGUANS. Fire elementals on which we have little hard information, except that they are more powerful than their brethren fire vampires. They are probably related to Fthaggua, and thus may be his greater servitors; possibly Fthaggua is merely one of this race.

See Fthaggua, Ktynga. (*S. Petersen's Field Guide to Creatures of the Dreamlands*, Petersen (C).)

FUNGI FROM YUGGOTH. See mi-go.

FURNACE OF YEB. Artifact which, according to *Necronomicon*, will emerge near the South Pole in the last days of our planet. The Furnace will aid in clearing off the Earth before the Great Old Ones return.

See Nug and Yeb, Yeb. ("To Clear the Earth", Murray.)

G

GELL-HO. See G'll-Hoo.

GEPH TRANSCRIPTIONS. Book of translations of the writings on the Broken Columns of Geph, probably made with the aid of Gordon Walmsley. The only known copy could be found in the library of British occultist Titus Crow, but others are likely to exist.

See Broken Columns of Geph. ("Name and Number", Lumley.)

GHADAMON. Great Old One who resides beneath a sterile lake in the underworld of the Dreamlands. This being appears as a bluish-brown slimy thing covered by malformed animal heads and orifices. The mi-go's laboratories created Ghadamon and placed him in the vast lake where he still dwells. Ghadamon desires to leave the Dreamlands for the waking world, but must possess a human to do so. After he has made the transition he will be escorted by deep ones to the House of Ghadamon under the sea, where he will feed and grow to be ready for the Great Old Ones' return.

The Spawn of Ghadamon are much like conical, wide-mouthed fish. Ghadamon's lake is full of such creatures. A way supposedly exists in which a dreamer can penetrate the water of the lake and evade the guardians, though no one now knows what this was.

("Pickman's Student", Herber (C).)

G'HARNE. Prehuman city located deep in the jungles of western Africa which, if *G'harne Fragments* is to be believed, has existed since the Triassic period. Beneath this city, native legend has it, the Great Old One Shudde-M'ell and his children, the cthonians, were imprisoned by the Elder Sign until they were freed by meddling shamans and natural disasters. The cult of Nophru-Ka fled to this city after their high priest's death; G'harne was the objective of Sir Wendy-Smith's last expedition, which left the noted archaeologist mentally unstable.

See Brotherhood of the Beast; cthonian; Davies, Chandler; Elder Sign; *G'harne Fragments*; Nophru-Ka, Shudde-M'ell; Wendy-Smith, Amery. (*Fungi From Yuggoth*, Herber (C); *The Burrowers Beneath*, Lumley.)

G'HARNE FRAGMENTS. Volume said to be a translation of certain shards possessed by a little-known African tribe. Where this group originally acquired the shards is unknown; according to the tribe's legends, these prized possessions were merely copied portions of a larger work of great power. Later examination has shown that parts of the document bear some resemblance to the characters in *Pnakotic Manuscripts*, and tests performed upon the originals, which are held at the British Museum, prove that these artifacts have somehow survived since the Triassic period.

In his expedition to the African interior, an explorer named Windrop somehow obtained the fragments from the tribe which owned them. Upon his return to civilization, he found that the curious inscribed dot-patterns could not be equated with the alphabet of any known language. His discovery was not taken seriously, and the explorer's shards became popularly known as "Windrop's Folly."

Sir Amery Wendy-Smith, the noted archaeologist who was the sole surviving member of an expedition to G'harne, became interested in the fragments. He was the first to make a serious effort to translate the fragments, and is known to have made a partial translation of them. It may have been Wendy-Smith who dubbed Windrop's discovery the "G'harne fragments", due to the reference to that city he found when he first broke the fragments' code. No one knows how much of the G'harne fragments Wendy-Smith translated, because his notes were lost in the curious collapse of his house, which caused his death. Some of his work may have survived him, since the noted occultist Titus Crow is known to have had a partial copy of the archaeologist's translation in his library, but this version remains relatively unknown.

The first reputable translation of the G'harne fragments was made in the 1970's by the Wilmarth Foundation. This work was based on the notes of Professor Gordon Walmsley of Goole, who had been ridiculed for his "spoof-notes", which he asserted were a translation of several chapters of this work. *G'harne Fragments*, which may have been written by the Elder Things, contains many references to Shudde-M'ell and his children, as well as a more or less accurate map of the solar system. Many locations mentioned within the book have been identified by some scholars as such sites as Stonehenge and Avebury.

See A'byy; G'harne; Thyoph; Walmsley, Gordon; Wendy-Smith, Amery. (*The Burrowers Beneath*, Lumley; "In the Vaults Beneath", Lumley; "Name and Number", Lumley; *The Transition of Titus Crow*, Lumley.)

GHAST. Bestial creature which is humanoid in shape with hoofed feet, kangaroo-like legs, and a noseless face. It is killed by direct sunlight, but can survive for many hours in illumination of lesser intensity.

Ghasts primarily dwell in the vaults of Zin, but have been known to issue from their homes to attack gugs or ghouls in the Underworld of the Dreamlands. If they are unable to find prey of this sort, they have no qualms about devouring each other. Despite their cannibalistic tendencies, ghasts often band together to raid outside their vaults.

See gyaa-yothn; Yoth; Zin, Vaults of. ("The Dream-Quest of Unknown Kadath", Lovecraft.)

GHATANOTHOA (also GHANTA, G'TANTA, TANOTAH, THAN-THA, GATAN, KAHUANTALOA, or KTAN-TAH). Great Old One who dwelt within the mountain Yaddith-Gho that stood within the now-sunken land of Mu. He had been left there by a colony of the fungi from Yuggoth. The people of Mu made many sacrifices to the god and his priests, fearing that Ghatanothoa would leave his home and seek prey among humanity if he was not placated. The sight of the Great Old One, which was said to petrify anyone who looked upon the god, was especially feared.

In his *Unaussprechlichen Kulten*, Friedrich von Junzt tells the tale of T'yog, the high priest of Shub-Niggurath who opposed Ghatanothoa and his servants. T'yog created a scroll covered with magical writings that would protect the holder from the effects of seeing Ghatanothoa, and resolved to climb the mountain to the god's resting place and confront the horror. Ghatanothoa's jealous priests opposed this and, when they could not prevent him from making his journey, secretly switched his magical scroll for a worthless one. T'yog never returned from his journey to the top of Yaddith-Gho, and his fate remains a mystery.

Due to T'yog's failure to destroy Ghatanothoa, the cult of this Great Old One gained even greater power. Ten thousand years after the high priest's ascent, the high priests finally possessed enough influence to close the temples of all of Mu's other deities. Zanthu, the newly-appointed high priest of Ythogtha, took umbrage at this decree, and unwittingly brought about the continent's destruction when he attempted to summon his own god.

Although the land of Mu sank beneath the ocean, entrapping Ghatanothoa, many branches of his cult still survive. According to von Junzt, traces of such worship have been found in Egypt, Atlantis, K'n-yan, Persia, Babylon, Africa, China, Mexico, and Peru. Most of Ghatanothoa's present-day worship occurs near the Pacific Ocean, beneath which Ghatanothoa is said to still be imprisoned. The god is still blamed for certain natural disasters, such as the offshore earthquake which took place in 1970 near Peru, and his cult hopes for a day when they will be able to free their master from his watery prison.

Along with Ythogtha and Zoth-Ommog, Ghatanothoa is one of the three "sons" of Cthulhu and Idh-yaa spawned near Xoth. Ghatanothoa is also served by the astral race known as the lloigor.

See Cthulhu, Dhoric shrine, elemental theory, Idh-yaa, Kn'aa, K'n-yan, *Legends of the Olden Runes*, Lloigor, Nath-feast, *Ponape Scripture*, T'yog, *Unaussprechlichen Kulten*, *Vatican Codex*, Yaddith-Gho, Ythogtha, Zanthu. ("The Thing in the Pit", Carter; "Out of the Aeons", Heald and Lovecraft; *House of the Toad*, Tierney; "The Return of the Lloigor", C. Wilson.)

GHISGUTH (also GHIZGHUTH or GHISGHUTH). Creature who was the child of Cxaxukluth, and who in turn sired the Great Old One Tsathoggua by his mate Zstylzhemgni. After his brother Hzi-ulquoigmnzhah left Yuggoth due to the cannibalistic depredations of their father, Ghisguth and his family remained a while longer in deep caverns where Cxaxukluth could not reach.

See Cxaxukluth, Zstylzhemghi. ("Some Observations on the Carter Glossary", Cockcroft.)

GHOORIC ZONE. Caverns on Thog, one of the moons of Yuggoth. There the fungi bloom and the shoggoths splash beside a foul lake.

("Discovery of the Ghooric Zone", Lupoff.)

GHORL NIGRAL. Book of which only one copy exists on Earth. Many aeons ago, *Book of Eibon* says, the great wizard Zkauba discovered *Ghorl Nigral*, or *The Book of Night*, and bore it away from the burrows of the dholes which had honeycombed his homeworld of Yaddith. The priests of Mu later obtained a copy of the book, and added chapters of historical data on that sunken land to the original.

Later, one copy of *Ghorl Nigral* was brought to our world and deposited in the lost city of Yian-Ho. It lay forgotten there for many years, until the noted German occultist Friedrich von Junzt and his friend Gottfried Mulder journeyed to a monastery high in the mountains of China. In a bargain with the holy men of that place, von Junzt was allowed to gaze upon *Ghorl Nigral*. The experience left a deep impression on von Junzt, and he discussed the book's contents at length with Mulder later on.

After the death of von Junzt, Mulder decided that it was of great importance to remember what his friend had learned from the dread volume he had found in China. Using hypnosis to recall his lengthy conversations with his friend, he made notes which later were incorporated into his book *The Secret Mysteries of Asia, with a Commentary on the* Ghorl Nigral. This volume, when published at Leipzig in 1847 at the author's expense, was immediately destroyed by the authorities, and Mulder fled to Metzengerstein, where he died in a sanitarium in 1858.

A copy of *Ghorl Nigral* is kept at Miskatonic University; this is most likely one of Mulder's edition. Access to the volume is very difficult, however, due to an incident that took place in the library's reading room some years ago.

See *Secret Mysteries of Asia with a Commentary on the "Ghorl Nigral"*; von Junzt, Friedrich Wilheim; Yian-Ho; Zkauba. ("The Thing in the Pit", Carter; "Zoth-Ommog", Carter; *Dreams and Fancies*, Lovecraft.)

GHOUL. Tomb-dwelling being which lives in both the waking world and the Dreamlands. Ghouls can be identified by their canine features, hoofed feet, rubbery skin, moldy odor, and disgusting habits. They tunnel beneath the graveyards of the world, bearing their trophies back through their burrows to the Dreamlands, where they devour their burdens and cast the remnants of their feast into the Vale of Pnath.

Little social organization exists among the ghouls, though they may at times follow one of their kind whom they respect. They are allied with the nightgaunts, and though individuals of the species may make deals with the Great Old Ones, ghouls as a whole do not commit themselves to any master. Ghouls are not necessarily unfriendly to humans who know them and take the time to learn their language of gibberings and meepings. On the other hand, they can be quite unfriendly to those who enter their delvings unbidden.

The exact origins of the ghouls are unknown, but it has been proven that over time a human can transform into one of these creatures. Proximity of other ghouls and a radical change in diet seem to bring about this metamorphosis. At times ghouls have stolen human infants and replaced them with young of their own kind, so that they might induct their hostages into their race.

Ghouls have existed for thousands of years, and have become monsters of legend in many parts of the world. They have attained special status in the myths of Arabia, where they are said to dwell in the desert and graveyards, preying on hapless passers-by.

See ankh; Baoht Z'uqqa-Mogg; ghast; Naggoob; nightgaunt; Nyogtha; Pnath, Vale of; tomb-herd. ("The Dream-Quest of Unknown Kadath", Lovecraft; "Pickman's Model", Lovecraft.)

GHROTH. Outer God known as the Harbinger. This being appears as a dark object the size of a planet with one huge red eye which it often closes when it wants to remain inconspicuous to lesser beings. At the time when the stars are right, Ghroth will travel through the universe, visiting each world where the Great Old Ones reside to awaken them. Ghroth has visited our world in the past, thereby causing the cycles of extinction usually believed to have been caused by meteors or comets.

See *Revelations of Glaaki*, shan. ("The Tugging", Campbell; *Spawn of Azathoth*, Herber (C).)

GLAAKI. Great Old One who dwells within a lake near the town of Brichester in England's Severn River Valley. One source cites New Britain Island in New Guinea as his dwelling-place, but this is probably apocryphal. Glaaki resembles a slug with three eyes on stalks and innumerable metal spikes rising from his back.

Before coming to Earth Glaaki dwelt on the worlds of Yuggoth, Shaggai, and Tond. Eventually he became imprisoned behind a crystal trap door beneath a city on an asteroid. When the meteor crashed into Earth, it created the lake where Glaaki now resides. Some insist that Glaaki had come to Earth before, through use of the Reversed Angles of Tagh Clatur by the priests of Sebek and Karnak. These "heretics" make note of a number of hybrid mummies discovered nearby with spines like Glaaki's. The Great Old One's influence on our world was negligible before the meteor's fall, however.

Glaaki's worship on Earth began around 1790, when a group of people led by Thomas Lee came from nearby Goatswood to the lake. This cult built a row of houses along the shore so they could be close to their god.

They remained until about 1860 or 1870, at which time all of them disappeared; some suggest that the people came to make Glaaki serve them, but were caught and made to serve him instead. Others have lived in this area since then, but few stay long, as they are frightened away by Glaaki's dream-sendings.

Glaaki commands a cult of undead slaves, which he creates by driving a spine from his back into a living body and injecting a substance from his body into its bloodstream. If the spine can be severed before the fluid is injected, the victim will die but will be spared from becoming Glaaki's slave. The fluid creates a network of tissue in the corpse's body, which Glaaki can then manipulate so that the zombie does his bidding. Although capable of independent thought and actions, these creatures must do Glaaki's bidding whenever he telepathically commands them. After sixty years a rapid rotting known as the Green Decay affects these servants whenever sunlight strikes them, so most of Glaaki's servants remain under shelter during the day.

Glaaki uses a special psychic "dream-pull" to call nearby humans to join his cult. This is usually ineffectual, as Glaaki's power does not extend far enough to reach anyone who is more than a few miles from the lake.

See Aklo Unveilings, Angles of Tagh Clatur, Green Decay, *Revelations of Glaaki*, tomb-herd, Tond, Yuggoth. ("The Inhabitant of the Lake", Campbell; "Glaaki", *Call of Cthulhu* rulebook, Petersen *et al*. (C).)

GLASS FROM LENG. Mysterious cloudy glass said to come from the Hyades to the Plateau of Leng. To be used, the glass must be mounted in a frame so that it appears to be a window. If the possessor desires to use it, he draws a pentagram in red chalk on the floor before the window, sits within the diagram, and says the words, *"Ph'nglui mglw'nafh Cthulhu R'lyeh wgah'nagl fhtagn."* The glass from Leng will then become clear and show some scene with Mythos significance to the person in the pentagram. The location viewed cannot be chosen by the user. The viewer must be wary, though, since beings on the other side can see through as well, and may pass through the magical gateway if they desire.

See moon-lens. ("The Gable Window", Derleth and Lovecraft.)

GLEETH. Moon god worshiped in the primal land of Theem'hdra. He is often said to be identical with Mnomquah, but in fact Gleeth was almost entirely blind and deaf to the prayers of his worshipers, as opposed to the other god. As such, he was only worshiped by the Suhm-Yi people, and had no formalized cult or priests.

See Monomquah, Theem'hdra. ("Isles of the Suhm-Yi", Lumley; *Mad Moon of Dreams*, Lumley.)

G'LL-HOO (also GELL-HO). Deep one city mentioned in several books of the Mythos and supposedly found in the ocean north of Britain, near the isle of Surtsey.

See deep one. (*The Burrowers Beneath*, Lumley.)

GLOON. A lesser Other God bound to a temple beneath the Atlantic Ocean. Gloon was imprisoned within this temple long before the sinking of Atlantis. Gloon appears to be a handsome youth wearing a laurel wreath while in his temple, though his true form is that of a wattled, sluglike horror.

Gloon has two servitors that may leave the temple to carry out his will. These servitors, which resemble Zoth-Ommog and may imply some connection between Gloon and that deity, take small statuettes of Gloon to places where humans may find them. When someone discovers one of these statues, he begins to have strange dreams of a sunken city, dominated by a huge basalt temple with a glowing light inside. These dreams become more and more vivid as time progresses. The dreamer is also doused with salt water, and sometimes seaweed, while asleep. The possessor of the statuette eventually goes insane, as his soul is taken back to the temple, where Gloon may torture it for a period of time before the life force dissolves completely.

("The City in the Sea", Thomas and Willis (C).)

GLOSSINA PALPALIS. Species of fly found in central Africa. It possesses a highly virulent bite, but the natives fear its supernatural powers even more. The soul of a person bitten by one of these insects will inhabit the fly's body until its death. The natives also associate this fly with the Fishers from Outside.

See Fishers from Outside. ("Winged Death", Heald and Lovecraft.)

GLYU'UHO. Naacal title for the star commonly known as Betelgeuse. According to those who believe in the Elder Gods, these beneficent beings came down from Glyu'Uho to battle the Great Old Ones. The Elder Gods may dwell in an alternate dimension known as Elysia; if this is true, there may be a gateway leading to this place near Glyu'Uho.

Glyu'Uho was also at one time the home of a race of amphibious beings who journeyed to Earth and built their stone cities here.

Strangely enough, these creatures were also imprisoned by the Elder Gods when they came to battle the Great Old Ones.

See Elder Gods, Great Old Ones, Rigel. ("The Horror in the Bridge", Campbell; "The Thing in the Pit", Carter; *The Lurker at the Threshold*, Derleth and Lovecraft; "The Lair of the Star-Spawn", Derleth and Schorer.)

GN'ICHT' TYAACHT. West African tree spirits which come forth at night from the trees called Nuwanda. When these beings are young, they move about a great deal, but as they grow older, they restrict their wanderings considerably.

The Gn'icht' Tyaacht customarily live in a stationary grove of trees. They may move in and out of their homes by melting into their trunks. If a Gn'icht' Tyaacht is injured, its tree also shows its injury. When a being is in the grove, the Gn'icht' Tyaacht may induce drowsiness in the interloper. The Gn'icht' Tyaacht never attack a being in the grove if they are left alone.

Once, witch doctors could tame the Gn'icht' Tyaacht by feeding them for five years with corpses dried of blood, and using certain rituals which are believed to have been lost as the tribes were decimated by the slave trade. The people of T'gaorl often summoned these spirits to do their bidding. The Gn'icht' Tyaacht still bear hatred for Cthugha due to his enslavement of them many years ago.

("The Horror of the Glen", Tamlyn (C).)

GNOPH-KEH. 1) Monsters from Greenland which, according to one chronicler, are horned and walk on two, four, or sometimes six legs. The voormis pushed the gnoph-keh into the polar wastes when the beast-men broke free of the Valusian serpent men and established their own kingdom. Sometimes Gnoph-Keh is also said to be an avatar of Rhan-Tegoth. See Rhan-Tegoth. ("The Scroll of Morloc", Carter and Smith; "The Lurker at the Threshold", Derleth and Lovecraft; "The Horror in the Museum", Heald and Lovecraft.)

2) Tribe of cannibals who dwelt in the north and who were destroyed when the inhabitants of Zobna came to their land and established the empire of Lomar. See Lomar, voormis, Zobna. ("Polaris", Lovecraft.)

GOATSWOOD. Village located in England's Severn River Valley, southwest of Brichester. Much like its neighbor Temphill, Goatswood was originally settled by former Templars in the first years of the 14th century. The people of the surrounding towns usually avoid Goatswood, as visitors there have been known to vanish without a trace. Many of the town's inhabitants are members of a strange religious cult which centered around goat worship and which holds a special glass-topped pylon known as the "moon-lens" in reverence.

The woods near Goatswood also have a bad reputation. In the 17th century, a coven met in a clearing deep in the forest, where they worshiped a stone which had fallen from the sky. After a while the people of the surrounding countryside grew nervous about this activity and called in Matthew Hopkins, the infamous witch hunter, who put all of the coven's members to death.

See Glaaki, moon-lens. ("The Insects from Shaggai", Campbell; "The Moon-Lens", Campbell; "The Curate of Temphill", Cannon and Price.)

GOD OF THE BLOODY TONGUE. See Nyarlathotep (God of the Bloody Tongue).

GODDESS OF THE BLACK FAN. Book in classical Chinese, and the central tome of Nyarlathotep's Cult of the Bloated Woman. The book is a series of connected poems, written by the monk Liu Chanfang, which deal with his liaisons with a mysterious divine woman who hides her face behind a mystic black fan. In the end the woman removes her mask, and when Liu sees what lies beneath, he guts himself with a sickle and scribes the final poem using his own blood. At least one copy of this book is held by the leaders of the Bloated Woman's cult.

See Nyarlathotep (Bloated Woman). ("Shanghai", DiTillio and Willis (C).)

GODS OF EARTH. See Great Ones.

GOF'NN HUPADGH SHUB-NIGGURATH. Term applied to certain worshipers of Shub-Niggurath whom the goddess has found especially worthy of her favor. In a special ceremony, the Black Goat of the Woods devours the cultist, transmogrifies him, and then regurgitates her victim. Following this ceremony the person may have sprouted horns, the feet of a goat, clawlike hands, or even less human traits, as well as been blessed with virtual immortality. It was sightings of these transformed worshipers which started the classical legends of satyrs, dryads, and other fantastic sylvan creatures.

See Shub-Niggurath. ("The Moon-Lens", Campbell.)

GOG AND MAGOG. Two tribes of evil men mentioned in the Bible. They are included here due to certain Islamic myths regarding them. According to legend, while Alexander the Great was searching for the Spring of Life, he was set upon by these people. Alexander beat them back into their mountain homes, and built a brass and iron barrier across the entrance. Since then, Gog and Magog have attempted to break through this wall. Each day, they lick the barrier until it has almost been destroyed. Then they cease their labors for the night, saying, "Tomorrow we shall break through!" Fortunately for mankind, they fail to add the traditional "God willing!", and each morning the barrier is back to its original strength. At the end of the world Gog and Magog will break through, drink up the Tigris and the Euphrates, and destroy all of humanity.

This story is interesting, as it includes many of the concepts of the Mythos. The idea of beings continually trying to break through the barriers between the worlds is reminiscent of the Great Old Ones attempting to break their own chains to emerge into the world. And is there a possible connection between Gog-Magog and Yog-Sothoth?

GOL-GOROTH. God of darkness who resembles a tremendous bird with one foot and one eye. He is said to dwell under the mountain Antarktos, somewhere near the South Pole, and is served by the shantaks.

Gol-Goroth was once worshiped in the city of Bal-Sagoth, located on an isle in the Atlantic Ocean. At every rising and setting of the moon, the god's priests sacrificed a victim and placed the heart upon Gol-Goroth's altar. Certain inscriptions within the ruins of Zimbabwe, supposedly built by the Fishers from Outside, bear the name of this god as well.

See Antarktos, Bal-Sagoth, Groth-golka, Quumyagga, shantak. ("The Fishers from Outside", Carter; "The Gods of Bal-Sagoth", Howard.)

GREAT ABYSS. Region in which Nodens is said to rule. According to Kenneth Grant, the Great Abyss is another name for the human subconscious; consequently, Nodens may be more important to humanity than was previously thought.

See nightgaunt, Nodens, Yog-Sothoth. (*Aleister Crowley and the Hidden God*, Grant; "The Dream-Quest of Unknown Kadath", Lovecraft.)

GORDON, ERNEST HENGIST. Author of several horror tales, including "Gargoyle" and "The Principle of Evil." While Gordon's work did receive some attention early in his career, his morbid choices of subjects soon drove away most publishers and readers. Due to this bias, Gordon was forced to publish *The Soul of Chaos* and his other three novels independently. After a while, Gordon disappeared and has not been heard from since.

See nightgaunt; *Soul of Chaos, The*. ("The Dark Demon", Bloch.)

GREAT DYING. Term applied to the return of the Great Old Ones, believed to have been coined by noted occultist J. Cornelius Wasserman.

See *Liber Damnatus Damnationum*; *Occult Foundation, The*. (*House of the Toad*, Tierney.)

GREAT NORTHERN EXPEDITION. Exploration team headed by Clark Ashton Scarsdale, which set out to Asia in 1933 to find the fabled Great White Space. Only one member of this expedition, Fredrick Plowright, returned.

See Croth, Great White Space, Trone Tables. (*The Great White Space*, Copper.)

GREAT OLD ONES. Ultrapowerful alien beings who have mastery over technology, magic, or some combination of the two. The Great Old Ones seem almost godlike in power, but are still subject to certain laws of nature. The physical appearances and individual abilities of the Great Old Ones may vary widely, but they seem to share several characteristics.

Millions of years ago the Great Old Ones came down from the stars to take up residence on Earth. (The Great Old Ones probably inhabit many other worlds like our own, and thus the large number of these beings who dwell here may not be a unique condition.) Little is known about this period, since few decipherable records survive. It was during this time that Cthulhu, the mightiest of the Great Old Ones, ordered his spawn to construct the city of R'lyeh upon a continent in the Pacific.

After thousands or millions of years, a great change occurred. The true cause of this alteration remains a mystery, though two theories have been constructed by scholars. The first hypothesis is that the Great Old Ones were at one time members of a company of beings titled the Elder Gods. Because they practiced black magic, or they stole certain of the Elder God's sacred records, or even that they had the temerity to attack the home of the Elder Gods themselves, the Great Old Ones were cast out by their brethren and imprisoned in various places on Earth, in the stars, and even in other dimensions. Having done this, the Elder Gods returned to their home near the star

Glyu'Uho, leaving the Great Old Ones within their prisons. There will come a time, though, when the Great Old Ones will break free of the strictures imposed by the Elder Gods, and they will come forth from their jails to challenge the supremacy of their captors once again.

The second theory states that, just as Earth has its seasons, the cosmos has its cycles, and as certain animals hibernate during winter, the Great Old Ones have gone into a long, deathlike slumber. For millennia they have dreamt in their tombs, awaiting the time when they will come forth again to conquer the world. For it shall be as the mad Arab Abdul Alhazred wrote:

> That is not dead which can eternal lie,
>
> And with strange eons even death may die.

When humanity first came into being, the dream-sendings of the Great Old Ones reached many of its members. Although some of these telepathic messages may have been distorted, creating the legends of the imprisoned titans and of sleeping heroes in many different mythologies, some clear visions managed to get through to especially sensitive humans. These chosen ones began a number of cults on Earth dedicated to the Great Old Ones. With the aid of the "Lesser Old Ones", alien creatures which do not sleep as their masters do but have limited power, these cults hope to reawaken the Great Old Ones so that their gods may be free once more and they shall receive the rewards, real or imaginary, of their labors.

More Great Old Ones exist than can be fully detailed in this entry, but a few of the more important ones are listed below. Great Cthulhu, the octopoid lord of the corpse-city of R'lyeh, sleeps yet beneath the Pacific Ocean. The toad-thing Tsathoggua drowses in the lightless caverns of N'kai. Hastur, Lord of the Interstellar Spaces, may dwell in outer space or might be imprisoned within the Lake of Hali, somewhere near Aldebaran. Ithaqua, the source of the northern Native American's legends of the Wendigo, is confined to the cold regions of our own planet and other worlds. Though some Great Old Ones might be free, the majority of these beings remain in their lengthy slumber.

The Great Old Ones should be distinguished from the Outer Gods, which includes such entities as Shub-Niggurath, Azathoth, Nyarlathotep, and Yog-Sothoth. Though the Great Old Ones have some limited power, the Outer Gods seem to represent personified cosmic forces, such as chaos and fertility, and are almost unlimited in range and ability. It should be noted, however, that some confusion may exist over the category in which a given creature should be placed, and many scholars have ignored this distinction entirely.

See Aklo, Angles of Tagh Clatur, Atlach-Nacha, Baoht Z'uqqa-Mogg, Black Brotherhood, *Book of Thoth*, Borea, Broken Columns of Geph, Bugg-Shash, Byatis, Celaeno, Chaugnar Faugn, Chthonioi, Cthugha, Cthulhu, Cyaegha, Eihort, Elder Gods, Elder Sign, elemental theory, Furnace of Yeb, Ghadamon, Ghatanothoa, Ghroth, Glaaki, Gloon, Great Dying, Hastur, Ithaqua, Leng, Lloigor, Nug and Yeb, Nyarlathotep, Nyogtha, Outer Gods, Pharos of Leng, Rhan-Tegoth, Shudde-M'ell, Thamuth-Djig, Torch of Nug, Tsathoggua, Ubbo-Sathla, Y'golonac, Yibb-Tstll, Yig, Ythogtha, Zarr, Zathog, Zhar, Zoth-Ommog. ("Zoth-Ommog", Carter; "The Return of Hastur", Derleth; "The Thing that Walked on the Wind", Derleth; *The Trail of Cthulhu*, Derleth; "The Call of Cthulhu", Lovecraft; "The Tale of Satampra Zeiros", Smith.)

GREAT ONES (also GODS OF EARTH). Title given to those deities of the Dreamlands which listen to the prayers of humanity. The Great Ones appear much like humans, but their pointed chins, long-lobed ears, and thin noses set them apart from mortals. At times these beings come down from their home atop Kadath to mate with human women to create demigods, and it is said that wherever the features of the gods are most prominent among the people, Kadath must surely be nearby. For the most part they are weak and forgetful, but they are infinitely preferable to the Other Gods which protect them.

According to some, the Great Ones are in fact the Elder Gods, and because of this will provide humanity no protection when the Great Old Ones awaken.

See Elder Gods, gug, Kadath in the Cold Waste, Nyarlathotep. ("The Dream-Quest of Unknown Kadath", Lovecraft; "The Other Gods", Lovecraft.)

GREAT RACE OF YITH. Time-travelling beings which dwelt on this world millions of years ago. The Yithians had no true physical forms, but took up residence in whatever bodies they desired. In the earlier days of our world, the Great Race lived in the bodies of immense cone-shaped creatures which they found here when they arrived from their home on the planet Yith. Upon their arrival the Yithians were forced to fight off the flying polyps which had in the past devoured the conical entities. With their mastery of technology, the Race beat back the invaders, imprisoning them beneath the ground. Periodic resurgences did occur, but these were quickly crushed by the Yithians.

After their victory over the polyps, the Great Race set about building cities with buildings thousands of feet tall, creating nuclear-powered vehicles and flying machines, and engaging in historical research. It was in the latter field that they made use of their extraordinary mental time-travel powers. To study the past, certain scientists would project their minds backward in time using a method much like astral projection. The Race was, however, unable to physically interact with the past.

A different technique was used to journey to the future. Usually, one of the exceptional members of the Race would send its mind into the future, selecting a body there from which it could study the time and displacing the host's mind into the Yithian's former body. The transition usually lasted for around five years, during which time the Yithian would grasp the basics of life in this new society, afterward embarking on an exploration of the history, sociology, and mythology of the culture. Meanwhile, the host's mind would write a history of its own time for the Great Race and, if cooperative, would be allowed to make excursions outside the cities, consult the Great Race's libraries, and speak with other visitors from different worlds and times.

After the Yithian had learned all it could about the period it was visiting, it would construct a device that sent its mind back to the original body. The alien mind would be hypnotized to forget the experience, and returned to its own time. One flaw in this procedure was that at times the alien would have visions of its imprisonment, and might even recall information about its world which it had learned from the Yithians. The Great Race considered these lapses to be annoyances and often dealt with them by repeated possession or through their operatives in that time, but did not cease in their research because of them.

The Great Race also started cults among the humans on Earth. These worshipers would aid Great Race visitors in becoming assimilated with their time period, silence those formerly possessed minds who remembered too much of their captivity, and protect the Yithians' agents from the cult of Hastur and the Yellow Sign, which desired the Great Race's secrets.

Around fifty million years ago, the flying polyps imprisoned by the Yithians rose up and defeated their ancient foes. The Great Race sent the minds of their brightest scientists into the bodies of the intelligent insectoids of Earth's future, ensuring their own survival, though their former borrowed bodies had been destroyed.

See Brothers of the Yellow Sign, *Eltdown Shards*, flying polyp, Nug-Soth, *Pnakotic Manuscripts*, Pnakotus, *Wondrous Intelligences*, Yekub. ("The Dreamer", Herber (C); "The Shadow Out of Time", Lovecraft.)

GREAT WHITE SPACE. Extra-dimensional belt which connects positions trillions of miles apart. The Old Ones use it often to journey through the universe, and hold it in reverence. The Earthly entrance to this place lies somewhere in the mountains of China or Mongolia, and a door five hundred feet high leads to a vast underground cavern with the Space at its far end. The Great White Space is protected by the minions of the Old Ones, so any journey there is inadvisable.

See Croth, *Ethics of Ygor*, Great Northern Expedition, Magnetic Ring. (*The Great White Space*, Copper.)

GREEN BOOK. Diary kept by an unnamed young girl, in which she tells of her many experiments in sorcery. Only one copy exists, but its contents have proved invaluable in investigating the Mythos.

See Aklo, Alala, Chian, Deep Dendo, Mao, Voor. ("The White People", Machen.)

GREEN DECAY. 1) Incantation from *Book of Eibon* that possibly converts its victim into a greenish pile of mold. See *Book of Eibon*. ("The Man of Stone", Heald and Lovecraft.)

2) Affliction suffered by the undead servants of Glaaki after they have served their master for sixty years or more. If one of these servants is exposed to direct sunlight, a rapid putrefaction sets in, quickly destroying the servitor. According to some, an extract made from those killed by the Green Decay is used in creating the zombies of Haiti. See Glaaki. ("The Inhabitant of the Lake", Campbell.)

GROTH-GOLKA. Bird god worshiped at one time by the people of the isle of Bal-Sagoth. Groth-golka could be an avatar of Gol-Goroth, who was also revered in the same land.

See Gol-Goroth. ("The Fishers from Outside", Carter; "The Gods of Bal-Sagoth", Howard.)

GUG. Huge black-furred being native to the Dreamlands. A gug's arms are split at the elbow, with each of its four forearms ending in a tremendous paw. The most hideous characteristic of a gug, though, is its face, with a pink eye on either side and its fang-lined mouth running vertically down its head.

The gugs once dwelt upon the surface of the Earth, where their great monoliths still remain. The Great Ones, however, grew frightened of the gugs' worship of Nyarlathotep and the Other Gods, and upon hearing one night of a great blasphemy performed by these creatures, banished them to caverns below the Earth's surface. Now the gugs live in a tremendous stone city quite near to the vaults of Zin, somewhere in the Dreamlands' Underworld. No gug has been sighted in the waking world.

See ghast, Koth, Sign of Koth, Zin. ("The Dream-Quest of Unknown Kadath", Lovecraft.)

GULF OF S'LGHUO. See S'lghuo, Gulf of.

GYAA-YOTHN. Animal resembling a human, save for its size, bestial appearance, and horn protruding from its head. The people of K'n-yan bred these from certain quadrupeds native to the caverns of Yoth and the remnants of various conquered peoples. These beasts are normally used for carrying burdens and as mounts. They do possess a rudimentary intelligence which proves useful to their masters. Some have speculated that the ghasts of the vaults of Zin beneath Yoth and the gyaa-yothn are related in some way.

See K'n-yan. ("The Mound", Heald and Lovecraft; *S. Petersen's Field Guide to Cthulhu Monsters*, Petersen.)

H

HALI (also HALEY). Place or person often linked with the King in Yellow and Hastur. Sometimes it seems to be the name of a wise man or prophet, though at other times it designates the lake which lies near the city of Carcosa. Three possible interpretations exist for this name.

1) Hali is a corruption of Ali ibn-Ridwan, an Arabian doctor, philosopher, and astrologer of the 11th century A.D. He was one of the foremost medical authorities of his time, but at the end of his life he went insane. Ibn-Ridwan was the author of over one hundred books on various topics, including philosophy and metaphysics. This Hali may be unconnected with the one mentioned in *The King in Yellow*, but it is likely that at least Bierce was aware of the Arabian doctor whose name he used in connection with Carcosa. ("The Death of Halpin Frayser", Bierce; "An Inhabitant of Carcosa", Bierce.)

2) According to Marion Zimmer Bradley, Hali is the Arabic name for the constellation Taurus, in which Aldebaran and the Hyades lie. Since these constellations are said to be the home of Hastur and the King, this explanation is also possible.

3) Hali might be a necromancer who lived in the Immemorial City on the planet of Carcosa. This Hali may be the one whose name has been given to the Lake of Hali. ("Carcosa Story about Hali" (fragment), Carter.).

See King in Yellow, *Revelations of Hali*, Thale, Uoht, Yellow Sign.

HALI, LAKE OF. Body of water where the cloud-waves break near the alien city of Carcosa. The Lake is the resting place of Hastur the Unspeakable One, and within its waters reside tentacled horrors whose faces are terrible beyond words. Those who gaze upon the Lake are visited by Hastur or his minions soon thereafter.

See Carcosa, Great Old Ones, Hali, Hastur, King in Yellow. ("The Yellow Sign", Chambers; "The Gable Window", Derleth and Lovecraft; "The Ring of the Hyades", Glasby; "Tatterdemalion", Love, Ross, and Watts (C).)

HAN (sometimes **DARK HAN**). Lesser deity of divination mentioned in *De Vermis Mysteriis*. In that book Han is mentioned in association with Yig, so there may be a linkage between the two. The Lakota plains tribe's personification of darkness is named Han, but whether this is the same as the Mythos being is uncertain.

("The Shambler from the Stars", Bloch.)

HAON-DOR. Powerful prehuman sorcerer who lived in ancient Hyperborea. He usually appears as a figure cloaked in shadow, but has also been known to manifest himself as a 15' rattlesnake. Haon-Dor once had a glimpse of the tablets of Ubbo-Sathla, and this vision left him fearful of the outdoors for the rest of his life. To control his phobia he took up residence beneath Mount Voormithadreth in Hyperborea, where he was accompanied by thousands of familiars. Later, Haon-Dor departed for the Hyperborean colony of Krannoria; when that colony was destroyed by Abhoth, he used Eibon's gateway to Saturn to escape the assault. He may now live on in the Dreamlands. Haon-Dor may be developing a way to reattain his former power in our world.

("The Descent into the Abyss", Carter and Smith; *Return to Dunwich*, Herber (C); "The Pits of Bendal-Dolum", Lyons (C); "The House of Haon-Dor", Smith; "The Seven Geases", Smith.)

HARAG-KOLATH. Underground city in southern Arabia to which Shub-Niggurath may have come when she left her former home on Yaddith. She waits here, served by her spawn, until Hastur is free to come to Earth once again.

See Shub-Niggurath. ("The Seed of the Star-God", Tierney.)

HASTUR (also **THE UNSPEAKABLE ONE, HE WHO IS NOT TO BE NAMED, ASSATUR,** or **KAIWAN**). Great Old One who resides or is imprisoned on a dark star near Aldebaran. He is related to Carcosa, the Yellow Sign, the Lake of Hali, and the King in Yellow. Paradoxically, the Unspeakable One also is sometimes referred to as the patron of shepherds. In his natural state, Hastur appears as an invisible force which can nonetheless be psychically sensed by those nearby.

The Tcho-Tchos and the people of K'n-yan are both known to worship Hastur. In the past he was also revered in Samaria, Attluma, and Hyboria. His cult is considered particularly abhorrent, even when compared with those of the other Great Old Ones. The members of the cult are dedicated to bringing Hastur to Earth, as well as to torturing Yithians and mi-go to gain knowledge of other times and places.

In addition to his cults, Hastur is served by the interstellar race known as the byakhee. Some say Hastur is also served by the mi-go and Ithaqua, but there is little evidence to support this. The Outer God Shub-Niggurath and Hastur are said to have mated, producing their own foul offspring called the Thousand Young. There seems to be some conflict between Hastur and Cthulhu; they are said to be half-brothers, and at times when the minions of the two beings have met, they have endeavored to destroy each other.

See Ajar-Alazwat, Alar, Aldebaran, Aldones, Brothers of the Yellow Sign, byakhee, Cthulhu, Demhe, elemental theory, Feaster from Afar, Great Old Ones, Hali, Ithaqua, King in Yellow, K'n-yan, *Legends of the Olden Runes*, L'mur-Kathulos, Magnum Innominandum, Nug and Yeb, Outer Gods, Pallid Mask, Ring of the Hyades, Sakkuth, *Sapientia Maglorum*, Shub-Niggurath, Tcho-Tcho, *Turner Codex*, Yellow Sign, Yhtill, Yog-Sothoth. ("Haita the Shepherd", Bierce; "The Gods", Carter; "The Return of Hastur", Derleth; "The Ring of the Hyades", Glasby; "The Mound", Heald and Lovecraft; "The Shadow Out of Time", Lovecraft; "The Whisperer in Darkness", Lovecraft; "The Seed of the Star-God", Tierney.)

HATHEG-KLA, MOUNT. Peak located in the Great Stony Desert beyond the town of Hatheg in the Dreamlands. On certain nights the gods of Earth come to Hatheg-Kla in their cloud-ships to dance upon its summit and recall the days of their youth.

Only two humans have climbed to the top of Hatheg-Kla to find the gods. One of these was Sansu, who according to *Pnakotic Manuscripts* found nothing at the top but wind and rock. The other was Barzai, a high priest of the gods, who vanished as he approached the peak.

See Atal, Barzai, *Pnakotic Manuscripts*, Sansu. ("The Other Gods", Lovecraft.)

HAUNTER OF THE DARK. See Nyarlathotep (Haunter of the Dark).

HE WHO IS NOT TO BE NAMED. See Hastur.

HIAMALDI, YOGI. From 1916-18 member of a Boston group dedicated to the study of psychic phenomena, and friend of Harley Warren and Etienne-Laurent de Marigny. This Indian mystic asserted that he was the sole living human to have travelled to the lost city of Yian-Ho, from which he bore the mysterious clock he later presented to de Marigny.

See time-clock, Yian-Ho. (*The Transition of Titus Crow*, Lumley.)

HOUNDS OF TINDALOS (also TIND'LOSI HOUNDS). Beings who come from the distant past, or possibly another dimension. The Hounds appear much like greenish hairless dogs with blue tongues, or possibly like black formless shadows; it is difficult to be sure of the Hounds' true forms. They dwell in Tindalos, a city of corkscrew towers, but have been known to go forth to other places and times to track their prey.

The Hounds of Tindalos are the embodiment of foulness, and lust after something of the pureness found within humanity. Sometime in the past an event took place in which the Hounds of Tindalos and humanity both took part (and upon which the tale of the Fall from Paradise is based), but humanity did not wholly participate. Thus some element of "pureness" remained with humans, but was lost to the Hounds. The Hounds hate all natural life because of this, seeking to destroy any such beings they encounter.

The Hounds may be attracted by attempts to psychically journey back in time. After an observer has been "scented", the Hounds can follow him through time and space until the person is caught and killed.

According to Halpin Chalmers, the noted occultist, these creatures have descended through "angled" time, while normal life has developed through "curves." This is not readily understood, but it is known that a hound must materialize itself through an angle; thus a person kept in a perfectly round room would be safe from the beast's attack. When this occurs, however, the hounds usually contact some of their metaphysical allies in the time period, such as the "satyrs" (possibly Shub-Niggurath's minions), to do away with these defenses in some way and allow them access to their prey.

One sage has hypothesized that the hounds are unable to enter our three dimensions, and anyone who is not travelling through time is safe from their depredations. Other occurrences of hound attack, however, seem to show that this is not the case. It may be that the hounds can only indirectly affect this dimension, which makes them no less of a threat.

Analysis of substances left after a Hound attack have revealed that the Hounds have no enzymes within their bodies. Enzymes are helpful in that they speed chemical reactions, yet their presence eventually causes a being to die. So, not only are the hounds masters of time travel, they seem to be immortal as well; whether or not this means that hounds cannot be permanently destroyed by violence or other means remains to be seen.

See Tindalos. ("The Hounds of Tindalos", Long; *Elysia*, Lumley; *The Transition of Titus Crow*, Lumley; *S. Petersen's Field Guide to Cthulhu Monsters*, Petersen (C).)

HOY-DHIN CHANT. Incantation found in *Necronomicon* and used by sorcerers to call the Black. The chant must be used in conjunction with other formulae found in *Cthaat Aquadingen*.

See Black, the; *Necronomicon* (Appendices); Sixth Sathlatta. ("The Horror at Oakdeene," Lumley.)

HYBORIA. Land in central Europe which prospered during the period between the destruction of Atlantis and the rise of civilization in Sumeria. The most famous hero of this age was Conan the Cimmerian.

See Cimmeria. ("The Hyborian Age", Howard.)

HYDRA (also MOTHER HYDRA). Tremendous deep one who is the mate of Dagon, as well as one of the deep ones' gods. She has much the same form as Dagon, and is revered by many of the same cults that worship her husband.

See Dagon, deep one, elemental theory, Lesser Old Ones. ("The Shadow over Innsmouth", Lovecraft.)

HYDROPHINNAE. Book on aquatic happenings penned by a Mr. Gantley. It appears in both Latin and English, though no publication date for either edition is known. This book details a wide variety of aquatic organisms, including a race of fish-like bipedal beings.

("The Aquarium", Jacobi; "Fischbuchs", Ross, *TU02* (C).)

HYPERBOREA. Fabled northern civilization that came to power during the Miocene Period, between nineteen and twenty-five million years ago. A long-eared, fair-haired people from the south originally populated Hyperborea; these settlers first traded with and later exterminated the subhuman voormis who had inhabited the area before them.

At this time in history, the northern lands were warm and fertile. Vast jungles, filled with exotic life ranging from sabre-toothed tigers to the last remaining dinosaurs, covered much of the continent. The people of Hyperborea were cultured and well-learned in the arts of science and magic. Their capital, first at Commoriom and later at Uzuldaroum, was a marvel to behold.

For many years after their arrival in Hyperborea the people of this region worshiped the toad god Tsathoggua, as the voormis had before them. Later the worship of this deity fell out of practice as the populace turned to more urbane deities. Soon the worship of Tsathoggua was so uncommon that when the priests of the elk god Yhoundeh declared an inquisition to deal with the Tsathogguan infidels, they were not opposed. Many of the black god's congregation were killed, and others fled the persecution to the southern colony of Krannoria. Though they were initially successful, Yhoundeh's clerics soon lost favor with the populace, and the worship of Tsathoggua began a short resurgence before the end of the Hyperborean civilization.

Of the many sorcerers who dwelt in Hyperborea, two are of especial note. The first, Zon Mezzamalech, who lived upon the northern peninsula of Mhu Thulan, is barely mentioned by the ancient texts despite his great feats. The second, Eibon, gained himself more renown. Though the exploits and astral journeys of this wizard are matters of legend, he is better known for penning *Book of Eibon*. Sadly, Eibon's career was cut short by Yhoundeh's inquisitors, who discovered that the sorcerer had made a pact with Tsathoggua. Though he was able to escape his would-be captors by magical means, Eibon was never again seen in Hyperborea.

Near the end of the Miocene Period glaciers began to roll over the northern portions of Hyperborea. Many of the land's lords and wizards fought to save their land from the cold, but their efforts were to no avail. After many centuries the ice covered all of Hyperborea. The lore of the lost continent was not forgotten, however; the Atlantean high priest Klarkash-Ton recorded the myths of Tsathoggua and the rest of the Commoriom myth cycle, and the Greeks believed that a race known as the Hyperboreans lived in a warm paradise far to the north.

During the Hyborian Age another kingdom named Hyperborea occupied the area around the present-day Gulf of Finland. A group of nomadic Hyborian tribesmen, who settled down there to build their great stone cities, became the founders of this new Hyperborea.

See Abhoth; Aphoom Zhah; Atlach-Nacha; *Book of Eibon*; Commoriom; Eibon; Haon-Dor; Klarkash-Ton; Kythamil; *Life of Eibon*; Mhu Thulan; Naacal; Nug and Yeb; *Parchments of Pnom*; *Pnakotic Manuscripts*; Ptetholite; Rlim Shaikorth; Sakkuth; Shub-Niggurath; Silver Key; Tsath-yo; Tsathoggua; Uzuldaroum; voormis; Voormithadreth, Mount; Yamil Zacra; Yhoundeh. (*Return to Dunwich*, Herber (C); "The Trail of Tsathogghua", Herber (C); "The Hyborian Age", Howard; "The Whisperer in Darkness", Lovecraft; "The Door to Saturn", Smith; "The Ice-Demon", Smith; "The Seven Geases", Smith; "The Tale of Satampra Zeiros", Smith; "Ubbo-Sathla", Smith.)

HYPNOS. Greek god of sleep, and the brother of Thanatos ("Death"). Hypnos dwells in the Corona Borealis, and concerns himself little with mortals. If a person does attract his attention in some unguessable way, Hypnos sends down a beam of red-gold light from his starry home to that person. The beam pulls the victim back to Hypnos, who may leave some token of this visitation behind.

See Crystallizer of Dreams. ("Hypnos", Lovecraft.)

HZIULQUOIGMNZHAH. Son of Cxaxukluth and paternal uncle of Tsathoggua. He resembles his nephew to some degree, save for the position of his head at the lower end of his body. After a brief sojourn on Yuggoth he left for Yaksh, where he was annoyed by the religious worship practiced by that world's curious inhabitants. A short while later he journeyed to Saturn, where he still resides.

See Cxaxukluth, Cykranosh, Ghisguth. ("Some Observations on the Carter Glossary", Cockcroft; "The Door to Saturn", Smith.)

I

IA. Word often used in rituals to the Great Old Ones and Outer Gods. It literally means "I hunger!" in the original Aklo, and may be linked to the cry of "IAO!" made by the worshipers of Dionysus.

("No Pain, No Gain", Adams, Isinwyll, and Manui.)

IB. City of gray stone, inhabited by strange frog-like beings known as the Thuum'ha, which once stood within the land of Mnar by a huge, still lake. In this city, which had existed for centuries before humans ever discovered it, these beings from the moon propitiated Bokrug the water lizard with curious rituals. The humans living in the nearby city of Sarnath, who felt uneasy about their neighbors, finally rose up and slaughtered the amphibians.

See Bokrug, Brick Cylinders of Kadatheron, *Ilarnek Papyri*, Lh-Yib, Mnar, Sarnath, Thuum'ha. ("The Doom that Came to Sarnath", Lovecraft.)

IBIGIB. Possible title of a book containing a number of references to the invocation of supernatural forces. The library of British occultist Titus Crow held a copy of this volume.

("The Caller of the Black", Lumley.)

IBN SCHACABAO. Arab scholar and author of the book *Reflections*, which Alhazred quotes at least twice in his *Necronomicon*.

See *Reflections*. ("The Plain of Sound", Campbell; "The Festival", Lovecraft; *The Burrowers Beneath*, Lumley.)

IDH-YAA. Monstrosity from the double star Xoth who is referred to in *Ponape Scripture* as Cthulhu's mate. The Great Old Ones Zoth-

Ommog, Ghatanothoa and Ythogtha came from the mating of Idh-yaa and Cthulhu. The ancient texts do not tell whether Idh-yaa came to Earth with her "husband."

See Cthulhu, Cthylla, Ghatanothoa, Xoth, Ythogtha. ("Out of the Aeons", Carter.)

ILARNEK PAPYRI. Manuscript, found only at the British Museum, that originates from Ilarnek in the land of Mnar. It tells the history of the two cities Ib and Sarnath.

See Ib, Sarnath. ("The Doom that Came to Sarnath", Lovecraft; *Beneath the Moors*, Lumley.)

ILEK-VAD. City of the Dreamlands. Ilek-Vad stands on a cliff of glass above a twilight sea in which the gnorri live, and its many high turrets and domes are famous throughout the lands of dream. Its king, who sits upon an opal throne, travels once a year to a temple on the river Oukranos, where he lived as a boy. The dreamer Randolph Carter may have become a king in this city following his disappearance.

See Carter, Randolph; de Marigny, Etienne-Laurent. ("The Dream-Quest of Unknown Kadath", Lovecraft; "The Silver Key", Lovecraft; "Through the Gates of the Silver Key", Lovecraft and Price.)

IN PRESSURED PLACES. Hartrack's book of undersea horror. ("De Marigny's Clock", Lumley.)

INGANOK (also INQUANOK). Onyx city located on the northern shore of the Dreamlands' Cerenerian Sea. This city trades mostly in onyx mined from the nearby quarries. On a hill in the city's center stands the Temple of the Elder Ones, which only the temple's priests and the Veiled King of Inganok himself are permitted to enter. Inganok is a very pleasant city, but its proximity to the Plateau of Leng keeps most travellers away.

See Quumyagga. ("The Dream-Quest of Unknown Kadath", Lovecraft.)

INNSMOUTH. Massachusetts town located at the mouth of the Manuxet River. At one time the town was a thriving seaport, but today it is almost deserted.

Innsmouth was founded in 1643, and soon became a major center of commerce on the Atlantic due to its large harbor. Ships from this town sailed all over the world, bringing back goods from many ports of call.

During the war of 1812 the captains of Innsmouth turned privateer and attacked the British fleets. Over the course of many skirmishes with the enemy, half of Innsmouth's sailors perished. This marked the end of the town's prosperity.

After the war Innsmouth's revenue came mainly from the mills built on the banks of the Manuxet, as well as from Captain Obed Marsh's successful trading in the Indies. Around 1840 Marsh lost the source of the gold upon which he had depended, and the town's economy went into a downward spiral. It was around this time that Marsh began the Esoteric Order of Dagon, a cult based on a combination of certain passages of Scripture and the beliefs of the Polynesian islanders whom Obed Marsh had visited. Some whispered that Marsh's Order possessed darker motives for its worship, and the Captain's trips to a formation in the harbor called Devil's Reef are legendary.

1846 was the year of Innsmouth's great plague. The exact disease responsible has never been identified, though it might have been a malady brought to the town on one of the remaining traders. What precisely happened during the plague remains a mystery, though evidently rioting and looting were widespread. When visitors from neighboring villages arrived they found half of the town's people dead, and Obed Marsh and his Order in firm control of the town.

Despite Innsmouth's curious newfound wealth in fishing and gold refining, the town's fortunes as a whole continued to decline. Also, degenerative traits began to turn up in the resident's children, most likely the aftereffects of the plague; during the Civil War, the town was unable to meet its quota of draftees due to these widespread deformities. Innsmouth remained under the Marsh family's rule for many years, and over time became shunned by the people of the surrounding countryside.

This state of affairs continued until 1927, when the government launched an investigation into supposed bootlegging taking place in the town. This inquiry culminated in a raid during the month of February, 1928, in which many of the town's abandoned buildings were dynamited, the Esoteric Order of Dagon was destroyed, and the bulk of Innsmouth's population was removed to military prisons. Rumors persist that a submarine fired torpedoes off of Devil's Reef for an unknown purpose. Innsmouth's remaining people attempted to rebuild their town, but this proved futile and it became a ghost town.

See *Book of Dagon*; Dagon; deep one; Devil's Reef; Esoteric Order of Dagon; Falcon Point; Innsmouth look; *Invocations to Dagon*; Marsh, Obed; Peaslee, Wingate; Waite, Asenath; Waite, Ephraim; Y'ha-nthlei. ("The Shadow over Innsmouth", Lovecraft; *Escape from Innsmouth*, Ross (C).)

INNSMOUTH LOOK. Hereditary condition which takes its name from the town of Innsmouth, Massachusetts, in which the majority of the population possessed this malady. An infected person seems normal at birth, but undergoes a slow, debilitating metamorphosis later in life. These changes often begin between the subject's twentieth birthday and middle age, though sometimes the disease's effects may be noticed earlier or later.

A person affected by the Innsmouth look is characterized by large, bulging eyes, scaly and peeling skin, a flattened nose, abnormally small ears, partially webbed fingers, and a wattling around the subject's neck. In the later stages the bone structure of the skull and pelvis shifts, forcing the victim to adopt a slow, shambling gait. The most advanced cases may involve the development of what appear to be rudimentary gills in the subject. Usually strange dreams of underwater realms and a growing obsession with the ocean accompany these physiological mutations. Often the person with the look drops out of sight after having the condition for many years; presumably the sense of self-preservation is overridden by the desire for the water, and he drowns himself while answering this call.

Sometimes a person with the Innsmouth look will progress only through the early stages of the malady, remaining in this state for the rest of his life. The exact cause of this is unknown. Also, proximity to the ocean or certain artifacts has been known to trigger the change in seemingly healthy individuals, though more research is needed before these factors can be predicted with any degree of certainty.

See deep one. ("The Shadow over Innsmouth", Lovecraft; *Escape from Innsmouth*, Ross (C.).)

INSECTS FROM SHAGGAI. See shan.

INUTO. Yellow-skinned people who destroyed the mighty Arctic civilization of Lomar, and from whom today's Eskimos are said to be descended.

See Lomar; Noton and Kadiphonek, Mounts; Olathoe. ("Polaris", Lovecraft.)

INVESTIGATION INTO THE MYTH-PATTERNS OF LATTER-DAY PRIMITIVES WITH ESPECIAL REFERENCE TO THE R'LYEH TEXT, AN. Book written by Professor Laban Shrewsbury, which was published in 1913 by Miskatonic University Press. In this book Professor Shrewsbury put forth his own conjectures regarding the rites and centers of the worldwide Cthulhu cult.

See *R'lyeh Text*; Shrewsbury, Laban. ("Zoth-Ommog", Carter; *The Trail of Cthulhu*, Derleth.)

INVOCATIONS TO DAGON. Manuscript written by Asaph Waite, a dweller in the town of Innsmouth, Massachusetts who died in the Federal raid of 1928. Evidence suggests that this manuscript was passed down in the family, though no outsider knows which member now possesses it. Miskatonic University also holds a few pages from this work. The invocations are mainly rituals and prayers dedicated to Father Dagon.

("Zoth-Ommog", Carter; *The Trail of Cthulhu*, Derleth.)

IOD. Being which is partly animal, vegetable, and mineral. Iod came down to Earth in the days of our world's youth. He was worshiped in Mu as the Shining Hunter, and the Greeks and Etruscans knew him in the guise of their gods of the underworld Trophonius and Vediovis, respectively. Iod the Source is still worshiped by beings beyond the farthest galaxies.

Some wizards have been able to summon Iod to do their bidding. Such conjurations are perilous, as the entity may hunt the wizard in order to devour his soul if not properly contained. No known volume contains the complete ceremony for calling up Iod, however.

See *Book of Iod, Book of Karnak*, Ixaxar. ("The Hunt", Kuttner; "The Invaders", Kuttner; "The Secret of Kralitz", Kuttner.)

IOG-SOTOT. See Yog-Sothoth.

IREM (also IRAM or possibly UBAR). Lost city located somewhere in the depths of the Arabian desert. Irem is the City of a Thousand Pillars, and is called "many-columned" in the Koran itself, where it has said to have been destroyed because of the sins of its inhabitants.

Two myths have been told about this city's origins. The first tells of Irem being built by creatures of great size and colossal strength. With our knowledge of the creatures of the Mythos, this should not be lightly dismissed. The second myth tells of Shaddad and Shaddid, two brothers and the joint rulers of the great city of Ad. After they had ruled Ad for a time, Shaddid died; following this tragedy, Shaddad became more egotistical, deciding to create an imitation of the celestial paradise on Earth. He gave orders to build a great city and garden in the desert of Aden, and named this new paradise Iram, after his great-grandfather Aram. When the garden was completed, Shaddad travelled with his entire entourage to view his new creation. A day's journey from the site, a "noise from heaven" destroyed him and all his courtiers. Another tale has it that creatures from the sky, who remain in the city to this day, killed or drove out all of the garden's inhabitants.

Abdul Alhazred was said to have opened up the first gate to allow the Great Old Ones' minions into this world in the ruins of Irem. It was also in this city where Hassan ibn Abbas received the insights later included in his book *Dreams of the Circle*, and Ludvig Prinn placed the beginnings of the cult of the worm-wizards in these ruins. Travellers lost in the deserts of Arabia have been known to stumble upon this city, later bearing their delirious tales back to civilization.

Over the gateway to Irem a tremendous hand is carved, which is said to reach for the artifact known as the Silver Key. A myth much like this is connected with the Alhambra in Granada. When a carven hand above a doorway in that palace grasps a long-lost key again, the palace will be instantly destroyed. This might have derived from an original myth relating to Irem.

Over the past year, we have heard much of the archaeological expedition to the lost city of Ubar, which is said by many to be Irem. At least one prominent archaeologist has said that Ubar and Irem are not one and the same, placing Irem in a different location. It may be too early to tell whether this site is the true Irem, but if it is the City of Pillars, its discovery might suggest that we are approaching the end-times.

See Abdul Alhazred, Black Litanies of Nug and Yeb, *De Vermis Mysteriis*, *Dreams of the Circle*, Lamp of Alhazred, Nameless City, Nephren-Ka, Nug and Yeb, "Saracenic Rituals", Ubar. ("The Lamp of Alhazred", Derleth and Lovecraft; *The Lurker at the Threshold*, Derleth and Lovecraft; "The Call of Cthulhu", Lovecraft; "The Nameless City", Lovecraft; "Through the Gates of the Silver Key", Lovecraft and Price; "Lord of the Worms", Lumley; "What Goes Around, Comes Around", Moeller, *TU08/9* (C).)

ISHAKSHAR. See Ixaxar.

ITHAQUA (also WIND-WALKER, DEATH-WALKER, and WENDIGO). Great Old One whose domain includes most of the northern regions of Earth. Ithaqua appears as a tremendous anthropomorphic shape with glowing carmine eyes and webbed feet, which walks through the air as if on solid ground. The Wendigo often emits eerie howling noises, but seeing the creature is worse; any who gaze upon Ithaqua are doomed to be taken by him. Ithaqua is probably one of a race of similar beings, as at least one encounter between Ithaqua and another wendigo has been reported. Only Ithaqua, however, has visited our world.

Like many of his fellow Great Old Ones, Ithaqua seems to be limited or imprisoned in a certain area. He was held at one time beneath a plateau on the world of Borea until he was able to effect his release. On our own planet Ithaqua is generally unable to leave the area between northern Manitoba and the North Pole, though in certain circumstances the Wind-Walker may travel further into the temperate zone. Whether Ithaqua may also manifest himself in the Antarctic is uncertain, as our exploration of that region has been limited. Ithaqua is not confined to our own world, however; he possesses the ability to fly through space, and is known to travel often to the world of Borea, which is located in a parallel universe. The Great Old One returns from his journeys elsewhere to Earth for one year in every five, when his cult experiences a stunning revival among the peoples of the north. Those in warmer latitudes who consider themselves safe from the Wind-Walker's wrath should beware, however; the Arctic boundaries do not constrain the servitor winds and other minions of Ithaqua, who may be sent anywhere in the world at their master's command.

The Native Americans of the regions where Ithaqua dwells know him as the Wendigo or Witiko. In their myths these monsters are human-like spirits who are taller than the mightiest trees and who live at the North Pole, coming south to catch and devour humans. According to legend, when two Wendigos meet they join in a titanic battle which ends in the destruction of one or both of the monsters.

The natives of Canada also say that the Wendigo sometimes touches the mind of a human. Such people usually become obsessed with cannibalism, and become so dangerous to their family and neighbors that they are often slain by their tribe. This "windigo psychosis" has recently come under intense scrutiny, however; it is likely that this "psychosis" is merely another cultural form of the witchcraft trials which took place in Europe and America. Possibly, though, there may be a small nucleus of cases which are directly caused by Ithaqua himself, as he creates more of his chosen servants.

Ithaqua is more widely feared than worshiped in the north; most of his worship died out in the early 19th century. The towns of Stillwater, the inhabitants of which all vanished in the space of one night, and Cold Harbor are current centers of his cult. In all instances these cults involved human sacrifice and kidnaping of those opposed to their worship.

The Wind-Walker is also responsible for a series of disappearances in Canada and the North. In most of these cases a person vanishes and nothing is heard of him for months or even years. Then he is found encased in shrouds of downy snow, with evidence of having fallen from a considerable height. Such victims may also be alive, babbling of the glories of Ithaqua, and have in some cases carried strange items which have plainly originated in widely-removed parts of the world. Those who have been in close physical proximity with the Wind-Walker are often able to endure the coldest temperatures without discomfort, or even transform into a creature physically resembling Ithaqua.

Some say that Ithaqua serves the Great Old One Hastur, but there seems to be little hard evidence to support this.

See Borea; Children of the Winds; Dromos; elemental theory; Great Old Ones; Hastur; Khrissa; Numinos; Ptetholite; Silberhutte, Hank; voormis, Wendigo. ("The Wendigo", Blackwood; "The Gods", Carter; "Ithaqua", Derleth; "The Thing That Walked on the Wind", Derleth; "Born of the Winds", Lumley; *Clock of Dreams*, Lumley; *In the Moons of Borea*, Lumley; *Spawn of the Winds*, Lumley; *Alone against the Wendigo*, Rahman (C).)

IXAXAR (or ISHAKSHAR). Artifact mentioned by Pomponius Mela in his *De Situ Orbis*. According to this authority the Ixaxar is an ebon stone with sixty characters inscribed upon it. A bestial people of Libya's interior holds the Ixaxar sacred, and holds sacrificial rites in its honor. This artifact's inscription deals with Iod the Hunter of Souls.

See Iod. ("The Hunt", Kuttner; "The Novel of the Black Seal", Machen.)

J

JERUSALEM'S LOT. Religious community founded on the coast of Massachusetts in 1710 by a splinter group of Puritans led by James Boon, a young charismatic preacher around whose meeting house the small town was constructed. The doctrines taught by Boon were strange even by modern-day standards; his sermons were filled with talk of demons, and Boon asserted his right to take any woman in the community to himself whenever he desired to do so. As a result, Jerusalem's Lot became a town filled with insanity and degeneration.

In 1789, when Boon, now an old man, was still the head of the community, the aged pastor gained a copy of Prinn's *De Vermis Mysteriis*. He incorporated this book into his services, and on Hallowe'en of that year he and his congregation attempted a ceremony contained within that volume. On that night, all of the people of Jerusalem's Lot vanished and were never seen again.

See *De Vermis Mysteriis*. ("Jerusalem's Lot", King.)

JIDHAUA. Nomadic people who dwell within the Gobi Desert of Mongolia. They are known to worship the Great Old One Shudde-M'ell.

See Shudde-M'ell. (*The Transition of Titus Crow*, Lumley.)

JOHANSEN NARRATIVE. Diary written by Gustaf Johansen, second mate of the ship *Emma*, in which he tells of his accidental journey to the risen corpse-city of R'lyeh on March 23, 1925, and what he encountered there.

See R'lyeh. ("The Call of Cthulhu", Lovecraft; *The Burrowers Beneath*, Lumley.)

JUK-SHABB. Great Old One resembling a shining sphere which constantly changes color and speaks with its worshipers telepathically. This being rules the world of Yekub and its centipede-like inhabitants. Though not necessarily malevolent toward humans, Juk-Shabb will protect any Yekubians who are harmed in its presence.

See Yekub. ("The Eyes of a Stranger", Aniolowski (C); "The Challenge from Beyond", Lovecraft *et al.*)

K

KA-RATH. See Quachil Uttaus.

KADATH IN THE COLD WASTE. Onyx fortress built by the Great Ones themselves, where they are protected or imprisoned by the Crawling Chaos Nyarlathotep. It may lie in the far north of the Dreamlands, beyond the Plateau of Leng; according to other tales, it may be found on a gigantic mountain chain in the Antarctic, somewhere near Mongolia, or in ruins far underground in modern-day Turkey. Wherever it is, Kadath is a terrible place for mortals to visit, as the gods do not take kindly to anyone invading their mountain retreat.

See Carter, Randolph; Cold Waste; Dreamlands; Great Ones; Leng; Ngranek; Yr-Nhhngr. ("The Seal of R'lyeh", Derleth; "At the Mountains of Madness", Lovecraft; "The Dream-Quest of Unknown Kadath", Lovecraft; *The Mind Parasites*, C. Wilson.)

KADIPHONEK, MOUNT. See Noton and Kadiphonek, Mounts.

KAGWAMON K'THAAT. Book penned by Adolphus Clesteros sometime during the 13th century. For reasons which are still unclear, Adolphus chose to write the volume's contents in a language of his own invention known as W'hywi. Only one copy exists, and its current whereabouts are uncertain. This volume probably deals to some degree with the cthonians and other such beings.

("Dark Carnival", Hargrave (C).)

KANT, ERNST. German baron and witch hunter who lived around the turn of the century, and father of Joachim Feery. The Baron dedicated his life to investigating the supernatural. In his later years, however, Baron Kant believed that his mind was being controlled by an alien being called Yibb-Tstll. Shortly thereafter he was confined to a Westphalian sanitarium, where he later died.

See Feery, Joachim; Yibb-Tstll. ("The Horror at Oakdeene", Lumley; "The Mirror of Nitocris", Lumley.)

KARA-SHEHR (Turkish for "The Black City"; known to Arabs as Beled el-Djinn, "City of Devils"). Deserted city located in the wastes of Arabia. In his *Necronomicon* Alhazred refers to it as the City of Evil. Refugees from Assyria whose homeland had been conquered by the Babylonians were the builders of Kara-Shehr. A magician named Xuthltan cursed the city when its king tried to learn the location of a great treasure from him, and the native tribes still shun the town's ruins.

Some have said that the Nameless City is identical with Kara-Shehr, but this is not the case. Kara-Shehr has been described as a relatively intact fortress built by humans, and the Nameless City was built by reptilian creatures and has been almost completely destroyed.

See Xuthltan. ("The Gods", Carter; "The Fire of Asshurbanipal", Howard; "The Nameless City", Lovecraft.)

KEEPER OF THE SILVER GATE. 1) Rank within the Masters of the Silver Twilight, above Knight of the Outer Void. 2) Book holding the tenets of that level of initiation.

See Masters of the Silver Twilight. ("The Hermetic Order of the Silver Twilight", Hutchinson (C).)

KEEPER OF THE YELLOW SIGN. Entity connected with Hastur and the Yellow Sign. Little is known about the Keeper, but keeping the Yellow Sign out of the hands of the uninitiated seems to be its duty. The Keeper possesses a human corpse to carry out its mission, leaving this body behind when it departs.

In one instance, a victim of multiple personality disorder in which one of his "selves" worshiped Hastur, while the other did not, attempted to call the Keeper to purge himself of his other side.

See Hastur, Yellow Sign. ("The Yellow Sign", Chambers; "The Madman", Harmon (C).)

KHRISSA. City of basalt which sat at the northern edge of the primal continent of Theem'hdra. Khrissa's priests avowed that only they could hold back the great glaciers from rolling over the rest of the world, and demanded hundreds of human sacrifices every year to aid them in their task. After a great war, however, savages from further south besieged Khrissa. The outcome of this siege has been lost to history, but Ithaqua took up his faithful ice priests to the moon Dromos circling Borea, where they have dwelt ever since.

See Dromos, Theem'hdra. (*In the Moons of Borea*, Lumley.)

KING IN YELLOW. 1) Play written in the late 19th century by an unknown playwright (possibly named Castaigne) who later attempted suicide. When first published the government and churches denounced this work, and the city of Paris banned the play. Since then other editions have been published secretly. Though this play contains much contradiction and allegory, it is a work which leaves none who read it unchanged.

During my research into this topic, I have found two different versions of this play, each having its own interpretation of the various elements mentioned in connection with the play. A synopsis of both is included herein, in the interest of completeness. Which one is truly correct is unknown; it could be that *The King in Yellow* is different for every reader.

A. The two-act play begins on another world in the city of Yhtill, under the stars of Aldebaran and the Hyades. The majority of the play concerns the intrigue in the royal court between the claimants to the throne of Yhtill — the Queen, Alar, Thale, Uoht, Cassilda, Aldones, and Camilla. The royal party hears of a mysterious stranger who wears a Pallid Mask and the horrid Yellow Sign, who comes to Yhtill at about the same time as a strange ghostly city is sighted across the Lake of Hali. The royal family questions this figure, but they learn nothing. After revealing at a masked ball that he in fact wears no disguise, the queen tortures the wearer of the Pallid Mask, also known as the Phantom of Truth, to death.

Following this affront, the dreaded mythical entity, the King in Yellow, appears in Yhtill as the mysterious city on the lake's far side disappears. The King states that Yhtill has passed away, and now only the city of Carcosa lies on the shore of the lake. All characters except the King go insane, die, or must helplessly await their fate.

B. In the second version, the setting is the city of Hastur, which has been at war with its neighbor Alar for countless years. The children of the ruling queen, Uoht, Thale, and Camilla, pester their mother Cassilda for the crown so that the dynasty might continue, but she puts off giving it away. Cassilda then learns that a figure wearing a Pallid Mask and bearing the Yellow Sign has been seen in Hastur. Counseled by the high priest Naotalba, she calls this stranger into the palace. The stranger, named Yhtill, offers the queen a chance to break free from the domination of the King in Yellow, who dwells in Carcosa across the Lake of Hali and rarely interferes in the works of humans. By wearing the Pallid Mask, he states, all those in the city may throw off the dread of the Yellow Sign as he has.

Believing what the stranger has told her, the queen holds a masquerade at which each person wears the Pallid Mask. When the time comes to unmask, Yhtill reveals that he wears no mask, and has come from Alar to wreak vengeance upon Hastur's people. This outrage does not go unnoticed by the King in Yellow, who comes to bear away Yhtill. The King promises Cassilda that he will allow the victor of the war between Hastur and Alar to rule the world, but on one condition: that the people of Hastur and their descendants wear their Pallid Masks for all time. As the play ends, the King in Yellow departs, leaving the courtiers in despair.

See Alar, Aldones, Camilla, Cassilda, Demhe, Hali, Hastur, Last King, Naotalba, Pallid Mask, Thale, Uoht, Yellow Sign, Yhtill. ("More Light", Blish; "In the Court of the Dragon", Chambers; "The Repairer of Reputations", Chambers; "The Yellow Sign", Chambers; "Tell Me, Have You Seen the Yellow Sign?", Ross (C).)

2) The King in Yellow is also the name for an avatar of Hastur, or possibly Nyarlathotep, which is the title character of this play. The King usually takes the form of a gigantic human dressed in tattered yellow robes and sometimes wearing the Pallid Mask. See Brothers of the Yellow Sign, Hastur, Nyarlathotep (Thing in the Yellow Mask), Sakkuth, Yellow Sign. ("More Light", Blish; "The Yellow Sign", Chambers; "Tatterdemalion", Love, Ross, and Watts (C).)

KINGDOM OF SHADOWS. Book in Latin written in the 17th century, of which very few copies still exist. The book tells of a being known as The Hanging One, and the Dark Stone which will release its power.

("Mansion of Madness", Behrendt (C).)

KINGSPORT. Town located north of Salem and Arkham on the coast of Massachusetts. In 1639 settlers from southern England and the Channel Islands founded Kingsport. The town quickly became a center for shipbuilding and overseas trade. At least four witches were hung in 1692, when witchcraft fervor struck the town. Thirty years later a raid was made upon the Congregational Church in response to rumors of pagan rituals being performed beneath it, and over thirty people were taken into custody. During the Revolutionary War many of Kingsport's merchants fought as privateers on the Colonial side, leading to a short blockade of the town by the British fleet. During the 19th century the sea trade in Kingsport declined and fishing became the port's major industry. At that time Kingsport's economy began to steadily fade until the first years of the 20th century.

Today Kingsport is a small seaside town in which the primary source of revenue is tourism. Kingsport boasts a large artistic community, and sailing and sightseeing are popular among its visitors. One point of especial interest is the Strange High House in the Mist, a one-story structure which stands atop one of the highest of the nearby cliffs.

See Martin's Beach; Miskatonic River; *Necrolatry*; *Necronomicon* (Appendices); Outer Ones; *Ponape Scripture*; Tulzscha; Waite, Asenath. ("The Festival", Lovecraft; "The Strange High House in the Mist", Lovecraft; *Kingsport*, Ross (C).)

KISH. 1) Catacombs where the Pharaoh Nephren-Ka held the Shining Trapezohedron and the mysterious mirror later connected with Nitocris. It was in these labyrinths that he did the horrible deed which caused later generations to strike his name from every monument.

This "Kish" is probably not the same as the Sumerian city of the same name, as Egypt never controlled the area in which these remains are located. See Nephren-Ka, Nitocris, Shining Trapezohedron, Sign of Kish. ("The Haunter of the Dark", Lovecraft; "The Mirror of Nitocris", Lumley.)

2) High priest of the city of Sarnath, which *Necronomicon* asserts was located in the Middle East. Just before his city's destruction, Kish and his congregation escaped the city, bearing with them the star-stones of Mnar. It may be that Kish and his followers escaped to Egypt, there constructing the catacombs which bear the hierophant's name. See Elder Sign, *Necronomicon* (Appendices), Sign of Kish, star-stone of Mnar. ("Zoth-Ommog", Carter.)

KITAB AL-AZIF. See *Al-Azif*.

KLARKASH-TON. High priest of Atlantis who is credited with preserving the Commoriom myth cycle of Hyperborea. In *The Sussex Manuscript*, Klarkash-Ton is said to be Yog-Sothoth himself; most likely this means that Klarkash-Ton was a manifestation of the Outer God, as it was revealed to Randolph Carter by Umr at'Tawil.

See Commoriom, Hyperborea, Luveh-Keraphf. ("Through the Gate of the Silver Key", Lovecraft; "The Whisperer in Darkness", Lovecraft; *The Sussex Manuscript*, Pelton.)

KN'AA. Kingdom of the sunken continent of Mu, mentioned in von Junzt's *Unaussprechlichen Kulten* as the original site of Ghatanothoa's worship on Earth.

See Dhoric shrine, Ghatanothoa, Nath-feast, Yaddith-Gho. ("Out of the Aeons", Heald and Lovecraft.)

KNIGHT OF THE OUTER VOID. Level of initiation within the Masters of the Silver Twilight.

See Masters of the Silver Twilight. ("The Hermetic Order of the Silver Twilight", Hutchinson (C).)

K'N-YAN. Blue-lit cavern located beneath Oklahoma. This immense underground land, despite its location, contains an amazing variety of plant and animal life, as well as a highly developed though decadent civilization of human-like beings.

The natives of K'n-yan appear to the untrained eye much like the Native Americans of the region; only their curious garb and tools set them apart from the surface-dwellers. In fact, these people may have been the ancestors of the Aztec people, since that tribe's mythology told of their origin in caverns to the north of their lands. The underground dwellers possess three abilities unavailable to those on the surface. First, they use telepathy for communication, with spoken language almost being a thing of the past. Second, they are able to dematerialize their bodies (and sometimes other objects) so that they may pass through solid objects almost effortlessly. Finally, the people of K'n-yan have the secret of immortality, so that death is an almost unheard-of occurrence among them.

At one time these people boasted many great works of art, technology, and science. Despite their former mighty accomplishments, the last recorded visitor to K'n-yan, Panfilio Zamacoma, who visited the land over four hundred years ago, reported that the inhabitant's civilization had stagnated, and the people had forgotten much of their former science. They put more value on experiencing new sensations through ritual torture, dreaming, and gladiatorial games than on their former pursuits. They still possessed many technological artifacts, however, such as disintegrating-ray projectors and forms of transportation, which they used in their day-to-day life.

According to Zamacoma, most of the population of K'n-yan lived in the central city of Tsath, whose inhabitants spent much of their time looking for novel experiences and emotions. To help them achieve these aims, they held great gladiatorial games, experimented with intoxicating substances, and held religious ceremonies to various deities. Of these gods, Yig and Tulu (Cthulhu) were the most important, but they also held rites in honor of Hastur, Shub-Niggurath, Ghatanothoa, Nug, and Yeb. At one time most of K'n-yan's people revered Tsathoggua, but after they discovered the true nature of his worship, they destroyed all of his temples and images.

Several passages connect K'n-yan with the surface. Once in a while a surface-dweller finds his way into the world of K'n-yan. The natives usually treat these people kindly, but forbid them from leaving the caverns to return home. In more recent years the people of K'n-yan have posted guards at these entrances to discourage the people on the surface from entering their land.

We have heard nothing of K'n-yan since the 16th century. If the older accounts are any indication, it would be unwise to investigate.

See Cthulhu, Ghatanothoa, gyaa-yothn, Hastur, Sansu, Tsath, Tsathoggua, y'm-bhi, Zuchequon. ("The Mound", Bishop and Lovecraft; "Out of the Aeons", Heald and Lovecraft; "The Cthulhu Mythos in Mesoamerican Religion", Tierney.)

KOSSUTH. See Sakkuth.

KOTH. 1) Black cyclopean city. No one knows precisely where this city is, but it is possibly that great city of the gugs sometimes seen by dreamers. A Dark Lord whose face is hidden resides there; this Lord might be Nyarlathotep, but this has not been confirmed. If a mortal comes to the city and beseeches him, the Dark Lord may bestow great riches and a lifespan of hundreds of years upon the petitioner. At the end of the person's life, the Dark Lord takes away his body and soul in exchange for services rendered. ("Dig Me No Grave", Howard.)

2) Being who lives in the Dreamlands and is known by the title "God of Dreams." He may also be the Dark Lord of the city of Koth. ("The Gods", Carter; "Dig Me No Grave", Howard.)

3) During the Hyborian Age, kingdom founded by the Hyborians which extended across what is today the Mediterranean Sea and the country of Italy. ("The Hyborian Age", Howard.)

See Sign of Koth, Uoht.

KTHANID. The mightiest of all the Elder Gods, who oppose the Great Old Ones. Kthanid is a tentacled horror much like Cthulhu, differing in appearance from the Great Old One only in his golden, peaceful eyes. This Elder God dwells in Elysia, where he presides over the entire land from his iceberg palace.

See Elder Gods. (*The Transition of Titus Crow*, Lumley.)

K'THOOLO OF SOUCHIS. High priest of the continent of Mu. He lived for half a million years, and was worshiped as a god by the people of this land. He survived the destruction of Mu by escaping to South America, but was killed in the end in present-day Mexico.

(*The Philosopher's Stone*, C. Wilson.)

K'THUN. A being whose odor or vapor is considered particularly abhorrent.

("The Horror in the Museum", Heald and Lovecraft.)

KTYNGA. Comet which is currently near the star Arcturus, and which will journey past our own world some four centuries from now. This body possesses some peculiar traits: It travels between solar systems instead of maintaining a steady orbit around a star, makes inexplicable changes in its trajectory, and may at times move faster than the speed of light.

When more closely observed, the comet appears to have a curious reddish-blue tinge, and seems to have an extremely high surface temperature. Upon Ktynga rests a tremendous building which houses the fire-being Fthaggua and his fire vampires, who guide the comet and use it to transport themselves between the stars.

See fire vampire, Fthaggua. ("Zoth-Ommog", Carter; "The Fire-Vampires", Wandrei.)

KUEN-YUIN. Cabal of Chinese sorcerers. The goals of the Kuen-Yuin are unknown; however, in one documented incident, they seemed bent on ruining the U.S. economy by the alchemical production of gold. They are said to control a hundred million people, body and soul, in their native China. The city of Yian serves as the headquarters of this organization. The Kuen-Yuin might be some of Cthulhu's cult leaders who live in the mountains of China, as detailed by Castro.

See Castro, Yian. ("The Maker of Moons", Chambers.)

KYTHAMIL (or KTHYMIL). Double planet that once circled the star Arcturus, and served as the dwelling place for certain fungoid beings. The worse-than-formless worshipers of the Great Old One Tsathoggua came to Hyperborea from this star.

("Shaggai", Carter; "Through the Gate of the Silver Key", Lovecraft and Price.)

L

LAKE OF HALI. See Hali, Lake of.

LAMP OF ALHAZRED. Device constructed by the mythical Arabian tribe of Ad, the builders of Irem, and possessed at one time by the mad Arab Abdul Alhazred. The Providence author Ward Phillips was the last to own this item, and it was disposed of following his disappearance. When filled with oil and lit, the Lamp projects images of Mythos-connected locations upon the walls and objects around it. It may also act as a gateway to various times and places, though this effect probably works only at certain times.

("The Lamp of Alhazred", Derleth and Lovecraft.)

LAN SHI. Being worshiped by an ancient Chinese cult. The worship of Lan Shi was begin by Cho Shek, a wizard who discovered references to a being known as Lan Shi on various ancient scrolls. He cast the rituals associated with this being, and called an unearthly beast into this dimension.

The fight between the two adversaries was prolonged and horrendous, but Cho Shek finally managed to capture and tame the beast. He then set it against the people of the region, and demanded that they pay tribute to him so that he would keep the monster from preying upon them. These peasants soon accepted their situation, starting a cult they hoped would placate the beast.

This cult became very powerful as more of the locals joined, but it also made enemies with many powerful people. These foes attacked on Midsummer's Eve, 1723, as the cult attempted to sacrifice one hundred people to summon Lan Shi. The cult's enemies beat back the worshipers, killed their leaders, and destroyed their temple. A few secret cells of this cult dedicated to summoning Lan-Shi once again still exist.

("The Vanishing Conjurer", Lewis and Price (C).)

LAST DAWN. Organization started by a group of Great Old One worshipers who infiltrated the Roman Catholic Church at the time of the Inquisition. These cultists used the Inquisition to further their own political power, and soon became a major force within the church.

Around the year 1500 there was a power struggle within the ranks of the Last Dawn. The victors, the Cassini family, foisted a new theology upon the organization. According to this new teaching, the horrors of the Mythos were visited upon humanity as God's punishment for modern man's lack of faith. Though upon close inspection this argument is full of logical fallacies, most of the Lasters, as they came to be known, accepted this new line of thought.

A few decades later the Last Dawn split with the Catholic Church, but they have continued their efforts to bring humanity to the light. Today the Last Dawn supposedly has cells on every inhabited continent, and operates under a rigid hierarchy led by a Hierophant said to live in a fortress in a high mountain chain (possibly the Andes or the Himalayas).

See Revelare Nuncius. ("The Last Dawn", Eastland, *TU07*.)

LAST KING. Title given sometimes to Aldones, a character from the play *The King in Yellow*, and sometimes to the King in Yellow himself.

See Aldones, King in Yellow. ("More Light", Blish; "Carcosa Story about Hali" (fragment), Carter; "The Repairer of Reputations", Chambers.)

LEGENDS OF LIQUALIA. Tome of aquatic horrors written by a Mr. Oswald. Titus Crow's library held a copy of *Legends*.

("De Marigny's Clock", Lumley.)

LEGENDS OF THE OLDEN RUNES. Manuscript found in a golden box thrown up from the depths of the Earth during the rising of the isle of Surtsey in 1963. A man named Thelred Gustau discovered the box and spent the next nine years translating the hieroglyphics on the documents within. When he released news of his discoveries to the world he was ridiculed, despite his formerly high scholarly reputation. Shortly thereafter Gustau vanished following a mysterious explosion in his study, and his work was only published in a very limited version.

The manuscript was said to have been the work of the sorcerer Teh Atht, a wizard of the primal land of Theem'hdra. The volume contained information regarding the land and inhabitants of Theem'hdra, and tales regarding some notable events in this land's history. Along with these there were notes regarding the worship of such beings as Ghatanothoa, Cthulhu, Hastur, and Yibb-Tstll. Some incantations were also included, such as a ritual intended to summon a byakhee, and another used to protect the user from all baneful influences.

See byakhee, Teh Atht of Kluhn, Theem'hdra. ("Introduction" to *The House of Cthulhu*, Lumley; "Name and Number", Lumley.)

LEGRASSE, JOHN RAYMOND. New Orleans police inspector who led a raid in 1907 against a bayou cult of particularly abhorrent nature. Legrasse could learn little of this sect, but his arrival at the American Archaeological Society Meeting in 1908 with a small idol taken in the raid was one of the first clues to the existence of the worldwide Cthulhu cult.

("The Call of Cthulhu", Lovecraft.)

LEMURIA. According to legend, land which sank beneath the Pacific Ocean thousands of years ago. The first human beings may have come into existence on Lemuria. This land might be identical with Mu or R'lyeh, but this remains unclear.

See Shamballah, Shining Trapezohedron. ("The Haunter of the Dark", Lovecraft.)

LENG (or PLATEAU OF LENG). Area quite close to Kadath in the Cold Waste, whose inhabitants perform rites to the Outer Gods and the Great Old Ones. The Plateau is usually placed in central Asia by scholars. However, reports from the Pabodie Expedition of 1930-31 place Leng somewhere in the frozen wastes of Antarctica, and experienced dreamers say it lies in the northern part of Earth's Dreamlands. Alhazred mentions it as a place where various alternate realities come together and things from Outside are wont to enter our dimension, which may explain these discrepancies.

No matter where it is, the Plateau should be avoided by the casual visitor, since its curious people, the Tcho-Tcho, do not take kindly to being visited. Many are said to belong to a cult which practices cannibalism and whose symbol is a winged hound. At one time these people built the great city of Sarkomand to the south of the Plateau, but today they are content to live in their small stone villages, carrying out their worship practices and serving their moon-beast masters.

A great stone temple surrounded by a ring of monoliths stands on this plateau. Within the labyrinthine corridors of this monastery are murals depicting the history of the Plateau's people. The only living thing to dwell in this place is its High Priest whose face, according to the experienced dreamer Randolph Carter, is not good to look upon.

See *Dhol Chants*; glass from Leng; Inganok; Kadath in the Cold Waste; Mnomquah; moon-beast; Nyarlathotep (The Thing in the Yellow Mask); Nyogtha; Pharos of Leng; shantak; Sung, Plateau of; Tcho-Tcho; Tsang, Plateau of; *Unaussprechlichen Kulten*; Yian-Ho. ("The Dweller in the Tomb", Carter; "Beyond the Threshold", Derleth; "At the Mountains of Madness", Lovecraft; "The Dream-Quest of Unknown Kadath", Lovecraft; "The Elder Pharos", Lovecraft; "The Hound", Lovecraft.)

LENG, PLATEAU OF. See Leng.

LESSER OLD ONES. Name given by Harold Hadley Copeland to the servitors of the Great Old Ones. Included among the Lesser Old Ones are Dagon and Hydra, as well as deep ones, fire vampires, mi-go, the nagaee, and cthonians. Unlike the Great Old Ones, the Lesser Old Ones are usually free to move about and do their masters' bidding.
See Great Old Ones. ("Zoth-Ommog", Carter.)

LETTERS OF NESTAR. Volume written by the Persian Nestar Mobedan Mobed in Pahlavi around the 6th century A.D. In this book are contained rituals for the summoning of Cthugha and his servitors.
See Nestar Mobedan Mobed. ("This Fire Shall Kill", Bishop (C).)

L'GY'HX. Planet known to humanity as Uranus, which is inhabited by a race of cubical, many-legged creatures made of metal who worship the curious bat god Lrogg.
Many years ago the shan arrived on this world in their teleporting temple of Azathoth. They were allowed by the natives to remain for a while. Soon, however, various individuals from both groups became converts to the religion of the other. In the end this caused a conflict that forced the Azathoth-worshiping shan to leave in their temple, leaving their heretical fellows on L'gy'hx with the natives.
See Nyarlathotep (Lrogg), shan. ("The Insects from Shaggai", Campbell.)

LH-YIB. "Sister city" of Ib. Its exact location is unknown, but according to the Brick Cylinders of Kadatheron it lies buried beneath the land of Cimmeria.

See Bokrug, Ib, Thuum'ha. (*Beneath the Moors*, Lumley.)

LIAO (also PLUTONIAN DRUG). Mind-altering substance that can be used to view other times, in the past or future. During his use of Liao, Lao Tze is said to have envisioned the universal concept of Tao, which served as the foundation of his thought.

Centuries ago a Chinese alchemist named Liao discovered the formula for this substance. The formula travelled from the East and reached the Saracens, from whom Ludvig Prinn gained his knowledge of the substance. This drug is extremely rare and is rarely used today.

See *De Vermis Mysteriis*, Pnakotic Pentagram. ("The Invaders", Kuttner; "The Hounds of Tindalos", Long; "Signs Writ in Scarlet", Ross (C); "The Plutonian Drug", Smith.)

LIBER DAMNATUS DAMNATIONUM. Volume written by Janus Aquaticus and published in London in 1647. It contains many magical ceremonies dedicated to the Great Old Ones, as well as information pertaining to the Great Dying, when the Great Old Ones shall return. In fact it seems that much of this book was shamelessly plagiarized for *The Occult Foundation*, the occultist Janus Wasserman's predictions on the future of humanity.

This volume may be the mysterious "Liber-Damnatus" alluded to in the correspondence of the reputed sorcerer Joseph Curwen and his colleagues. If so, it may contain a formula which allows a sorcerer to become immortal through the actions of one of his descendants, along with an incantation for contacting Yog-Sothoth.

("The Case of Charles Dexter Ward", Lovecraft; *House of the Toad*, Tierney.)

LIBER IVONIS. Caius Phillipus Faber's Latin translation of *Book of Eibon*.

See *Book of Eibon*.

LIFE OF EIBON. Book by Cyron of Varaad, which deals with the Hyperborean sorcerer Eibon and the world in which he lived.

See Eibon. ("The Fishers from Outside", Carter.)

LITHARD. Species of draconian beings which dwelt on the world of Thak'r-Yon. When their sun exploded, the lithards were taken to Elysia by the Elder Gods, where they are used for transportation by the land's other inhabitants.

(*The Transition of Titus Crow*, Lumley.)

LIVRE D'IVON. French translation of *Book of Eibon*.
See *Book of Eibon*.

LIYUHH. Little-known German translation of *R'lyeh Text*, including notes on the text. At least one copy is held by an unnamed private collector.

See *R'lyeh Text*. ("Darkness, My Name Is", Bertin.)

LLOIGOR (also LLOIGORNOS). 1) Being who is the twin of Zhar. Lloigor is imprisoned beneath the Plateau of Sung in Burma, but can manifest itself elsewhere when Arcturus, from whence it came, is above the horizon. In its natural form Lloigor is a huge winged mass of wailing tentacles which uses winds to trap and seize its foes. See elemental theory; Sung, Plateau of; Twin Obscenities; Zhar. ("The Sandwin Compact", Derleth; "The Lair of the Star-Spawn", Derleth and Schorer; *The Sussex Manuscript*, Pelton.)

2) Immaterial beings composed of some unknown type of psychic energy, but who manifest themselves at times in tremendous reptilian bodies. Long ago they came down from the Andromeda Galaxy and ruled over the land of Mu, using human slaves to further their designs. As time progressed, however, the lloigor slowly lost power and withdrew into the ground, leaving their slaves free to leave Mu and populate the Earth.

The lloigor still survive today, but are unable to muster enough strength to overthrow humanity. They can still use their power in underground places to demagnetize compasses, affect photographic equipment, and exert psychokinetic force on people and objects. If the lloigor require more energy than this, they may draw more power from the sleeping inhabitants of nearby populations. Those whom the lloigor drain awaken the next day feeling ill, but have recovered their vitality by the end of that day. Using the energy so gained, the lloigor can cause a ship or plane to disappear for a short length of time (causing the "lost time" effect often reported in UFO encounters), or create a huge explosion which leaves great crevices in the ground and pools of blue-green water in its radius. Many believe that the Llandalffen explosion and the detonation near Al-Kazimiyah in Iraq were caused by the lloigor.

The lloigor's mental influence extends to the people who live near them, and rampant crime and degradation are often found in regions inhabited by them. Sometimes the lloigor recruit the most degenerate members of the population to do their bidding in the upper world. Though these individuals often believe that they will gain great power from their masters, they mean nothing to the lloigor, who casually dispose of them if they prove unnecessary or troublesome.

At times the lloigor have been known to take on material form, creating bodies which resemble the dragons of legend. This may explain why myths of huge reptilian beings are prevalent in many cultures but no physical traces of any such entities have been found. Taking this hypothesis further, the lloigor are possibly the basis for the lake and sea monsters which have been sighted for millennia yet have never been caught or dissected.

The lloigor are filled with a never-ending pessimism. Their minds are not divided into the id, ego, and superego, as those of humans are. As a consequence of this, they are unlikely to put any of their plans into action. Still it should be realized that they can be dangerous foes to those who learn of their existence.

Centers of lloigor activity include Al-Kazimiyah in Iraq, Wales, Lebanon, Ceylon, and Providence, Rhode Island. The lloigor are servitors of the Great Old One Ghatanothoa, but the extent of his control over them is unknown. They may be linked to the Great Old One Lloigor in some way. See Ghatanothoa. (*Call of Cthulhu* rulebook, Petersen *et al.* (C); "The Return of the Lloigor", C. Wilson.)

L'MUR-KATHULOS. Being associated with the League of Hastur. In ancient times initiates would undergo the most excruciating tests to become one of his pupils. There might also be some connection between this being and Kathulos, a sorcerer from the lost continent of Atlantis.

("Skull-Face", Howard; *The Sussex Manuscript*, Pelton.)

LOMAR. Northern land of ancient legend (though whether located in the Dreamlands or the waking world, none can say), which is said to have risen from the depths of the ocean. The founders of Lomar were humans who came from the land of Zobna to the north, slaying the cannibalistic gnoph-keh who lived there to establish their own kingdom. The capital of this land was Olathoe, which lay between the mountains of Noton and Kadiphonek. The people of

Lomar were quite accomplished; they raised great monuments out of marble and devoted their time to studying the *Pnakotic Manuscripts* and the annals of their Zobnarian forebears. Despite their high level of civilization, they were destroyed by the primitive Inutos, leaving no trace of their splendor.

See gnoph-keh; Inuto; Noton and Kadiphonek, Mounts; Olathoe; *Pnakotic Manuscripts*; Tsathoggua; Zobna. ("The Dream-Quest of Unknown Kadath", Lovecraft; "Polaris", Lovecraft; "Through the Gates of the Silver Key", Lovecraft and Price.)

LROGG. Two-headed bat deity worshiped on the world of L'gy'hk (Uranus) by that world's metallic beings and certain rebellious insects from Shaggai. The Uranians sacrifice to Lrogg once a year by removing the legs from a conscious native. Some say that Lrogg is in fact a minor avatar of Nyarlathotep.

See L'gy'hx, Nyarlathotep (Lrogg). (*Ye Booke of Monstres*, Aniolowski (C); "The Insects from Shaggai", Campbell.)

LUD. See Nodens.

LUVEH-KERAPHF. Atlantean high priest of Bast who is credited with writing *Black Rites*. He lived at much the same time as the infamous Klarkash-Ton.

See *Black Rites*. ("The Mannikin", Bloch.)

M

MAGELLANIC CLOUDS. Pair of galaxies neighboring our own. Wilmarth once hinted at the secret behind these stellar phenomena mentioned by one of his correspondents, but no record of this revelation remains.

("The Whisperer in Darkness", Lovecraft.)

MAGIC AND THE BLACK ARTS. Book by "Kane" that contains a passing reference to B'moth, the Devourer.

See B'moth. ("The Scourge of B'moth", Russell.)

MAGNETIC RING. Great field which circles the farthest galaxies of the cosmos. It is mentioned in *Ethics of Ygor*, and may be linked with the Great White Space.

See *Ethics of Ygor*, Great White Space. (*The Great White Space*, Copper.)

MAGNUM INNOMINANDUM (roughly "One-Who-Is-Not-To-Be-Named"). Great nameless deity mentioned in the incantation to summon a star vampire in *De Vermis Mysteriis*. This mysterious being was also worshiped long ago by the Miri Nigri. Though the title of this entity seems to connect it with the Great Old One Hastur, it is more likely a title of Chaugnar Faugn.

See Chaugnar Faugn, *De Vermis Mysteriis*, Hastur, Miri Nigri. ("The Shambler from the Stars", Bloch; *The Horror from the Hills*, Long; *Dreams and Fancies*, Lovecraft.)

MAO. Ceremony that may be found in *Necronomicon* that aids in communication with the beings from the Gulf of S'lghuo. After using the incantation the caster falls asleep and may speak with the Gulf's inhabitants in his dreams. The Mao ritual is dangerous if used over long periods, though, and the people in the Gulf prefer other methods of speech.

See *Necronomicon* (Appendices). ("The Plain of Sound", Campbell; "The White People", Machen.)

MAPULO. Object created by deep ones to control the shoggoths allied with them. These protoplasmic bodies take several months to create. They are held in the controller's hands, and put him in telepathic rapport with the shoggoth. The mapulo have a small chance of eating the commander, and there is no way to get rid of them, except for burning. The mapulo processes the commander's lactic acid, so that they have no need of sleep or rest — fortunately enough for them, since the slightest misstep by the controller could result in disaster.

See shoggoth-twsha. ("Shanghai", DiTillio and Willis (C).)

MARK OF CTHULHU. Abnormalities which Cthulhu bestows upon his most devout priests. A person bearing the Mark of Cthulhu appears mostly human, but on some part of his body pale, worm-like tentacles have sprouted, sometimes replacing one of the person's organs.

("The Fairground Horror", Lumley.)

MARSH, OBED (?-1878). Innsmouth's most prominent merchant-captain and founder of that town's Esoteric Order of Dagon. Obed's three ships, *Columbia*, *Hetty*, and *Sumatra Queen*, did a brisk business in the Pacific trade beginning in 1820 and lasting for almost twenty years. As a result of this prosperity the Marshes became Innsmouth's most powerful family.

On one of his early trips Captain Marsh stumbled across a group of Polynesian islanders who possessed a large number of golden ornaments. According to Walakea, the tribe's chieftain, these had been brought to them by a race of fish beings in exchange for sacrifices made by the people. For a few rubber and glass trinkets, Marsh procured a large amount of the natives' gold. In the following years he visited the islanders many times, trading for more gold and listening to their legends.

When Marsh journeyed to this island in 1838, however, he found that all of the natives had been killed, and that his source of revenue was lost. The repercussions of this disaster were felt throughout Innsmouth, and the town soon plunged into a depression.

It was then that Marsh began to preach a new religion based on the Polynesians' beliefs. If the people of Innsmouth followed the gods of his islander friends, he proclaimed, they would become rich and the nets of the fishermen would always be full. After a while Marsh's Esoteric Order of Dagon became so popular that all of Innsmouth's churches were forced to close down due to either lack of worshipers or the Order's strongarm tactics. During the chaos instigated by the plague of 1846, in which half of the town's people died, Marsh became the town's de facto leader, a post which he held until his death in 1878. Following his demise, the Marsh family kept its hold on local power until the government raids of 1927-28.

See *Book of Dagon*, Devil's Reef, Esoteric Order of Dagon, Innsmouth. ("The Shadow over Innsmouth", Lovecraft; *Escape from Innsmouth*, Ross (C).)

MARTIN'S BEACH. Oceanside village located a few miles north-east of Kingsport. Its only notable landmark is the Wavecrest Inn, a popular resort site. In 1922, Martin's Beach was scandalized by the inexplicable drownings of several men in the same night.

("The Horror at Martin's Beach", Greene and Lovecraft; *Kingsport*, Ross (C).)

MASON, KEZIAH. Supposed witch from Arkham, Massachusetts, who was apprehended during the witch scare of 1692. Keziah Mason confessed freely to her crimes, saying that the Devil had given her the secret name of Nahab and taken her to secret rites at various isolated locations. To aid in her mischievous deeds she had been given a familiar named Brown Jenkin, who took the form of a rat with the face of a human. She had also discovered certain combinations of lines and angles which could allow a person to travel great distances at will.

Having heard her testimony, the judges condemned Keziah to death. Shortly thereafter, she escaped from her cell, leaving nothing behind but a mysterious drawing upon the wall of her prison.

See Arkham. ("The Dreams in the Witch-House", Lovecraft.)

MASSA DI REQUIEM PER SHUGGAY ("Requiem for Shaggai"). Opera written in Italian by Benvento Chieti Bordighera in 1768. Bordighera, a gifted young composer, was born in Rome in 1746, and made many travels throughout Europe. Only one performance of the opera was made, but this was enough for Pope Clement XIII to ban the opera in 1769. Bordighera was imprisoned for heresy in 1770, and was executed the following year.

Many professional musicians have declared the score to be unplayable, since certain parts seem to have been written for unknown instruments and notes that cannot possibly be made. Copies may be found at the British Museum, Bibliothèque Nationale, and the Vatican Library, and others are held by private collectors in India, Japan, and the United States.

The opera tells the story of the destruction of Shaggai, and the journeys of its former inhabitants throughout space. It also details the insects from Shaggai's worship of Azathoth and a being known as Baoht Z'uqqa-Mogg, the Bringer of Pestilence. Performing the entire opera will result in the summoning of Azathoth.

See Azathoth, Baoht Z'uqqa-Mogg, Shaggai, shan. ("Fade to Grey", Aniolowski (C); "Mysterious Manuscripts", Aniolowski *et al.*, *TUO3* (C); *Keeper's Compendium*, Herber (C).)

MASTERS OF THE SILVER TWILIGHT. Organization founded in 1657. Its primary goal is to raise the corpse-city of R'lyeh from the ocean and to bring Cthulhu from his tomb, so that he may kill and destroy all humanity. This society is primarily found in America and Europe.

See *Catechism of the Knights of the Outer Void*, Keeper of the Silver Gate, Knight of the Outer Void, Son of Yog-Sothoth. ("The Coven at Cannich", Clegg (C); "The Hermetic Order of the Silver Twilight", Hutchinson (C).)

MAZE OF THE SEVEN THOUSAND CRYSTAL FRAMES. Concept alluded to by Abd al-Azrad, but whose true meaning is unknown. Some cults are believed to have travelled its ways. It may give access to a new level of reality that gives the traveller more occult knowledge, yet also makes him more likely to be subjugated by the Great Old Ones. The 3333rd frame is supposed to consist of many mouths that moan and gibber, and this frame is very hard to pass.

("The Inhabitant of the Lake", Campbell.)

MERCY HILL. Area of Brichester deriving its ironic nickname from the town gallows which were located there at one time. Mercy Hill is now primarily suburbs, and is distinguished by a hospital at the peak of the hill. This area is considered a rough part of town, though, and is avoided by all "respectable" people.

Folk legend holds that some children who dwell on Mercy Hill have been affected by a number of unpleasant dreams, and this serves to keep many away from this area. The author of the twelfth volume of *Revelations of Glaaki* lived in this area, and the reclusive cult leader Roland Franklyn had his headquarters at the base of Mercy Hill.

See Brichester; Franklyn, Roland. ("Cold Print", Campbell; "The Franklyn Paragraphs", Campbell; "The Inhabitant of the Lake", Campbell; "Return of the Witch", Campbell.)

MHU THULAN. Utmost northern portion of Hyperborea. Connected with the rest of Hyperborea by a peninsula, this land makes up much of present-day Greenland. The great wizards Zon Mezzamalech and Eibon were both said to have lived in Mhu Thulan.

See Cykranosh, Eibon, Hyperborea, Zon Mezzamalech. ("The Door to Saturn", Smith; "Ubbo-Sathla", Smith.)

MI-GO (also FUNGI FROM YUGGOTH). Race of beings which dwell on many worlds and have an outpost on Pluto, otherwise known as Yuggoth. These beings resemble winged crustaceans with egg-shaped heads which constantly change color (their means of communicating with each other). Some breeds are able to fly to other worlds, stars, and realities, though others must use other ways (such as magical gateways) to attain this goal. All these physical attributes, however, may be changed at a whim, for the fungi are masters of surgery.

The mi-go originally came to Earth during the Jurassic period, fighting off attacks from the Elder Things in order to settle in the northern hemisphere, where for the most part they have remained ever since. The fungi show a great deal of interest in our planet, because Earth contains deposits of certain minerals that are not found in other parts of the universe. To obtain these minerals the fungi have set up mining bases in the Andes, the Appalachians, and the Himalayas. Such bases are usually well hidden, and the mi-go usually recruit members of the local population to help them keep their activities secret. Word of their actions usually spreads despite this secrecy, and references to these curious creatures are often found in the legends of the countryside surrounding the creatures' lairs.

One of the mi-go's most amazing feats of technology involves a device known as a brain-cylinder. Through their surgery, the fungi can remove the brain of any being and transplant it into a curious metal cylinder, leaving the body in a state of suspended animation until the mind's return. The brain can observe and interact with its surroundings via certain apparati connected with the cylinder, and may be taken by the mi-go on trips back to Yuggoth, other stars inhabited by the fungi, and even other dimensions and times. This procedure is usually reserved for those especially favored or hated by the mi-go.

The mi-go who dwell within the Himalayas have been known to cover their bodies with the pelts of various animals. According to some, this is the source of the legends of the Abominable Snowman. The mi-go's surgical propensities also suggest that they may be responsible for the ongoing cattle mutilations reported in the south-western U.S.

See Big Dipper, Brothers of the Yellow Sign, Elder Things, Ghadamon, Ghatanothoa, Hastur, Lesser Old Ones, N'gah-Kthun, Seed of Azathoth, Shining Trapezohedron, Shub-Niggurath, Winged Ones, Yog-Sothoth, Yuggoth. ("The Temple of the Moon", Aniolowski and Szymanski (C); "The Dweller in the Crypt", Carter; "At the Mountains of Madness", Lovecraft; "The Whisperer in Darkness", Lovecraft; "Convergence", Tynes, *TU07* (C).)

MIGHTY MESSENGER. See Nyarlathotep.

MILLION FAVORED ONES. Beings said to be Nyarlathotep's spawn, although this relationship is most likely only symbolic. These Favored Ones are said to come from all the worlds of the universe and serve their lord Nyarlathotep unswervingly.

("The Million Favored Ones", Carter; "The Whisperer in Darkness", Lovecraft.)

MIRI NIGRI. Creatures created by Chaugnar Faugn from amphibian tissue. These beings worshiped their maker, first living near his home in the Pyrenees and destroying an invading Roman force, and later bearing Chaugnar to his new home on the Plateau of Tsang. The Tcho-Tcho people were created by the intermingling of Miri Nigri with normal humans.

See Chaugnar Faugn, Tcho-Tcho. ("The Curse of Chaugnar Faugn", Barton (C); *The Horror from the Hills*, Long.)

MISKATONIC RIVER. Body of water which springs from the hills to the west of Dunwich, Massachusetts. The river flows east past Dunwich and continues in that direction for many miles before turning to the southeast a few miles south of Bolton. Next the Miskatonic runs through the town of Arkham and continues on its way until it empties into the sea just north of Kingsport.

The Miskatonic's name may have came from a Native American tribe known as the Misqat, an offshoot of the Massachusetts Indians who lived within this valley.

See Arkham, Dunwich, Kingsport. ("With Malice Afterthought", Anderson and Lehmann (C); *Tales of the Miskatonic Valley*, Aniolowski *et al.* (C); "Dreams in the Witch-House", Lovecraft; "The Dunwich Horror", Lovecraft.)

MISKATONIC UNIVERSITY. Institution of higher learning located in Arkham, Massachusetts. The origins of this university remain shrouded in obscurity. One history holds that this school began as the Salem Academy in 1690, which moved to Arkham in 1776 and was renamed Miskatonic Liberal Seminary. Another states that Miskatonic Liberal College was founded in 1765 with a bequest from Jeremiah Orne, one of Arkham's foremost merchants.

At first classes were held in only one building on College Street, but Miskatonic College grew so quickly that soon after the Revolutionary War, the people of Arkham presented their former town common to the school in recognition of its achievements. In 1861 Miskatonic College combined with Elder Faith Seminary to became a university, and in 1880 its world-famous medical school opened.

Over the years Miskatonic University has gained a great deal of prestige, and is often considered to be one of the Ivy League schools. Even now, over two hundred years after its foundation, Miskatonic remains at the fore in scholarship and research. Its forays into the far parts of the world, such as the Pabodie Expedition of 1931 and the later Australian excavations of 1935, though not entirely successful, have earned the university acclaim from the scientific community.

Of especial note to the visiting scholar is the University's library, which includes the largest collection of rare occult material in the western hemisphere. Also of interest is the Miskatonic University Exhibit Museum, which is known to hold some intriguing artifacts of an unknown culture, and the Nathaniel Derby Pickman Nuclear Laboratory.

See Arkham; Armitage, Henry; *Black Book of the Skull*; *Book of Eibon*; *Celaeno Fragments*; Crow, Titus; *Cthulhu Among the Victorians*; *Cultes des Goules*; *De Vermis Mysteriis*; Derby, Edward Pickman; Dunwich; Dyer, William; *Ghorl Nigral*; *Investigation into the Myth-Patterns of Latter-Day Primitives with Especial Reference to the R'lyeh Text, An*; *Invocations to Dagon*; *Necrolatry*; *Necronomicon* (Appendices); Pabodie Expedition; Peaslee, Nathaniel; Peaslee, Wingate; *Pnakotic Manuscripts*; *Revelations of Hali*; *Seven Cryptical Books of Hsan*; Shrewsbury, Laban; Starkweather-Moore Expedition; *True Magik*; *Tunneler Below, The*; *Turner Codex*; *Unaussprechlichen Kulten*; Waite, Asenath; Wilmarth, Albert; Wilmarth Foundation. (*Arkham Unveiled*, Herber (C); "To Arkham and the Stars", Leiber; "At the Mountains of Madness," Lovecraft; "The Dreams in the Witch-House", Lovecraft; "The Dunwich

Horror", Lovecraft; "The Shadow out of Time", Lovecraft; Miskatonic
U. Graduation Kit, Petersen and Willis (C).)

MLANDOTH. Being mentioned in von Konnenberg's *Uralte
Schrecken*. According to this investigator, all of the world's myths of
gods could be traced in the beginning back to Mlandoth. Unfortunately, von Konnenberg had to concede that he did not know whether
Mlandoth was a creature, an impersonal force, or even a location. It
would seem that Mlandoth could be identical with Azathoth or
Yog-Sothoth, but *Uralte Schrecken* is unclear on this point.

See Ngyr-Khorath, *Uralte Schrecken*. ("Where Yidhra Walks", DeBill.)

M'NAGALAH. Being appearing as a mass of entrails, eyes, and
tentacles. Its name is mentioned in *Revelations of Glaaki*.

See *Revelations of Glaaki*. ("The Tugging", Campbell.)

MNAR. Land located within the Dreamlands, though according to
others it is actually present-day Saudi Arabia. Wherever it may be, Mnar
is a very ancient land which is touched little by time. Upon the winding
river Ai in the land of Mnar, the towns of Thraa, Ilarnek, and Kadatheron
were reared. The great cities Ib and Sarnath were built within the land
of Mnar. A type of mysterious gray stone was taken from Mnar by an
unknown being(s), who created a large number of the artifacts called the
"star-stones of Mnar", small carven pieces of rock emblazoned with the
Elder Sign.

See Brick Cylinders of Kadatheron, Elder Sign, Ib, *Ilarnek Papyri*,
Sarnath, star-stone of Mnar. ("The Lurker at the Threshold", Derleth
and Lovecraft; "The Doom that Came to Sarnath", Lovecraft; *The
Burrowers Beneath*, Lumley; *The Transition of Titus Crow*, Lumley.)

MNOMQUAH. God worshiped in both Theem'hdra and in Earth's
Dreamlands. In Theem'hdra, Mnomquah was often connected with
the moon deity Gleeth, but the two were entirely different beings.
Gleeth was the blind, deaf god who did not answer his worshiper's
prayers; Mnomquah's great influence made his cult rich and powerful.

In the Dreamlands, Mnomquah is worshiped by the curious moon-
beasts, as well as their servitors from the Plateau of Leng. According
to these, Mnomquah is imprisoned within the Black Lake of Ubboth
at the moon's core, but will one day be freed from his prison. Then
Mnomquah will come down to Sarkomand to mate with his wife Oorn,
and the two will rule the world together.

See Gleeth, Oorn, Ubboth. ("Introduction" to *The House of Cthulhu*, Lumley; *Mad Moon of Dreams*, Lumley.)

MONSTRES AND THEIR KYNDE. Book believed to have been compiled in the 16th century from a number of Mythos texts. The only known copy was stolen from the British Museum in 1898. We know little of what this book contains, but it says much about the Dragon Kings, a line of cannibalistic warlords who ruled over Britain in prehistoric times.

("Sacraments of Evil", Behrendt (C); *Keeper's Compendium*, Herber (C).)

MOON-BEAST. Slippery white toad-like creature with pinkish tentacles protruding from its snout. Moon-beasts are native to the Earth's Dreamlands, and even there they prefer to dwell on the dark side of the moon, so they are rarely encountered.

Unlike the same body in the waking world, the dark side of the Dreamlands moon has vast forests and oily seas, providing an ideal habitat for the moon-beasts. Here these creatures have reared great cities, built with the labor of many different slave races. They ply the oceans of their home in great black galleons, which may also fly them through space to other worlds. In addition to this body, the moon-beasts are known to have colonies on Earth, especially on the nameless rock in the Cerenarian Sea.

The moon-beasts are clever, and realize that the civilized folk of the Dreamlands would not abide their presence if they came to trade openly. Therefore they have enslaved many of the people from the Plateau of Leng. The Lengites can usually pass for humans, if the proper attire is worn. These almost-human agents usually disembark at ports to sell the rubies mined by their masters and obtain slaves with their profits, though the moon-beasts themselves remain belowdecks during this time.

The things from the moon are known to be allied with the cats from Saturn, and at times serve Nyarlathotep as well.

See Leng, Mnomquah. ("The Dream-Quest of Unknown Kadath", Lovecraft.)

MOON-LENS. Device built by certain worshipers of Shub-Niggurath and stationed in Goatswood. The mysterious glass from Leng is believed to have been used in its construction. The lens is usually set on a high tower with several mirrors positioned about it to concentrate a beam of moonlight on a certain spot.

The moon-lens is used so that Shub-Niggurath may be summoned at the full moon, as well as at the dark of the moon, the normal time for her summoning.

See Goatswood, Shub-Niggurath. ("The Moon-Lens", Campbell; "Dark Harvest", Ross, *TU08/9* (C).)

MOTHER HYDRA. See Hydra.

MOUNT ANTARKTOS. See Antarktos, Mount.

MOUNT HATHEG-KLA. See Hatheg-Kla, Mount.

MOUNT KADIPHONEK. See Noton and Kadiphonek, Mounts.

MOUNT NOTON. See Noton and Kadiphonek, Mounts.

MOUNT VOORMITHADRETH. See Voormithadreth, Mount.

MTHURA. Dark world whose inhabitants are of a crystalline nature. Long ago, wizards of Yaddith often visited this place while they were searching for the formulae that would save their home world. Mthura is the home of the Great Old One Q'yth-az.

See Q'yth-az. ("An Early Frost", Aniolowski; "Shaggai", Carter; *Visions from Yaddith*, Carter; "Through the Gates of the Silver Key", Lovecraft and Price.)

MUM-RATH PAPYRI. Documents translated by Ibn Shoddathua which are said to deal with the Great Old Ones in some way.

("The Fairground Horror", Lumley.)

MY UNDERSTANDING OF THE GREAT BOOKE. Book in English written by Joachim Kindler and published in the city of Buda in 1641. This book contains much speculation into life and the state of the universe, as revealed in a Gothic copy of *Necronomicon* to which Kindler suggests he had access. According to his book, this *Necronomicon* includes an in-depth analysis of all concepts included therein, making it even more horrible than the original Arabic.

See *Necronomicon* (Appendices). ("The Lurker in the Crypt", Miller (C).)

MYLAKHRION. Greatest magician to have ever lived in the long-lost land of Theem'hdra. Despite his great mastery of the sorcerous arts, he became obsessed with the idea of immortality. Through his magic Mylakhrion could prolong his life for hundreds or even thousands of years, but eternal life continued to elude him.

After many years of futile research, Cthulhu contacted him and offered Mylakhrion his long-sought goal in exchange for freeing the Great Old Ones from their prisons. When Mylakhrion refused to follow through on his part of the bargain, Cthulhu destroyed him.

See Exior K'mool, Teh Atht of Kluhn, Theem'hdra. (*Elysia*, Lumley; "Mylakhrion the Immortal", Lumley; "The Sorcerer's Book", Lumley.)

N

NAACAL. Language mentioned in *Unaussprechlichen Kulten* and connected with the lost continent of Mu by James Churchward. This tongue possibly originated in Hyperborea, and served as the sacred language of the priests of Mu. Naacal is now known only to a handful of lamas in the Himalayas, and can be split into two dialects, common and hieratic Naacal. The originals of *Ponape Scripture* and the Zanthu Tablets were written in hieratic Naacal.

See Glyu'Uho, *Ponape Scripture*, Zanthu Tablets. ("The Dweller in the Tomb", Carter; "The Ring of the Hyades", Glasby; "Out of the Aeons", Heald and Lovecraft; "Through the Gates of the Silver Key", Lovecraft and Price.)

NAACAL KEY. Unpublished work by Churchward outlining the translation of the Naacal tongue.

("The Fishers from Outside", Carter.)

NAGAAE. Amphibious creatures living somewhere in western Germany. A nagaae has the body and hind legs of a frog, but has four arms like those of a human. Its head bears two bulging eyes and a slitted mouth from which two forked tongues occasionally flicker. The nagaae moves by pushing itself along with its two hind feet, leaving a wide furrow in its wake.

The nagaae are the servitors of the Great Old One Cyaegha, and often attend its rituals.

See Cyaegha. ("Darkness, My Name Is", Bertin.)

NAGGOOB. Personage known as the "Father of Ghouls", and head
of the servitors of Nyogtha. Usually the ghouls are considered to serve
no one; it is possible, though, that this particular one may have gained
some sort of ascendancy of the ghoulish population.

("Zoth-Ommog", Carter.)

NAMELESS CITY. Ruins buried somewhere within the Arabian
desert, near Hadramaut. Before the coming of humanity to this region,
a race of reptilian humanoids, possibly a branch race of the deep ones or
the serpent men, reared their metropolis in this barren land. When
humans appeared in the Middle East and constructed the city of Irem,
the reptiles withdrew to their deepest cavern-temples, carving through
the rock to an underground paradise promised to them by their prophets.
All the inhabitants of the Nameless City departed to this subterranean
world, leaving their city uninhabited. Today only a few walls and cavern
shrines remain.

Though it has been empty for centuries, the natives of this region
still shun the Nameless City. Before he wrote *Necronomicon*, Abdul
Alhazred spent much time here, blackening the city's reputation
even further. According to Professor Shrewsbury, the forces of evil
took Abdul Alhazred to this city following his illusory "demise"
in Damascus.

See Abdul Alhazred, Kara-Shehr. (*The Trail of Cthulhu*, Derleth;
"The Lurker at the Threshold", Derleth and Lovecraft; "A History of
the *Necronomicon*", Lovecraft; "The Nameless City", Lovecraft; "The
Return of the Deep Ones", Lumley.)

NAOTALBA. 1) High priest of Yhtill in the play *The King in Yellow*.

2) A king of Carcosa who sent the "record-keepers" out from the
library of Celaeno to the far corners of the earth, to disseminate the
knowledge of the Great Old Ones.

See King in Yellow. ("Tell Me, Have You Seen the Yellow Sign?",
Ross (C); *House of the Toad*, Tierney.)

NASHT AND KAMAN-THA. Two mysterious individuals
dressed as Egyptian priests who are encountered by dreamers in the
Cavern of Flame. These two individuals decide whether a visitor is
worthy to enter the lands of dream, and may be asked about the
Dreamlands and the ways of its gods. Nasht and Kaman-Tha are
revered as gods in some parts of the Dreamlands.

See Dreamlands. ("The Dream-Quest of Unknown Kadath", Lovecraft; "Passing of a Dreamer", Myers.)

NATH. Location known as the Land of the Three Suns. The history of this place is detailed in *Chronike von Nath*. Nath may be identical with the infamous Vale of Pnath, but the descriptions of the two places seem greatly different. Another possibility is that it is a world home to the Elder Things, as one dreamer records such a world as having three suns and documents of that race speak of artifacts known as the "Spheres of Nath."

See *Chronicles of Nath*; Nath-feast; Pnath, Vale of; Spheres of Nath; *Tunneler Below, The*. ("Dreams in the Witch-House", Lovecraft; "The Tree on the Hill", Lovecraft and Rimel; "In the Vaults Beneath", Lumley.)

NATH-FEAST. Celebration performed in the land of Kn'aa. It is probably connected with the worship of Ghatanothoa.

See Ghatanothoa. ("Out of the Aeons", Heald and Lovecraft.)

NECROLATRY ("Worship of the Dead"). Book written by Ivor Gorstadt and published in the year 1702 in Leipzig. The Hoag family of Kingsport once held a copy of *Necrolatry*, which is now presumably in the library of Miskatonic University, to which the family's books and papers have been donated.

(*Dreams from R'lyeh*, Carter.)

NECRONOMICON. See Appendices.

NEMESIS OF FLAME. Being mentioned in some references. It may be symbolically referring to fire's role as the great destroyer and purger of evil.

("The Last Test", Castro and Lovecraft.)

NEPHREN-KA (also THE BLACK PHARAOH). Last pharaoh of Egypt's Third Dynasty. Legend has it that Nephren-Ka was a mighty sorcerer, the greatest of Egypt's priest-kings. He came to Egypt from the lost city of Irem, and revived worship of Nyarlathotep in that land. During his reign the priesthoods of Bast, Anubis, and Sebek flourished. The Black Pharaoh is also credited with the discovery of the Shining Trapezohedron. This artifact he kept in the darkened labyrinths of Kish, where he performed abominable rites involving the mysterious stone.

There was great discontent within the populace due to these changes, and soon thereafter the people of Egypt were in revolt. In the end Sneferu, the founder of the Fourth Dynasty who had received aid from the goddess Isis, prevailed over the Black Pharaoh. Nephren-

Ka made his way toward the coast, in order to escape to a "western island." Enemy forces cut him off, however, somewhere near the site of modern-day Cairo. The evil pharaoh and his priests buried themselves within an underground vault whose location has remained a secret to this day. Following his rival's death Sneferu had Nephren-Ka's name stricken from all records and monuments, an effort which was not wholly successful in the end.

No one truly knows what happened to the remaining followers of the Black Pharaoh. Some say they were pushed south into the swamps beyond the Sudan. Others assert that the cultists travelled to Britain, and a third school of thought holds that the magicians remained in Egypt, carrying on their worship in secret.

The final resting place of Nephren-Ka likewise remains a mystery. Records of the time state that the Collapsed Pyramid at Meidum and the Bent Pyramid of Dhashur were both built for the internment of Nephren-Ka, and that he rests in the Bent Pyramid. No explorers of this pyramid have found any trace of his remains, however. In the chapter "Saracenic Rituals" of his *De Vermis Mysteriis*, Ludvig Prinn adds the last chapter to this tale. He declared that in his travels to Arabia and Egypt, he had encountered the last remnants of the Black Pharaoh's cult. These cultists asserted that in the depths of his hidden funeral vault, Nephren-Ka sacrificed one hundred victims to Nyarlathotep. In exchange for this gift, the Mighty Messenger bestowed the gift of prophecy upon his servant. Nephren-Ka spent the last days of his life inscribing the future of the world on the walls of his tomb. He then died. After seven thousand years, the Black Pharaoh will arise again to bring the worship of Nyarlathotep back to Earth.

See Blind Ape of Truth; Kish; Nitocris; Prinn, Ludvig; "Saracenic Rituals"; Shining Trapezohedron. ("Fane of the Black Pharaoh", Bloch; "Cairo", DiTillio and Willis (C); "The Haunter of the Dark", Lovecraft.)

NESTAR MOBEDAN MOBED. Self-proclaimed Zoroastrian prophet of the 6th century. He and his followers mocked the excesses of the more orthodox priests, departing into the wilderness soon thereafter. Twenty years later they returned in great numbers to Nestar's home city, which they assaulted in order to attain and immolate the Tower of Gold, as they called the priests' temple. The city guard slew Nestar, however, and most of his worshipers were captured and killed.

The remnants of Nestar's followers returned to their secret dwellings in the hills, where they discovered Nestar's letters of instruction to his people. Following his commands, the majority of the cult emigrated to India, where they remain to this day. It is rumored that other branches survive elsewhere, but this has not been confirmed.

See Cthugha, *Letters of Nestar*. ("This Fire Shall Kill", Bishop (C); *Keeper's Compendium*, Herber (C).)

N'GAH-KTHUN. 1) Prehuman city in which the high temple of the Elder God Ulthar was built. Once every thousand years the rulers and priests of all of Earth's empires would come here to the ritual of B'kal to call the avatar of Ulthar to our world. See B'kal, Ultharathotep. ("The Whisperer in Darkness", Lovecraft; *The Sussex Manuscript*, Pelton.)

2) The leader of the mi-go. ("Zoth-Ommog", Carter.)

N'GAI, WOOD OF. The most sacred of all of Nyarlathotep's places of worship, said to be located somewhere in northern America.

See Nyarlathotep (Dweller in Darkness). ("The Dweller in Darkness", Derleth.)

N'GRAL KHUL ("Talons of the Dark"). Set of serpentine tablets bearing Aklo inscriptions. These two tablets are the sources of the spells calling and dismissing the Black Demon, one of Nyarlathotep's forms.

See Aklo, Nyarlathotep (Black Demon). ("One in Darkness", Isinwyll and Lyons (C).)

NGRANEK, MOUNT. Dormant volcano located on the southern isle of Oriab in Earth's Dreamlands. Its peaks are rugged and bare, and only lava-cutters climb them to find rock to make their famous carvings. The place has a bad reputation, for many have vanished without a trace while climbing Mount Ngranek. On the mountain's far side, legend has it, long ago Earth's gods carved a huge stone face before they returned to their homes on Kadath.

("The Dream-Quest of Unknown Kadath", Lovecraft.)

NGYR-KHORATH. Being which, according to von Konnenberg's *Uralte Schrecken*, haunted the spaces in which our solar system was formed before it existed, and still dwells there even today. Von Konnenberg asserts that Ngyr-Khorath is but a manifestation of what he calls Mlandoth.

See *Uralte Schrecken*, 'Ymnar. ("Where Yidhra Walks," DeBill.)

N'HLATHI. Centipede-like beings which inhabit the Valley of
Dreams at the base of the Purple Mountain in Elysia. They spend most
of their time hibernating in tunnels, hidden behind metal doors
bearing glyphs which even Elysia's greatest sages are unable to deci-
pher. These creatures are undoubtedly intelligent, but attempts to
communicate with them have been futile. Once every ten thousand
years the poppies bloom in the Valley of Dreams, and the n'hlathi
emerge to feed upon their seeds, returning afterwards to their homes
to hibernate once more. The only time when this cycle is known to
have been broken was the uprising of the Great Old Ones.

(*Elysia*, Lumley; *The Transition of Titus Crow*, Lumley.)

NIGHT-GAUNT. First novel written by Edgar Gordon, which Charnel
House Publishers of published. The novel was excessively morbid and was
a commercial failure, necessitating the future private publication of Gordon's works.

See Gordon, Edgar Hengist. ("The Dark Demon", Bloch; "The
Winfield Inheritance", Carter.)

NIGHTGAUNT. One of a race of beings found in both the Dreamlands and the waking world. Anatomically they are much like humans,
save for their whale-like skin, huge bat wings, horns, and a blankness
where their faces should be. (How these beings are able to sense their
surroundings without the customary organs has not been determined.)
Sometimes they carry tridents, but otherwise they bear nothing.

Nightgaunts are usually found in desolate places, as far from
humanity as possible. If a traveller intrudes upon their territory, the
nightgaunts ambush him and carry him through the air, tickling their
victim with their large barbed tails if he struggles. Those who
continue to fight back are dropped from a great height; those who do
not are taken to strange and dangerous places, and then abandoned
there (in the Dreamlands, the Vale of Pnath is a particular favorite).
The 'gaunts have also served as steeds for the ghouls on certain
ventures, and there has been at least one instance in which nightgaunts
have willingly served a human master.

Nightgaunts are said to serve Nodens, Lord of the Great Abyss, but are
allied to some degree with the ghouls, the deity Yibb-Tstll, and possibly
Yegg-ha as well. This brings up an interesting point. Usually, Nodens is
classified as an Elder God, and Yibb-Tstll is one of the Great Old Ones. Yet
nightgaunts have been known to serve both of these beings. Are there two
different factions among the nightgaunts, each serving a different master?
Or have scholars misclassified Yibb-Tstll or Nodens?

The summoning of a nightgaunt requires the use of a stone bearing the Elder Sign at night, but nothing else is known of this procedure.

See ghoul; Nodens; Pnath, Vale of; Yegg-Ha; Yibb-Tstll. ("The Winfield Inheritance", Carter; "The Dream-Quest of Unknown Kadath", Lovecraft; *Dreams and Fancies*, Lovecraft; "The Horror at Oakdeene", Lumley; *Hero of Dreams*, Lumley.)

NITHON. According to some sources, one of the moons of the great world Yuggoth.

("Star-Winds", Lovecraft; "The Discovery of the Ghooric Zone", Lupoff.)

NITOCRIS. Sixth Dynasty queen of Egypt. During her reign she revived the worship of Nyarlathotep. Her cruelty knew no bounds; she is said to have invited many of her officials and priests to a lavish banquet hall one night and then flooded the area, inundating the revelers. She is also known to have owned for a brief time the Shining Trapezohedron.

One of the blackest tales of the reign of this queen involves the so-called "Mirror of Nitocris." The queen unearthed this artifact from the vaults of Kish, where legend told that Nephren-Ka had left it, and Nitocris used it in many ways. She often left a condemned prisoner in a room with the mirror for one night; in the morning, the victim had vanished completely.

At the end of her reign Nitocris was buried alive within her tomb, the exact location of which has never been revealed.

See Kish, Nyarlathotep, *People of the Monolith*, Shining Trapezohedron. ("Imprisoned with the Pharaohs", Houdini and Lovecraft; "The Mirror of Nitocris", Lumley.)

N'KAI (possibly also N'KEN). Dark cavern-world beneath Yoth, and the home of the Great Old One Tsathoggua. The images of Tsathoggua which adorned Yoth's temples were taken from this land. A later exploration from the caves of K'n-yan found only certain amorphous servitors of Tsathoggua which oozed down stone troughs and worshiped the toad god's many idols. The expedition's survivors sealed off the passage. Since then, there have been several attempts to discover the location of this entrance, but none have been successful.

See K'n-Yan, Tsathoggua, Yoth. ("The Mound", Bishop and Lovecraft; "The Grinning Ghoul", Bloch.)

NODENS (also NUADA, LUD, and NUD). Former head of the Celtic pantheon. He lost his arm in battle, and a new silver one was forged for him. Due to his disability, however, he stepped down as head of the Celtic gods. He had a holy site in Lydney, on the banks of the Severn River.

In the Cthulhu Mythos Nodens is known by the epithet "Great Lord of the Abyss", and is sometimes considered to be one of the Elder Gods. He is usually represented as standing with an oaken staff in one hand on a seashell chariot drawn by fantastic beasts. Nodens has been known to take worthy individuals on trips with him across space and time, but this occurs only rarely. Nodens is also said to be the lord of the nightgaunts.

According to some, Nodens last came to Earth billions of years in the past, and was worshiped by certain beings of whom we know nothing. He left when the Great Old Ones arrived, and he and his worshipers made their way to the far future, when Nodens would once again walk the lands of Earth. This myth holds that Nodens and Yog-Sothoth are opposed to one another. This is hard to reconcile with the other known manifestations of Nodens, unless Nodens has avatars which visit our planet periodically.

In other stories Nodens has been entrusted to guard the prisons of the Great Old Ones by the gods of Earth. There will come a time, though, when Nodens himself will cease his vigilance and sleep. Then the Great Old Ones will be freed from their tombs.

See Elder Gods, Great Abyss, nightgaunt, Yog-Sothoth. ("Glimpses", Attansio; "The Dream-Quest of Unknown Kadath", Lovecraft; "The Strange High House in the Mist", Lovecraft; "The House of the Worm", Myers.)

NOPHRU-KA. High priest of a powerful cult of Nyarlathotep in Egypt during the Fourteenth Dynasty who attempted to overthrow the old regime and become the new pharaoh. To accomplish these ends he called down monsters from the stars which would wreak havoc across the land. In the confusion, Nophru-Ka and his cultists would attack the pharaoh and set up their own government. Nyarlathotep himself smiled on their venture and promised to send a messenger to aid them.

The current pharaoh learned of the plot, and his assassins tracked down Nophru-Ka and killed him as he knelt to pray in his cult's most sacred temple. As he lay dying, Nophru-Ka pronounced a curse upon the head of the pharaoh and the ruling line of Egypt. The high priest's followers, demoralized by their leader's death, were driven to the south until they arrived at the ruined city of G'harne. The threat to the pharaoh had been averted.

See Brotherhood of the Beast, G'harne, Nyarlathotep, Nyarlathotep (The Beast). (*Fungi from Yuggoth*, Herber (C).)

NOTES ON THE CTHAAT AQUADINGEN. Volume by Joachim Feery. This book is very rare, as are most of Feery's limited editions. If it is anything like his *Notes on the* Necronomicon, it is a set of annotated quotes taken from *Cthaat Aquadingen*.

See Feery, Joachim. ("The Fairground Horror", Lumley.)

NOTES ON THE NECRONOMICON. Book written by Joachim Feery, an occult scholar who died mysteriously in 1934. His *Notes on the* Necronomicon is the best known of the many limited-edition books he privately published. Despite his claims of obtaining the occult knowledge he put in his books through dreams, no one raised any doubts of his knowledge of the paranormal.

Two editions of *Notes on the* Necronomicon were published, the first containing all of Feery's researches, the second an abridged and edited printing. This slim volume contains many quotes from *Necronomicon*, as well as Feery's commentaries upon the texts. Many of the quotes within differ significantly from the original volume, as Feery inserted much material he asserted he had received in dreams into these extracts.

See Feery, Joachim; *Necronomicon* (Appendices); Original *Notes on the* Necronomicon. ("Aunt Hester", Lumley; "Name and Number", Lumley.)

NOTH-YIDIK. Being whose children are considered especially repulsive, even by the worshipers of the Great Old Ones.

("The Horror in the Museum", Heald and Lovecraft.)

NOTON AND KADIPHONEK, MOUNTS. Two mountains in the land of Lomar which flanked the pass that led to the city of Olathoe. The Inutos came through this pass and, catching the Lomarians unaware, destroyed them and their city.

See Lomar. ("Polaris", Lovecraft.)

NUG. Creature who may be the "Grandfather of Ghouls", but who is probably the twin of Yeb instead.

See Black Litanies of Nug and Yeb, Nug and Yeb, Torch of Nug, Yeb. ("The Mound", Bishop and Lovecraft; "The Descent into the Abyss", Carter and Smith.)

NUG AND YEB. Two minor Mythos entities whose true origins and significance remain a mystery. They are said to be the children of Shub-Niggurath and Yog-Sothoth, and in turn have given birth to Cthulhu and Tsathoggua by way of asexual fission. The link to

Tsathoggua is unlikely, however, as the Hyperborean *Parchments of Pnom* deal at some length with the genealogy of this Great Old One, making no reference to either of these entities. On the other hand, others allege that Nug and Yeb are the spawn of Shub-Niggurath and Hastur the Unspeakable; this seems more likely, considering that these beings are often mentioned together, but is not commonly accepted.

Nug and Yeb were worshiped together in Irem, Mu, and K'n-yan. In Irem, their shrine has been found bearing the yin-yang symbol, implying that the two beings may represent cosmic opposites of some sort. Their rites were said to be especially abhorrent. The two have been entrusted with the task of clearing off Earth to make it ready for the Great Old Ones' return.

See Black Litanies of Nug and Yeb, Furnace of Yeb, K'n-yan, Nug, Shub-Niggurath, Torch of Nug, Yeb. ("Carcosa Story about Hali" (fragment), Carter; "The Mound", Bishop and Lovecraft; "Out of the Aeons", Heald and Lovecraft; *Selected Letters*, Lovecraft; "To Clear the Earth", Murray.)

NUG-SOTH. 1) Magician from fourteen thousand years in the future whose mind was at one time captured by the Great Race of Yith. ("The Shadow Out of Time", Lovecraft.)

2) Race of magicians who at one time lived on the planet of Yaddith. They were humanoid in shape, encased in carapaces, and bore the snouts of tapirs. On their home world the Nug-Soth built a highly advanced civilization, in which travel through space and other dimensions was an everyday occurrence. When the dholes came to Yaddith, however, the Nug-Soth were unable to save their world, and they scattered themselves throughout the cosmos. See Shub-Niggurath, Yaddith. ("Visions from Yaddith", Carter; "Through the Gates of the Silver Key", Lovecraft and Price.)

NUMINOS. Borea's closest moon, which Ithaqua has populated with many sorts of animals and plants. Numinos is mostly covered with ocean, and is home to many fierce bands of Norsemen whose culture is much like that of Earth's Vikings. Almost all the world's inhabitants revere the Wendigo unswervingly, having seen the destruction he wrought upon them many years before; one small colony of rebels does live on the Isle of Mountains, though.

See Borea. (*In the Moons of Borea*, Lumley.)

NYARLATHOTEP (also THE CRAWLING CHAOS or MIGHTY MESSENGER). The mighty soul and messenger of the Outer Gods. He is said to dwell in a cavern at the center of the world, accompanied by two mindless flutists, yet he often sends messages and performs services for the Other Gods throughout space and time. Nyarlathotep answers to the every whim of his masters, though he is contemptuous of them as well.

The Crawling Chaos is also said to act as an intermediary between the Great Old Ones and their worshipers, as well as carrying tidings between the Great Old Ones themselves; however, only a few such cases have been reported. In fact, Nyarlathotep may be a personification of the telepathic powers of the Great Old Ones. However, he seems to have a distinct personality which the Old Ones' inhuman minds might find difficult to duplicate.

Nyarlathotep has been worshiped under several guises in all parts of the world, but he is usually connected with Egypt. He was one of the greatest gods in the land of the Nile, where he was the ruler of the underworld, the master of the night, and the patron of sorcerers. After many years, however, the people of Egypt grew frightened of the dark god and struck out all references to him, reassigning his attributes to other gods, such as Set and Thoth. Though the enemies of the cult tried to suppress the memory of Nyarlathotep, he was still remembered, and there were resurgences of his worship throughout Egyptian history, especially during the time of Nephren-Ka, Nophru-Ka, and Nitocris.

Nyarlathotep is called the "all-seeing eye" in Prinn's *De Vermis Mysteriis*, and knows much about magic and technology. He sometimes appears to a chosen person, and gives him a useful incantation or piece of machinery. Unfailingly, these gifts lead only to the madness and destruction of their wielders. Nyarlathotep seems to gain great pleasure from watching these victims destroy themselves.

The Outer God is credited with eventually bringing destruction to humanity and Earth. Several prophesies state that Nyarlathotep will come in the last days, dressed in red and with wild beasts following him, licking his hands. He will journey among the cities of the world, giving demonstrations of science and magic. Then "quaking auroras will roll down on the citadels of man", and humanity will be destroyed as he turns the entire universe into a graveyard. Nyarlathotep has aided in the construction of the first nuclear weapons, so this prophecy may already be coming true.

Nyarlathotep's true form is a noxious expanse of yellowish slime, but to carry out the bidding of the Other Gods, he can take any one of his thousand forms. He has used only a few during his journeys to our world; those which are known are listed below.

AHTU (Congo): In this form Nyarlathotep appears as a huge mound of viscous material, with several golden tentacles sprouting from its central mass. Ahtu's worshipers are usually deformed or mutilated natives, though some Europeans have also attained membership. He is called by using a golden bracelet usually separated into two parts, to prevent Ahtu from being summoned by accident. See *Dhol Chants*. ("Than Curse the Darkness", Drake; "Dead of Night", Herber (C).)

THE BEAST (worldwide): This form of Nyarlathotep manifests itself though a great monument somewhere in the world. It is the focus for a worldwide brotherhood which seeks to find a successor to their high priest Nophru-Ka, whom the Pharaoh's assassins killed during Egypt's Fourteenth Dynasty. See Brotherhood of the Beast, Nophru-Ka. (*Fungi from Yuggoth*, Herber (C).)

THE BLACK DEMON: This form is not known to be worshiped anywhere. It is a black-furred, snouted monster which fears the light (though it is not harmed by it). The formula for summoning it may be found on the N'gral Khul. The being may be controlled by a summoner using certain talismans, though the user runs a chance of being attacked himself. The Black Demon is much like the Dark Demon in form, but is much less intelligent than the other avatar is. See N'gral Khul. ("One in Darkness", Isinwyll and Lyons (C).)

BLACK MAN (England): A hairless man with dead black skin and hooves on his feet. The Crusaders brought the worship of Nyarlathotep in this form back to Europe, the descendants of whom began the European witch cults in which the Black Man played an important role. See Payne, Hesper. ("The Faceless God", Bloch; "The Dreams in the Witch-House", Lovecraft.)

BLACK PHARAOH (Egypt): A man of proud Egyptian features, garbed in prismatic robes and wearing the headpiece of a pharaoh. This form may be identical with that of the Black Man, and is much like the occultist Aleister Crowley's description of Aiwaz, the spirit which dictated *Book of the Law* to him. See ankh. ("The Dream-Quest of Unknown Kadath", Lovecraft.)

BLACK WIND (Kenya): This cult is the same as that of the God of the Bloody Tongue. At times Nyarlathotep takes the form of the Black Wind, a great storm which can destroy crops, forest, and houses for miles around when he manifests. ("Kenya", DiTillio and Willis (C).)

BLOATED WOMAN (China): In this form Nyarlathotep appears as a huge, obese woman, with five mouths and many tentacles. It carries the mystical Black Fan, with which it magically hides its unseemly bulk from humans until it has ensnared them. This cult has deep roots in China. See

Goddess of the Black Fan, Tale of Priest Kwan. ("Shanghai", DiTillio and Willis (C).)

BRINGER OF PESTS (Egypt): Worshiped in Egypt's Twelfth Dynasty, this manifestation can only be described as a horde of huge spitting supernatural locusts. It is not worshiped today by any known cult. ("The Ten Commandments of Cthulhu Hunting", Monroe and Petersen (C).)

CRAWLING MIST (Dreamlands): A sickly-colored fog which springs up without warning and moves purposefully toward the Messenger's destination. (*Elysia*, Lumley.)

DARK DEMON: A form of Nyarlathotep which occasionally manifests itself through a contactee. It appears much as the Black Demon (a snouted, clawed, black-furred being), but is larger and more cunning. It sometimes seduces those steeped in studies of black magic, promising them glory if they will allow it to enter their bodies. Of course, no reward comes to those possessed by this form of Nyarlathotep. ("The Dark Demon", Bloch.)

DARK ONE (California, Louisiana): Some Mythos cults are visited by Nyarlathotep in the semblance of an 8' tall, totally black man without a face, who can pass through any material barrier at will. ("Mr. Skin", Milan.)

DWELLER IN DARKNESS (Wood of N'gai): In the Wood of N'gai, Nyarlathotep's sacred wood, the Crawling Chaos takes the form of a wailing, faceless monstrosity which constantly puts out and reabsorbs various appendages. While in this form Nyarlathotep can temporarily transform into any shape he desires. This avatar usually only manifests itself at night. ("The Dweller in Darkness", Derleth.)

EFFIGY OF HATE (Africa): One African tribe worshiped the Mighty Messenger in this form, which manifested itself through their war totems. This winged monstrosity allowed its cultists to relive past battles and change the course of their history, a power which in the end did them no good. ("Regiment of Dread", Gillan (C).)

THE FACELESS GOD (Ancient Egypt): In the elder days of the Egyptian civilization the people worshiped Nyarlathotep in the form of a winged sphinx with a featureless head which bore the triple crown of a deity. The Faceless God manifested itself at times through the bodies of its idols. The other priesthoods later suppressed this cult, it becoming nearly forgotten in the millennia following its dissolution. This avatar may be identical with Nyarlathotep's Beast aspect. ("The Faceless God", Bloch.)

THE FLOATING HORROR (Haiti): This form of Nyarlathotep must manifest itself through the body of a specially chosen and prepared host, from whom it springs when the host body has been killed. It appears as a red-veined jellyfish-like floating organism of a bluish color.

This avatar is connected with certain fringe voodoo cults. ("The Star-Pools", Attansio.)

GOD OF THE BLOODY TONGUE (Kenya): For the rituals of the Cult of the Bloody Tongue, Nyarlathotep takes the form of a huge monster having a huge red tentacle where the face should be. The cult primarily consists of natives, and its center is the Mountain of the Black Wind. This form is also known as the Howler in Darkness. See Cult of the Bloody Tongue. ("Kenya", DiTillio and Willis (C).)

GREEN MAN (Celts): A figure which appears as an effigy of a man constructed of parts from various plants. The Green Man is usually dormant, awakening only to answer questions as an oracle or to accept a sacrifice. ("Eyes for the Blind", Hallett and Isinwyll (C); *Keeper's Compendium*, Herber (C).)

HAUNTER OF THE DARK (Australia, Yuggoth): This cult originated on Yuggoth, but was prevalent during the latter part of Egypt's Third Dynasty. Nyarlathotep appears as a huge bat-like thing with a tri-lobed eye. This manifestation of Nyarlathotep must be kept in darkness, or it will be destroyed.

A sacred item of the cult is the Shining Trapezohedron, which allows the Haunter to enter this dimension. A modern-day cult in Australia numbers Aborigines and slum-dwelling members of other races in its ranks, and is symbolized by a spiralling sign. The cult had a small branch in Providence known as the Starry Wisdom Church, but the city leaders closed it down in 1877. This form of Nyarlathotep is also known as Sand Bat, Face Eater, Father of All Bats, Dark Wing, and Fly-The-Light. See Fly-the-Light, Shining Trapezohedron, Starry Wisdom Cult. ("City in the Sands", DiTillio and Willis (C); "The Haunter of the Dark", Lovecraft; *The Book of Ceremonial Magic*, Waite.)

HORNED MAN (Celts): The Celts worshiped this aspect of Nyarlathotep. Resembling a human male with the horns of a stag, it can only be seen by those under the influence of hallucinogens. (*Return to Dunwich*, Herber (C).)

LROGG (Uranus): On the world of L'gy'hx (Uranus), Nyarlathotep is worshiped as a two-headed bat, to whom the natives sacrifice one of their number every year. See Lrogg. (*Ye Booke of Monstres*, Aniolowski (C); "The Insects from Shaggai", Campbell.)

MANY-LEGGED GOAT: This form is only known from ceremonies dedicated to the Crawling Chaos. (*A Night in the Lonesome October*, Zelazny.)

MESSENGER OF THE OLD ONES: This avatar resembles a tremendous black mass which moves through the sky, constantly throwing out streamers with which it seems to pulls itself through the air. The Messenger only appears for extremely important events, such as the emergence of Cthulhu from his tomb. (*Ye Booke of Monstres*, Aniolowski (C); "The Rise of R'lyeh", Petersen (C).)

SHUGORON (Malaysia): A black humanoid figure represented as playing a sort of horn. This being is revered by the Tcho-Tcho people of Malaysia, who call it and send it against those who have offended them. ("Black Man with a Horn", Klein; *Escape from Innsmouth*, Ross (C).)

SKELETAL HORROR (Egypt): This rare manifestation resembles a 12' tall living skeleton with the head of a human embryo and tremendous claws on its hands. Nyarlathotep only comes in this form when he transforms from one of his other avatars due to an attack. ("Thoth's Dagger", Hamblin (C).)

SKINLESS ONE (Middle East): In the guise of a flayed, skinless corpse, Nyarlathotep is revered by a particularly despicable cult in Turkey and the surrounding area. (*Horror on the Orient Express*, Gillan *et al.* (C))

SMALL CRAWLER (India): This form consists of a dwarfed human figure, with four arms and three tentacles for legs. Little else is known of it, except that it is mentioned in *Cthaat Aquadingen* and has a small following in India. See *Cthaat Aquadingen*. ("Kenya", DiTillio and Willis (C).)

THING IN THE YELLOW MASK (Dreamlands): An entity draped in yellow silk, it visited the abandoned city of Ygiroth on Mount Lerion, and may dwell in the nameless monastery on the Plateau of Leng. Although most consider the King in Yellow to be an avatar of Hastur, this may provide an alternate explanation. See King in Yellow. ("In 'Ygiroth", DeBill; "The Dream-Quest of Unknown Kadath", Lovecraft; "The Elder Pharos", Lovecraft.)

THOTH (Egypt): This hypothetical form, resembling an ibis-headed human, may be the guise which Nyarlathotep adopted for use among the early Egyptians. ("Thoth's Dagger", Hamblin (C).)

WAILING WRITHER: A column of whirling black tentacles and screaming mouths. This particular form of Nyarlathotep has been known to possess a chosen victim, later bursting apart its host's body on its departure. Though it is alluded to in some Hindu tales, the Writher has no known earthly worshipers. (*Escape from Innsmouth*, Ross (C).)

See Abbith; Blind Ape of Truth; Byagoona; Cthugha; Dreamlands; elemental theory; Fable of Nyarlathotep; Great Old Ones; gug; Kadath in the Cold Waste; Koth; Million Favored Ones; moon-beast; *Necronomicon* (Appendices); Nephren-Ka; N'gai, Wood of; Nitocris; Nophru-Ka; Other Gods; Outer Gods; Sakkuth; shantak; Sharnoth; Sign of Eibon; Thasaidon; Yegg-ha; 'Ymnar. ("The Faceless God", Bloch; "The Shadow from the Steeple", Bloch; "The Lurker at the

Threshold", Derleth and Lovecraft; *Masks of Nyarlathotep*, DiTillio and Willis (C); *Fungi from Yuggoth*, Lovecraft; "Nyarlathotep", Lovecraft; "The Rats in the Walls", Lovecraft; *The Burrowers Beneath*, Lumley; *Elysia*, Lumley.)

NYHARGO CODE. Arabic script which should be written on a wall using blue and green chalk. Its powers and uses are unknown.
("Lord of the Worms", Lumley.)

NYHARGO CODEX. Book written in English and published in 1879. Lord Waite, an amateur archaeologist, transcribed this book; he believed the book to be a translation of writings he discovered within certain ruins in central Africa. The rest of his expedition died on their way back to civilization, so only Waite remained to affirm the veracity of these inscriptions. As such, the academic community looked upon the book as the work of a crank. Shortly thereafter Waite committed suicide, was murdered, or was killed in a freak accident at a train station.

Besides the rumor that the book contains much information about the living dead, the contents of this volume remain a mystery.
("Dead of Night", Herber (C).)

NYHARGO DIRGE. Chant contained within *Cthaat Aquadingen*. It may be used to destroy zombies and other of the living dead which possess a physical body.
(*Keeper's Compendium*, Herber (C); "Billy's Oak", Lumley.)

NYLSTROM. City in Mongolian desert about a hundred miles from Zak. It consists of mud-baked huts, some small trees, and a brackish lake. The gaunt people here are likely to have eye disease, but are very friendly to visitors.
See Zak. (*The Great White Space*, Copper.)

NYOGTHA (also THE THING THAT SHOULD NOT BE). Great Old One who dwells deep beneath the earth, or possibly within a dark world circling Arcturus. He can only manifest himself through certain openings to the upper world. Such openings have been found in Massachusetts, Romania, New Zealand and the Plateau of Leng, but they undoubtedly exist in other places as yet undiscovered.

Nyogtha is not thought to have an active cult, though solitary sorcerers have invoked him to gain personal power. He has been connected with at least one of the witches executed in the Salem witch trials, and there have been other instances scattered worldwide. Nyogtha is also known to be served by some cults associated with ghouls.

One theory about Nyogtha suggests that he has some link with the Elder Things. It is said that Nyogtha appealed to these aliens to aid his growth, and the Elder Things agreed, hoping to control him. However, as they had feared, Nyogtha began to break away from their control. In response, they constructed a huge magical shield which kept him imprisoned in a cavern on his native New Zealand, unable to reach his full maturity. This theory does not explain how Nyogtha has manifested himself elsewhere in the world.

No matter what his nature, Nyogtha is relatively easy to drive off. Use of an ankh, the Vach-Viraj Incantation, or the Tikkoun Elixir will cause him to return to the caverns from whence he came.

See ankh, *Black God of Madness*, elemental theory, Naggoob, Tikkoun Elixir, Ubbo-Sathla, Vach-Viraj Incantation. ("Zoth-Ommog", Carter; "The Stairs in the Crypt", Carter and Smith; "Castle Dark", Herber (C); "The Salem Horror", Kuttner; *The Thing at the Threshold*, McConnell (C).)

O

OAKDEENE SANITARIUM. English mental institution located near Glasgow. Despite the high quality of care given to the inmates, the Sanitarium is best remembered for the scandal caused by the death of some inmates the night of January 1, 1936.

See *Cthaat Aquadingen*, *Visions from Yaddith*. (*The Burrowers Beneath*, Lumley; "The Horror at Oakdeene", Lumley.)

OATHS OF DAGON. Vows taken by worshipers of Dagon to ensure loyalty to their god and his cult. The first is taken by all cultists; this oath ensures that the person will not allow the Order to come to harm. The second is intended for more devoted members, and calls that person to actively aid the deep ones in their projects. The third oath is only taken by a few, and couples the oath-taker with a companion deep one, with whom the person must have children to perpetuate the deep one race.

See Dagon, deep one. (*Escape from Innsmouth*, Ross (C); "The Shadow over Innsmouth", Lovecraft.)

OCCULT FOUNDATION, THE. Book published in the late 1980's by the eminent occultist J. Cornelius Wassermann. In it Wassermann describes his beliefs on the nature of the Primal Ones, and their eventual goals as they relate to humanity. The book sold well in certain of the darker occult circles, but the Wiccans and other groups were successful in banning its author from attending any of their meetings.

The book contains much information about the Great Dying, how this will be brought about, and the benefits that will accrue to the Great Old Ones' worshipers when the promised resurrection occurs.

See Great Dying, *Liber Damnatus Damnationum*. (*The House of the Toad*, Tierney.)

OF EVILL SORCERIES DONE IN NEW-ENGLAND OF DAEMONS IN NO HUMAN SHAPE. Anonymous pamphlet printed in colonial times which deals with reputed sorcerers and mysterious events in New England, especially the case of Richard Billington of New Dunnich, Massachusetts.

See Billington, Richard. ("The Lurker at the Threshold", Derleth.)

OLATHOE. Capital city of the land of Lomar. This town's buildings were all of marble, and the images of grave bearded men adorned the peaks of pillars set throughout the city. Olathoe was a center for culture and learning, until the Inutos came from over the mountains and destroyed the people of Lomar.

See Lomar; Noton and Kadiphonek, Mounts. ("Polaris", Lovecraft.)

OLD ONES. See Elder Things.

OORN. Great Old One who dwells in the Dreamlands, in the ruins of Sarkomand. She is said to be the mate of the moon god Mnomquah, who will come to earth to join her when he breaks free of his lunar prison.

See Mnomquah. (*Mad Moon of Dreams*, Lumley.)

OOTH-NARGAI. Valley in the Dreamlands in which King Kuranes constructed the timeless city of Celephais.

See Celephais. ("Celephais", Lovecraft.)

ORIGINAL *NOTES ON THE* NECRONOMICON. The first printing of Joachim Feery's *Notes on the* Necronomicon. It contains much material expurgated from the later version.

See Feery, Joachim; *Notes on the* Necronomicon. ("Name and Number", Lumley.)

OSSADAGOWAH. Being said to be the child of Tsathoggua. Ossadagowah appears as a great toad-like creature or a misty shape with a tentacled face. He dwells in the stars, and can only come to

Earth if summoned. The Native American tribes of Massachusetts once knew how to call down Ossadogowah, but most of these did not use this knowledge, considering it an evil act.

See Tsathoggua. ("The Lurker at the Threshold", Derleth and Lovecraft.)

OTHER GODS. Group of beings, including Nyarlathotep, who protect the lesser gods of Earth in the Dreamlands. These may be merely the Outer Gods, or they may include other entities unknown to us.

See Azathoth, Gloon, Great Ones, gug, Nyarlathotep, Outer Gods, Seed of Azathoth. ("The Dream-Quest of Unknown Kadath", Lovecraft; "The Other Gods", Lovecraft.)

OTHUUM. Mythos "demon" whose true nature is uncertain. In some references he seems to be one of the servants of Great Cthulhu, and dwells beneath the waves striving for his master's return. In others, Othuum is the "Great Master of Those Who-Wait-Without", thus at least in title resembling Yog-Sothoth and his fellows.

See *Othuum Omnicia*. ("The Last Rite", Lumley; "Rising with Surtsey", Lumley.)

OTHUUM OMNICIA. Book in Latin which details the proper worship of the being Othuum. The locations of only two copies are known: one located in the British Museum, and another in a private collection somewhere in Hungary.

See Othuum. ("The Last Rite", Lumley; "The Second Wish", Lumley.)

OTHUYEG. Great Old One resembling an eye surrounded by innumerable tentacles, a form which bears much physical similarity to that of Cyaegha. Othuyeg and his spawn, which have been created in their parent's image, dwell beneath the ground within the fabled Seven Cities of Gold in the fabled land of Cakatomia, awaiting the time when they may issue forth to reconquer the surface world.

Othuyeg is mentioned in *Black Book of the Skull* and *Necronomicon*, but no other references in Mythos books have been found. Othuyeg desires to open up a gate so Zathog and the Zarrians may invade this planet, but how the Great Old One hopes to achieve this goal is unknown.

See *Black Book of the Skull*. ("The Seven Cities of Gold", Burnham.)

OUTER GODS (possibly also **OTHER GODS**). Group of beings who are differentiated from the Great Old Ones because they are personifications of cosmic forces, while the Great Old Ones can be compared to immensely powerful, yet limited, alien beings. This distinction is not recognized by all scholars, and it is not always clear where a certain entity should be placed. Some entities who are generally categorized with the Outer Gods are Azathoth, Yog-Sothoth, Shub-Niggurath, and Nyarlathotep. Others who may be included in their number are Tulzscha, Daoloth, and Abhoth.

It is unknown whether there is any connection between the Great Old Ones and the Outer Gods. There are close links between Shub-Niggurath and Hastur (an Outer God and a Great Old One, respectively), and Nyarlathotep has acted in the interests of the Great Old Ones at least twice. The extent of any further interaction is unknown.

See Azathoth, *Book of Azathoth*, Ghroth, Great Old Ones, Ia, Leng, Nyarlathotep, Other Gods, Shub-Niggurath. (*The Lurker at the Threshold*, Derleth and Lovecraft; *The Clock of Dreams*, Lumley; *Elysia*, Lumley; *The Transition of Titus Crow*, Lumley; "The Cthulhu Mythos", Petersen.)

OUTER ONES. Book in Latin which deals with Azathoth, his spawn, and the deity Tulzscha. The only known copy may be found in Kingsport, Massachusetts.

("The Seventh House on the Left", Ross, Kingsport (C).)

P

PABODIE EXPEDITION. Scientific journey to Antarctica financed by Miskatonic University and nominally headed by Professor William Dyer, from that institution's Department of Geology. The primary purpose of this expedition was to collect fossil specimens from the Antarctic rock. To this end Professor Frank Pabodie of Miskatonic's Department of Engineering invented a drill capable of boring deep into the rock to extract specimens.

After a good deal of unremarkable explorations, a biology professor named Lake set off on a side expedition to a site to the northwest of the main camp, where he hoped to find an explanation for certain strange impressions which had been found during the previous drillings. According to reports made to the outside world, the expedition exceeded the team's expeditions; they had discovered a range of mountains taller than the Himalayas, as well as the fossilized remains of creatures which seemed to be part animal and part plant.

At this point our information is fragmentary and unsatisfactory. It is likely that an epidemic of madness overtook the scientists camped near the mountains, and all of them save one were killed by one another. Following this tragedy, the rest of the expedition's members gathered what little data they had already discovered and returned to Miskatonic. Many were later diagnosed with *dementia Antarctica* and were confined to institutions for a brief while.

Shortly after his return Professor Dyer published his account of the "true" occurrences of the Pabodie Expedition with hopes of discouraging further scientific visits to Antarctica. This manuscript, however, was held in low esteem by the scientific community.

See Dyer, William; Elder Things; Leng; Miskatonic University; Starkweather-Moore Expedition. (*Alone Against the Dark*, Costello (C); "At the Mountains of Madness", Lovecraft.)

PALLID MASK (also PHANTOM OF TRUTH). Entity connected with the King in Yellow. In the play of the same name, the Pallid Mask acts as the messenger sent by Hastur to the city of Yhtill. Other references cite the Pallid Mask as the semblance the King in Yellow puts on when dealing with mortals.

See King in Yellow, Yhtill. ("The Yellow Sign", Chambers; "Tatterdemalion", Love, Ross, and Watts (C).)

"PAPYRUS OF THE DARK WISDOM". Name applied to the third section of *Book of Eibon*. In this portion of his magnum opus, the Hyperborean wizard gives the history of the many different alien beings who came to Earth before the coming of humanity. Von Junzt later paraphrased this material in his *Unaussprechlichen Kulten*.

See *Book of Eibon*; *Unaussprechlichen Kulten*; von Junzt, Friedrich. ("Something in the Moonlight", Carter; "Papyrus of the Dark Wisdom", Carter and Smith.)

PARCHMENTS OF PNOM. Volume written by Pnom, Hyperborea's leading genealogist and seer, in his homeland's "Elder Script." In it is given the lineage of Tsathoggua, as well as many powerful exorcisms intended for use against the spirits of the cold north.

See Nug and Yeb. ("Some Observations on the Carter Glossary", Cockcroft; "The Coming of the White Worm", Smith.)

PAYNE, HESPER (?-1692). Witch executed during the Arkham witch trials. Several people admitted they had seen Payne in the woods with other witches and the Black Man, a figure identified with Satan. She was also accused of having a familiar, in the form of a goat-like being named Specter. Her confession was extracted after the torturers had branded a strange seal over her heart. Just before being hanged, she cursed three town fathers and said that one day she would return.

See Arkham; Nyarlathotep (Black Man). ("Season of the Witch", Launius (C).)

PEASLEE, NATHANIEL WINGATE. One-time professor of political economics, and later psychology, at Miskatonic University. Peaslee was born in Haverhill, Massachusetts. No details of his early life are known, but it is known that he became a professor of political economics at Miskatonic in 1895. He married Alice Keezar in the following year, and over the next decade they had three children.

In 1908, Professor Peaslee underwent a mysterious seizure followed by a bout of amnesia. For the next five years he embarked upon a study of history, anthropology, and mythology, undertaking many voyages to all parts of the world to consult various sources of esoteric information in an apparent attempt to regain his memory. During this period his wife divorced him, and she and all of his children refused to have anything to do with him. Many psychologists studied him, but confessed that they were baffled by his condition. This state of affairs concluded in 1913, when Peaslee inexplicably returned to a healthy state of mind. At this time his son Wingate was returned to his custody.

Peaslee then seemed completely normal, but was soon plagued by nightmares of alien creatures and tremendous stone cities. These visions forced him to abandon the professorship which the University had returned to him, and he spent the next few years attempting to discover the roots of his affliction. While searching through other cases Peaslee found many striking parallels between his own condition and those of many others. These findings were published in several academic journals, and in 1922 the University awarded him a professorship in Miskatonic's Department of Psychology in recognition of his achievements.

Along with his son Wingate and Professors Dyer, Freeborn, and Tyler, Peaslee travelled to Australia in 1935 to aid in excavations of a supposed ruined city in the desert. A month and a half later he left the diggings, following an attempt to cease excavations in a certain area of the desert. Following this incident, he had his conclusions about his former condition, entitled *The Shadow Out of Time*, privately published by Golden Goblin Press of Philadelphia in 1936.

See Great Race of Yith; Peaslee, Wingate; Wilmarth, Albert. ("The Shadow Out of Time", Lovecraft; *The Burrowers Beneath*, Lumley; *S. Petersen's Field Guide to Cthulhu Monsters*, Petersen (C).)

PEASLEE, WINGATE (1900-1980). Son of Nathaniel Peaslee and psychology professor at Miskatonic University.

Wingate was only eight when his father underwent his mysterious change in personality. Though he and the rest of his family were repulsed by the change, the young boy remained faithful to his father, and was returned to the elder Peaslee's custody when his father's condition reversed itself. His father's affliction encouraged Wingate to study psychology, and after he had completed his graduate work, the young man gained a professorship at Miskatonic University.

Wingate accompanied his father upon the Australian expedition of 1935. Despite his father's request, he and his colleagues continued their excavations of a seemingly prehuman city. Fortunately, nothing went amiss, and the team returned to Miskatonic unscathed by the horrors Nathaniel avowed he had seen.

Following a celebrated career as an instructor at Miskatonic, Peaslee took up the post of director of Miskatonic's Wilmarth Foundation, a group dedicated to fighting the forces of the Mythos. Although he and his men had great success initially, in the end Peaslee died while engaged in a bombing operation in the waters off of Innsmouth, Massachusetts.

See de Marigny, Henry-Laurent; Wilmarth Foundation. ("The Shadow Out of Time", Lovecraft; *The Burrowers Beneath*, Lumley; *The Transition of Titus Crow*, Lumley.)

PENTACLE OF PLANES. Artifact or diagram said to be useful in protection from summoned beings, especially Daoloth. It consists of many black plastic pieces which, when placed together, keep anyone inside the pentagram from harm, though it is possible for the person to voluntarily let part or all of a summoned being inside.

See Daoloth, Saaamaaa Ritual. ("Render of the Veils", Campbell.)

PEOPLE OF THE MONOLITH. Volume of poetry written by Justin Geoffrey, a noted Baudelairean poet and correspondent of Edward Derby. Its title poem is thought to be connected in some way to the author's descent into insanity.

Justin Geoffrey wrote the poem "People of the Monolith" after a trip to a location in Hungary known as Xuthltan in 1922. After his return to America, Geoffrey dropped out of sight for three years, finally turning up in Chicago in 1925 with the poems that would comprise his only volume. He went mad shortly after his reappearance, and died while in an asylum in 1926.

Erebus Press published the volume in 1926, shortly before the author's mental decline. At least one copy was bound in the skin of a monstrous creature of the inner earth, but the bindings of most of the other copies are conventional. This collection contains the poems "The People of the Monolith", "Out of the Old Land", and an untitled poem dealing with the Egyptian queen Nitocris.

See Black Stone. ("New York", DiTillio and Willis (C); *Keeper's Compendium*, Herber (C); "The Black Stone", Howard; "The Thing on the Roof", Howard; "The Thing on the Doorstep", Lovecraft.)

PHANTOM OF TRUTH. See Pallid Mask.

PHAROL. A fanged, black entity with tentacles in place of arms. Eibon mentions in his *Book* that he sometimes summoned this being to answer certain perplexing questions in the course of his studies.

See Eibon. ("Shaggai", Carter.).

PHAROS OF LENG. Edifice found in the heart of the Plateau of Leng, and possibly identical with the fabled black monastery of that region. The Pharos often emits a bluish light which can be seen for miles. It is told in *Necronomicon* that the Pharos of Leng will give the signal for the Great Old Ones to re-emerge, but this will only happen after Earth is cleared off.

("The Dream-Quest of Unknown Kadath", Lovecraft; "The Elder Pharos", Lovecraft; "To Clear the Earth", Murray.)

PHILETAS, THEODORUS. Scholar of Constantinople who translated *Kitab Al-Azif* from Arabic into Greek, and bestowed upon this work the title *Necronomicon*.

See *Al-Azif*, *Necronomicon* (Appendices). ("History of the *Necronomicon*", Lovecraft.)

PH'NGLUI MGLW'NAFH CTHULHU R'LYEH WGAH'NAGL FHTAGN. Rough phonetic rendering of a R'lyehian phrase often used in the rites of Cthulhu. It may be roughly translated as, "In his house at R'lyeh dead Cthulhu waits dreaming."

See glass from Leng, Seal of R'lyeh. ("The Call of Cthulhu", Lovecraft.)

PICKMAN, RICHARD UPTON (1884-1926?). Salem painter considered by some to be one of the greatest who ever lived. Pickman is especially remembered for his works depicting strange bestial monsters in graveyards and cellars. His techniques made the monstrosities he painted appear extremely lifelike, and although his works received a cool reception by the public, they were highly prized by certain collectors.

In 1926 Pickman disappeared from his home in Boston. Some assert that he committed suicide, but others believe that he dwells somewhere in the Dreamlands. From what we know of that magical land, both of these theories may be true.

See *Necronomicon* (Appendices). (*Strange Eons*, Bloch; "The Dream-Quest of Unknown Kadath", Lovecraft; "Pickman's Model", Lovecraft.)

PLATEAU OF LENG. See Leng.

PLATEAU OF SUNG. See Sung, Plateau of.

PLATEAU OF TSANG. See Tsang, Plateau of.

PLUTONIAN DRUG. See Liao.

PNAKOTIC. Language mentioned in passing in an obscure reference. It may be this tongue in which the first parts of *Pnakotic Manuscripts* were written, and thus it might be Yithian in origin.

See *Pnakotic Manuscripts*. (*Dagon*, Chappell.)

PNAKOTIC MANUSCRIPTS (also *PNAKOTIC FRAGMENTS*). Book of uncertain age. The *Manuscripts* (or at least, their first five chapters) are said to have been written by members of the Great Race of Yith, who preserved these volumes of the *Manuscripts* at their City of the Archives known as Pnakotus, from which the book derived its name. The people of Lomar preserved this knowledge, who passed it on to Hyperborea, where it was rewritten in the tongue of that land and passed on by a secretive religion to the rest of the world. The first portions of the manuscript are written in a curious sort of cuneiform and dot-group glyphs, which bear resemblance to many patterns carved in rock which have been found throughout the world.

The *Manuscripts* originally appeared in scroll form. All editions of this version are said to be lost, though one may still exist in the Temple of the Elder Ones in Ulthar. Greek and English translations were made in later times. Although it is rumored that the *Manuscripts* were published in English during the 15th century by an anonymous translator, others hold that this document has only been circulated in the original manuscript form. *Pnakotic Manuscripts* may be found at Miskatonic University, and a photostatic, expurgated copy is also held at the British Museum.

Contained in this volume is information about the Great Race of Yith, the nature of Chaugnar Faugn and Yibb-Tstll, the journey of Sansu to the top of Mount Hatheg-Kla, rituals of Rhan-Tegoth's worship, and the location of Xiurhn. Some of the oldest portions of the *Manuscripts* are no longer legible; in these sections are characters which greatly resemble the 50' high symbol found at the summit of Mount Hatheg-Kla following the disappearance of the High Priest Barzai. Some have pointed to parallels between this document and *Eltdown Shards* as well.

It is said that *Pnakotic Manuscripts* has some sort of Guardian, and that those who would read this work must pay the Guardian's price. This Guardian may be entirely fanciful, or even symbolic, but the reader should beware.

See A'byy; Barzai; *G'harne Fragments*; Hatheg-Kla, Mount; Lomar; Pnakotic Pentagon; *Pnakotica*; Pnakotus; Priests of the Ivory Blade; shan. ("Zoth-Ommog", Carter; "The Horror in the Museum", Heald and Lovecraft; *Keeper's Compendium*, Herber (C); "Ulthar and Beyond", Herber (C); "At the Mountains of Madness", Lovecraft; "The Dream-Quest of Unknown Kadath", Lovecraft; "The Other Gods", Lovecraft; "Polaris", Lovecraft; *Selected Letters V*, Lovecraft; "The Shadow Out of Time", Lovecraft; "The Diary of Alonzo Typer", Lovecraft and W. Lumley; *The Burrowers Beneath*, Lumley; "The Asylum", McCall (C); "Xiurhn", Myers; *The Keep*, F. Paul Wilson.)

PNAKOTIC PENTAGON. Warding sigil said by Ludvig Prinn to be efficacious against intrusions by beings from outside during the use of Liao. In addition, the people of Hyperborea used the Pentagon to seal the tombs of wizards and prevent them from coming forth again. The source of this sign may in fact be *Pnakotic Manuscripts*.

("The Stairs in the Crypt", Carter and Smith; "The Invaders", Kuttner.)

PNAKOTICA. Title given to the Greek scrolls bearing the original text of *Pnakotic Manuscripts*.

See *Pnakotic Manuscripts*. (*Keeper's Compendium*, Herber (C).)

PNAKOTUS. City built by the Great Race millions of years ago in the Australian desert. Its name, given to it by later races, roughly translates as "City of the Archives." According to von Junzt, this city lent its name to *Pnakotic Manuscripts*, which were brought to this city by the Yithians.

See *Pnakotic Manuscripts*. ("Zoth-Ommog", Carter.)

PNATH, VALE OF. Valley located in the Dreamlands' Underworld. Here lie the gnawed bones tossed into the great crevasse by the ghouls who feast on a nearby plateau. The Vale is inhabited by gigantic worm-like creatures known only as bholes, which no one has ever seen.

Nightgaunts delight in leaving hapless travellers in this place, for unless the ghouls deign to help them, the bholes will sense their vibrations and come to the surface to engulf them.

See *Book of Eibon*, ghoul, Nath, nightgaunt. ("The Dream-Quest of Unknown Kadath", Lovecraft.)

PNIDLEETHON. World circling the star Yamil Zacra. The inhabitants of this world are of some of the mightiest and most evil sorcerers in the universe. Even the greatest wizards from other worlds must first be deemed worthy by Avalzant, the Warden of the Fiery Change, and then proceed through a long series of initiations before being accepted into their ranks. In all of Earth's history, only four beings have been given this honor.

See Yamil Zacra. ("The Infernal Star" (fragment), Smith.)

PONAPE SCRIPTURE. Manuscript researched or discovered by Captain Abner Ezekiel Hoag in the Carolines circa 1734. This Kingsport, Massachusetts seafarer had pioneered the rum and copra trade in these isles. During his travels Hoag discovered a book written on parchment made from palm leaves and bound in the wood of a long-extinct cycad. According to legend, the high priest of Ghatanothoa, Imash-Mo, and his successors wrote this book in the hieratic Naacal tongue; not knowing the language himself, Hoag received help from his servant Yogash in translating the volume's contents. When he attempted to have the volume published he met with condemnation from the religious leaders of the time, who were especially concerned with the references to the being Dagon found within the *Scripture*.

Having been surreptitiously circulated in certain occult circles, *Ponape Scripture* was finally published in the late 18th century, after Captain Hoag's death, in a slightly abridged version. The original can still be found at the Kester Library in Salem. This book was the subject of Harold Hadley Copeland's *The Prehistoric Pacific in Light of the "Ponape Scripture"*, published in 1911.

Among other things, the *Scripture* tells of the lost continent of Mu and the mighty wizard-priest Zanthu.

See Copeland, Harold Hadley; Idh-yaa; Naacal; Zanthu. (*Dreams from R'lyeh*, Carter; "The Dweller in the Tomb", Carter; "The Fishers from Outside", Carter; "Out of the Ages", Carter; "The Ponape Scripture: A Brief History" in *Kingsport*, Ross (C).)

POSEIDONIS. The last isle of Atlantis to sink beneath the ocean. Its high temple is supposedly still seen by lost ships sailing in the Atlantic.

See *Yhe Rituals*. ("The Strange High House in the Mist", Lovecraft; "The Death of Malygris", Smith.)

POTT, JOHANNES HENRICUS. Author of an untitled Latin manuscript turned down by publishers in the German city of Jena, handwritten copies of which have circulated secretly among certain cults. Ultimate Press at one time considered publishing this volume, but whether they actually followed through with their promise is unknown.

The book is said to contain some sort of "immortality" formula (which may not be complete enough to be performed with the information in the book alone), as well as the rather curious notion that deformed entities reside in all darkened places.

("Cold Print", Campbell; "The Mine of Yuggoth", Campbell; "A Word from the Author" in *The Inhabitant of the Lake*, Campbell.)

POWDER OF IBN-GHAZI. Magical dust which allows the user to see the invisible for the space of ten heartbeats.

("The Dunwich Horror", Lovecraft.)

PRIESTS OF THE IVORY BLADE. High ministers of a religion that venerated Yibb-Tstll. This group is mentioned in the *Pnakotic Manuscripts*, but it is doubtful that these priests exist today.

("Ulthar and Beyond", Herber (C).)

PRINN, LUDVIG (sometimes LUDWIG; ?-1542). Sorcerer whose most famous work is the book *De Vermis Mysteriis*.

The true origins of Ludvig Prinn are unknown. He declared that he had lived for centuries and was the sole survivor of the Ninth Crusade; though it is true that there is an entry for a Ludvig Prinn among the records of the Crusades, this claim is entirely unfounded.

Even if his tales of his past exploits were untrue, it is a definite fact that Prinn did make many trips throughout the world of his time. He spent much time as a captive of Syrian warlocks in the Jebel Ansariye, learning much from their dealings with the djinn. He also made trips to Alexandria, supposedly spoke with the priests of the Black Pharaoh Nephren-Ka, and dwelt for a time in the ruins of the city Chorazin on the Lake of Galilee.

At the end of his career Prinn returned to his homeland of the Flemish countryside, taking up residence first in Bruges, then in Ghent, and finally in a pre-Roman tomb in a forest near Brussels. In the nearby towns, many said that the eccentric hermit had dealings with invisible familiars. Soon Ludvig Prinn was imprisoned by the Roman Inquisition on charges of sorcery.

While imprisoned, Prinn wrote the book *De Vermis Mysteriis*. Somehow, in the dead of night, he managed to smuggle the volume past his guards to be published. Shortly thereafter he was executed.

See Byatis, Chorazin, *De Vermis Mysteriis*, deep one, Irem, Jerusalem's Lot, Liao, Nephren-Ka, Nyarlathotep, Pnakotic Pentagon, "Saracenic Rituals", Shub-Niggurath. ("Darkness, My Name Is", Bertin; "The Shambler from the Stars", Bloch; "Lord of the Worms", Lumley.)

PTETHOLITE. Ancient prehuman tribe that worshiped the Great Old Ones, especially Ithaqua, and who often called down demons upon their enemies. The legends of Hyperborea state that the Ptetholites sent their summonings against Edril Ghambiz of Esipish. Unfortunately, Edril sent the magic of the tribesmen back upon its callers, possibly causing the unknown doom which overtook these people in the end. The only records left behind by the Ptetholites were the Broken Columns of Geph, as well as the Sixth Sathlatta, which they invented.

See Black, the; Broken Columns of Geph; Sixth Sathlatta. ("The Caller of the Black", Lumley; "The Horror at Oakdeene", Lumley; *Spawn of the Winds*, Lumley.)

PUSLT. Unit of time comprising three and one quarter Earth years. It is this length of time that the priests of Chig on Tond spend performing their worship ritual.

See Chig. ("The Inhabitant of the Lake", Campbell.)

Q

QUACHIL UTTAUS (also TREADER OF THE DUST). A being who usually appears as a 4' tall shriveled human mummy whose limbs are stiff and immovable. The Treader has some control over time, and his appearance is signaled by local temporal anomalies; everything within a limited area will age at an accelerated rate. After many "years" have passed within this space, Quachil Uttaus will arrive, riding down from the sky on a beam of gray light. Any person whom he touches will turn into dust instantaneously. Sometimes Quachil Uttaus alights upon the person's remains, leaving two tiny footprints in the dust. It is from this habit that Quachil Uttaus derives his epithet.

Quachil Uttaus is mentioned in no book save *Testament of Carnamagos*, which is the only source of his summoning formula. This volume also contains a method by which a sorcerer may make a pact with the Treader by saying the words "Exklopios Quachil Uttaus." Quachil will arrive and then twist the caster's spine in return for making him immortal. If the Forbidden Words are said again near a bargainer, Quachil Uttaus will come and destroy his one-time servant.

A being very similar in appearance and nature to Quachil Uttaus was worshiped in Egypt under the title Ka-Reth, the Keeper of the Dust.

See *Testament of Carnamagos*. ("The Keeper of the Dust", Brennan; "The Condemned", Herber (C); "The Treader of the Dust", Smith.)

QUUMYAGGA. Sire of the race of shantaks, and the greatest of Gol-Goroth's servitors. At one time this creature dwelt beneath Mount Voormithadreth. It may be Quumyagga who dwells within the innermost dome of the great palace of Inquanok in the Dreamlands, and who troubles the dreams of those who gaze too long upon that edifice.

See Gol-Goroth, shantak. ("The Fishers from Outside", Carter; "The Descent into the Abyss", Carter and Smith.)

Q'YTH-AZ. Great Old One who takes the form of a colossal amalgamation of crystals. Q'yth-az dwells on the world of Mthura, and can only travel from its home under very specific circumstances.

Q'yth-az has been known to broadcast its telepathic messages to those who are in close contact with crystals. If the person contacted agrees to aid the Great Old One, Q'yth-az may manifest itself on this world when Mthura can be seen in the sky. When it arrives, the crystalline entity grows and attempts to transform everything around it into mineral matter. If Mthura is hidden by clouds or travels below the horizon, however, Q'yth-az must return to its home world.

See Mthura. ("An Early Frost", Aniolowski.)

R

RAM WITH A THOUSAND EWES. Being invoked in certain of Shub-Niggurath's rituals. It is most likely Shub-Niggurath's male incarnation.

See Shub-Niggurath. (*The Transition of Titus Crow*, Lumley; "The Holiness of Azedarac," Smith.)

RAMASEKVA. Asura, or demon, mentioned in a few Hindu legends. This multi-limbed being is in actuality an avatar of Yog-Sothoth, and may be contacted through the use of a hallucinogenic drug. It is not known whether a cult to Ramasekva exists.

See Yog-Sothoth. ("Mr. Corbitt", DeWolfe (C).)

REFLECTIONS. Book written by Ibn Schacabao and referred to in *Necronomicon*. The only known surviving copy is held at the British Museum.

Contained within this book is the famous line, "Happy is the town where no wizard hath lain, and happy is the town at night whose wizards are all ashes." The rest of our information about *Reflections* is fragmentary, but it also contains a description of the beings of the Gulf of S'lghuo. This may also be the volume by Schacabao mentioned in the correspondence of Joseph Curwen which described the face of Yog-Sothoth.

See Ibn Schacabao. ("The Plain of Sound", Campbell; "The Case of Charles Dexter Ward", Lovecraft; "The Festival", Lovecraft; *The Burrowers Beneath*, Lumley.)

REMNANTS OF LOST EMPIRES. Volume written by Otto Dostmann and published in Berlin by Der Drachenhaus Press in 1809. In this book Dostmann deals with the Black Stone, which he states Attila's troops erected as a victory marker, as well as the Fishers from Outside.

("The Fishers from Outside", Carter; "The Black Stone", Howard.)

REVELARE NUNCIUS (also REVEL NUNCIO or REVELERS). Organization backed by the Roman Catholic Church and dedicated to the investigation of occult matters which might prove dangerous to the Church. Formed in 1701 as a response to the de Medicis' calls for action against the Last Dawn, it became that organization's greatest foe.

The Revelare Nuncius, now known as the Revel Nuncio, still survives today. Though it is made up mostly of Catholic priests, it also accepts other Catholics or Christians of other denominations into its ranks.

See Last Dawn. ("The Last Dawn", Eastland, *TU07* (C).)

REVELATIONS OF GLAAKI. Set of books detailing the practices of the cult of Glaaki. These eleven volumes were originally handwritten by various worshipers of that deity who dwelt in England's Severn River Valley near Brichester. An escaped member of the cult secretly leaked the manuscript to a publisher, who printed *Revelations* in 1865. The worshiper who transcribed the books chose to leave out several portions, and *Revelations* was released in a nine-volume set. Most of them were bought up by members of Glaaki's cult, so very few non-initiates were able to obtain copies.

In the 1920's a Brichester bookseller discovered a twelfth volume of *Revelations*. All copies of this book are believed to be destroyed — fortunately, because this is the only volume which mentions the abhorrent deity Y'golonac. Rumor has it that a later edition put out by Ultimate Press contained fifteen or more volumes, but this has not been verified.

Copies of *Revelations* are relatively rare. The handwritten original may still be kept at the former base of the English Glaaki cult, but all of this organization's members vanished around 1870. Brichester University held a mostly complete nine-volume edition from the estate of Professor Arnold Hird for a time, but the books later disappeared.

This set of books deals mostly with rites of Glaaki but sometimes tells of other entities, including Daoloth, Ghroth, and the inhabitants of

S'lghuo. It is a strange and confusing book; the topics and handwriting vary widely, as different writers replaced those who had kept the records before them.

See Brichester, Crystallizer of Dreams, Daoloth, Ghroth, Glaaki, Mercy Hill, M'nagalah, Saaamaaa Ritual, Tond, Vulthoom, yarkdao, Y'golonac. ("Cold Print", Campbell; "The Inhabitant of the Lake", Campbell; "The Plain of Sound", Campbell; "Behold, I Stand at the Door and Knock", Price.)

REVELATIONS OF HALI. Book by the famous prophet translated by the medium E. S. Bayrolles. *Revelations* was later published by Golden Goblin Press of New York in 1913. Although a copy is kept at Miskatonic University, nothing is known of its contents.

("An Inhabitant of Carcosa", Bierce; "Typo", Winkle.)

RHAN-TEGOTH. Great Old One who came down from Yuggoth to Earth, taking up residence in the Arctic three million years ago. The sacrifices his primitive followers made maintained the Old One's strength and vigor. Later on, the people of the region forgot Rhan-Tegoth, and their former "god" lapsed into hibernation.

During the early 20th century the curator of a London waxworks museum launched an expedition up the Noatak River, from Fort Morton to the great ruined city where Rhan-Tegoth once lived. Finding the dormant god on a tremendous ivory throne, he took it back with him to London. This explorer disappeared shortly thereafter, however, and the current whereabouts of Rhan-Tegoth are unknown.

According to some, this Great Old One may be awakened by the following chant:

Wza-y'ei! Wza-y'ei!

Y'kaa haa bho-ii,

Rhan-Tegoth — Cthulhu fhtagn —

Rhan-Tegoth,

Rhan-Tegoth,

Rhan-Tegoth!

The mythical beast Gnoph-Keh is sometimes said to be an avatar of Rhan-Tegoth. No evidence has been found to verify this, and it is more likely that the gnoph-keh are a species of Arctic monster. Also, the gnoph-keh were active at times when Rhan-Tegoth still sat dreaming on his throne.

Some say that if Rhan-Tegoth can be destroyed the Great Old Ones can never return to life. The destruction of a being like Rhan-Tegoth, however, would probably be beyond the abilities of humanity. Even if it were possible, the supposition that his destruction would stop the Great Old Ones sounds like wishful thinking.

See gnoph-keh, *Pnakotic Manuscripts*, Yuggoth. ("The Gods", Carter; "Some Observations on the Carter Glossary", Cockcroft; "The Horror in the Museum", Heald and Lovecraft.)

RHYDAGAND. Painter mentioned in *Book of Eibon*. Rhydagand could paint a picture and then, while sleeping near the painting, travel to the place pictured.

See *Book of Eibon*. ("Pickman's Student", Herber (C).)

RIGEL. Star traditionally connected with the Elder Gods, though not to such a great degree as Glyu'Uho.

("Lair of the Star-Spawn", Derleth and Schorer.)

RING OF EIBON. Artifact owned or created by the mighty Hyperborean wizard Eibon. It later became the possession of the le Chaudronnier family of Averoigne in medieval times, but its current owner is unknown. The ring was forged of a reddish gold, and set with a large purple stone. When held over burning amber, a demon from within the gem would come forth to answer whatever questions its summoner might have.

See Eibon. ("The Beast of Averoigne", Smith.)

RING OF THE HYADES. Piece of jewelry which is believed to have originated within the Hyades, and is kept in a great cavern which only the greatest sorcerers may enter. By speaking the runes carven upon the Ring, the wearer may transport himself to the Outer Gulfs of the universe. This device also will protect its owner from the creatures in these regions, such as Hastur, but provides no protection from Shub-Niggurath or her minions.

("The Ring of the Hyades", Glasby.)

RLIM SHAIKORTH. Creature mentioned in *Book of Eibon*. Rlim Shaikorth is said to have been much like a immense white worm in form. At one end he had a wide mouth and two empty eye sockets from which blood constantly dripped. He was practically omniscient and mighty in the ways of magic. This creature was not native to our world, and may have arrived on Earth along with his master, Aphoom Zhah.

Rlim Shaikorth appeared on Earth when Hyperborea was still a mighty world power. In his ice citadel of Yikilth, the White Worm travelled south from the Pole, blasting all of the lands he sailed past with a great cold which killed all that it touched instantly. Only a few survivors, the Ylidheem, remained; these were great wizards whom Rlim Shaikorth had transformed so that they might live comfortably in the cold to render him worship. According to Eibon, the cold from Yikilth destroyed many of Hyperborea's finest cities, and the end of the world seemed certain. One day, though, the unnatural cold ended as Yikilth melted away. What happened to Rlim Shaikorth still remains a mystery, though Eibon's book provides one possible answer: Rlim Shaikorth may seem to be independent, but in fact he serves the fire-being Aphoom Zhah, who dwells in the ice mountain of Yarak at the northern pole.

See Aphoom Zhah, *Book of Eibon*, Yikilth, Ylidheem. ("Zoth-Ommog", Carter; "The Light from the Pole", Carter and Smith; "The Coming of the White Worm", Smith.)

R'LYEH (also ARLYEH). Sunken alien city beneath the southern Pacific (though others place it near Ponape, or even off the coast of Massachusetts). Cthulhu and his minions built R'lyeh millions of years before the earliest recorded history. Cthulhu and his children lived in R'lyeh, sallying forth to battle the Elder Things and other alien entities. Then a catastrophe occurred. According to some scholars, the stars moved to a particular astrological configuration; others assert a great cosmic war occurred; still others believe the creation of the moon was the cause of this event. Whatever the reason, R'lyeh sank beneath the waves of the Pacific Ocean, becoming the tomb of Great Cthulhu.

Though R'lyeh has sunk deep beneath the Pacific Ocean, there have been certain times when the city (or at least its highest mountain) has breached the surface of the sea, only to sink down again after a short period of time. These occasions have been connected with outbreaks of religious fervor, insanity, and natural disturbances about the world. The interested reader should obtain the works of Professor George Angell of Brown University as well as the Johansen Narrative for more information on these events.

From the descriptions of the corpse-city of R'lyeh which have come down to us, we learn that its buildings are made of colossal green stones which fit together in a non-Euclidean manner. In a mighty mausoleum at the top of the tallest mountain, Great Cthulhu sleeps, held within his tomb by an Elder Sign. Only the ignorant or foolhardy would open the door of this tomb; in all of history, this has only occurred a few times, and the results were disastrous.

See *Book of Dagon*, Cthulhi, Cthulhu, Great Old Ones, Johansen Narrative, Lemuria, Masters of the Silver Twilight, *Ph'nglui mglw'nafh Cthulhu R'lyeh wgah'nagl fhtagn*, *R'lyeh Text*, Seal of R'lyeh, Yhe, Ythogtha, Zoth-Ommog. ("The Black Island", Derleth; "The Seal of R'lyeh", Derleth; *The Lurker at the Threshold*, Derleth and Lovecraft; "The Call of Cthulhu", Lovecraft; "The House of Cthulhu", Lumley.)

R'LYEH TEXT. Book said to have originally been transcribed on great tablets by the spawn of Cthulhu themselves and to be preserved in scroll form somewhere in the depths of China. It is said that both English and German translations were smuggled out of China, and these few copies are the most likely to be encountered in the western world (although one Latin copy is said to exist). The book reportedly deals with the proper worship of Cthulhu and his kindred.

See *Investigation into the Myth-Patterns of Latter-Day Primitives with Especial Reference to the* R'lyeh Text, *An*; Liyuhh; R'lyeh; *R'lyeh Text Commentary*. ("Darkness, My Name Is", Bertin; "The Return of Hastur", Derleth; "Black Devil Mountain", Hargrave (C).).

R'LYEH TEXT COMMENTARY. Book in classical Chinese which explains several of the passages within *R'lyeh Text*. This volume also contains a sketchy map of R'lyeh.

See *R'lyeh Text*. ("Shanghai", DiTillio and Willis (C).)

S

SAAAMAAA RITUAL. Incantation said by Carnacki, the noted ghost hunter, to have been used by the "Ab-Human priests" in their worship. Its last line is said to be unknowable by humans. Whether this is true or not, the second line of the Saaamaaa Ritual is mentioned in *Revelations of Glaaki* as an ideal way to create the Pentacle of Planes, which guards against the uncontrolled manifestation of Daoloth during the summoning of that Outer God.

See Daoloth. ("The Whistling Room", Hodgson; "The Gates of Delirium", Sumpter (C).)

SADOGUI. See Tsathoggua.

SAINT TOAD. Title sometimes given to the Great Old One Tsathoggua. See Tsathoggua. (*The Illuminatus! Trilogy*, Shea and R. Wilson.)

SAKKUTH (also KOSSUTH). Being who serves both Hastur and Shub-Niggurath. According to the magi of Roman times, Sakkuth came to Earth once every thousand years, possessing the body of a human for his purposes. Sakkuth spread dissension in the lands through which he travelled, and is believed to be responsible for the Dark Ages which followed the destruction of Atlantis and Hyperborea. While on this planet Sakkuth would try to summon his masters to Earth, where they would mate and give birth to the spawn that would gain dominion over the world.

Sakkuth seems in many ways to be similar to Nyarlathotep, but may also be another name for the King in Yellow.

See Ajar-Alazwat, Hastur, Shub-Niggurath. ("The Seed of the Star-God", Tierney.)

SANBOURNE INSTITUTE OF PACIFIC ANTIQUITIES. Anthropological society in Santiago, California devoted to the study of the various cultures of the Pacific. Carlton Sanbourne II, a man whose father had made a fortune in the tuna-packing industry, was the founder of this institute. Upon his death he bequeathed to the Institute all of his money, his house and grounds, and a great number of Polynesian artifacts, which formed the Institute's core collection.

Despite the amount of scholarly research credited to its staff, the Sanbourne Institute is best remembered by the public for the circumstances surrounding the donation of the Copeland Bequest, which may have been responsible for the death of Copeland himself and the madness of two of its caretakers.

See Copeland, Harold Hadley; *Unaussprechlichen Kulten*; Zanthu Tablets. ("The Dweller in the Tomb", Carter; "Out of the Aeons", Carter; "Zoth-Ommog", Carter.)

SAND-DWELLER. Creature who resembles an emaciated, grit-encrusted human with a head like that of a koala. Sand-dwellers live in the American Southwest, and possibly in other desert areas elsewhere in the world. These creatures live in bands and are usually nocturnal, remaining in their caverns until they leave to hunt at nightfall. The sand-dwellers may serve creatures which thrive deeper within their grottoes.

("The Gable Window", Derleth and Lovecraft.)

SANSU. Inhabitant of the Dreamlands. Sansu was one of the only two people in history to scale Mount Hatheg-Kla, though he found nothing at the top. The things he saw on a journey to K'n-yan drove him insane in the end.

See Hatheg-kla, Mount; *Pnakotic Manuscripts*. ("K'n-yan", DeBill; "The Other Gods", Lovecraft.)

SAPIENTIA MAGLORUM ("Wisdom of the Magi"). Volume written in Greek and Latin by the great Persian magus Ostanes. Even in Roman times the volume was quite rare; aside from at least one copy held at Ephesus, editions could also be found in Italy and Samaria, though these were almost impossible to find or to consult.

Within this volume Ostanes recorded the rituals necessary to raise Kaiwan (Hastur) and Shupnikkurat (Shub-Niggurath), a formula to propitiate Fortuna, the Roman god of luck, and the true reason that Herostratos burned down the temple of Artemis at Ephesus which Croesus had financed.

("The Seed of the Star-God", Tierney.)

"SARACENIC RITUALS". The most famous chapter of Ludvig Prinn's *De Vermis Mysteriis*. It contains the secrets learned by the author during his captivity under the wizards of Syria — or so Prinn asserted. Not only is this chapter contained in *De Vermis Mysteriis*, a "Clergyman X" made another translation during the 19th century. This holy man, however, omitted several passages from his version out of pious horror. A copy of this pamphlet is kept at the British Museum Library.

This chapter deals with the efreet and djinn of the Arabian deserts, as well as with the pharaoh Nephren-Ka, the priesthoods of the Egyptian gods Sebek and Bast, and the worm-wizards of many-columned Irem.

See *De Vermis Mysteriis*, Nephren-Ka. ("The Brood of Bubastis", Bloch; "Fane of the Black Pharaoh", Bloch; "The Secret of Sebek", Bloch; "The Shambler from the Stars", Bloch; "Lord of the Worms", Lumley.)

SARNATH. City built near a great lake in the land of Mnar by a group of nomads. Sarnath lay quite near to another city, Ib, in which a species of amphibious creatures dwelt. The people of Sarnath hated the creatures who dwelt in Ib, and decided that their neighbors must be destroyed. One day the warriors of Sarnath marched on Ib, slew all of its inhabitants, and bore the statue of Bokrug worshiped by the people of Ib back to Sarnath.

After this victory, Sarnath conquered many of the nearby nations and became rich and powerful. A thousand years later, however, a great calamity befell, and the city of Sarnath disappeared in one night.

A ruined city named Sarnath does exist in India; these two sites are probably not identical, though, since the Indian Sarnath's ruins still exist, while only an idol of Bokrug survived the destruction of Mnar's Sarnath.

See Bokrug, Ib, *Ilarnek Papyri*, Kish, Mnar, Shub-Niggurath, Sign of Kish, Thuum'ha. ("The Doom that Came to Sarnath", Lovecraft.)

SARNATH-SIGIL. See Elder Sign.

SATHLATTAE. Set of formulae, at least one of which may be found in *Cthaat Aquadingen*. Little is known about any of these, save for two. One, the Ninth Sathlatta, served as a potent protection from baneful magics in Theem'hdra. The other, the Sixth Sathlatta, is important enough to receive its own entry.

See Sixth Sathlatta. ("Billy's Oak", Lumley; "Cryptically Yours", Lumley.)

SCARSDALE LIGHTS. Phenomena first sighted in 1932. These mysterious lights in the sky were given their name because of the theories of Professor Clark Ashton Scarsdale, who hypothesized that they were the symbols of the resurgence of the Old Ones.

(*The Great White Space*, Copper.)

SCRIPTURE OF KLEK. Book of which little is known, save that Yohk the Necromancer consulted it.

("Yohk the Necromancer", Myers.)

SEAL OF R'LYEH. Insignia bearing a picture of Cthulhu standing over the city of R'lyeh and encircled by the motto, *"Ph'nglui mglw'nafh Cthulhu R'lyeh wgah'nagl fhtagn."*

See R'lyeh. ("The Seal of R'lyeh", Derleth.)

SECRET MYSTERIES OF ASIA, WITH A COMMENTARY ON THE GHORL NIGRAL. Volume by Gottfried Mulder, an associate of Friedrich von Junzt, who accompanied the eccentric scholar on many of his journeys. During a journey to China, von Junzt consulted a copy of *Ghorl Nigral* held in a monastery. He later spoke much of that volume's contents to Mulder.

In the years following von Junzt's death, Mulder began to realize how crucial the revelations given to him had been. Making use of self-hypnosis, he reconstructed many of the hints he had been given, and incorporated them into his *Secret Mysteries of Asia*. Following the volume's Leipzig printing in 1847, most copies were seized and destroyed by the government. Mulder escaped to Metzengerstein, where he was incarcerated and finally passed away. The locations and contents of this volume are not common knowledge, though one is probably held at Miskatonic University Library.

See *Ghorl Nigral*; von Junzt, Friedrich. ("Zoth-Ommog", Carter; *Dreams and Fancies*, Lovecraft.)

SECRET WATCHER, THE. Book by Halpin Chalmers, a noted occultist and one-time Curator of Archaeology at the Manhattan Museum of Fine Arts, who was found murdered in his apartment following a bout of insanity. This volume, published by London's Charnel House Publishers, seems to deal with some type of psychic journey undertaken by the author.

See Chalmers, Halpin. ("The Winfield Inheritance", Carter; *The Horror from the Hills*, Long; "The Hounds of Tindalos", Long.)

SEED OF AZATHOTH, THE. A greenish, glowing material whose source is the spawn of Azathoth that the Outer God occasionally throws off while dancing at his court. Some of these, in their flights through the cosmos, later become part of some of the objects known to humans as comets. When one of these seeds lands on a planet, it burrows into the ground until it reaches the planet's heart. There it may hatch and form another of Azathoth's spawn, cracking the planet open. A seed landing upon the world of Thyoph destroyed that world, creating our asteroid belt. Another Seed may have caused the Tunguska explosion, but if this is true, its effects were halted before much damage could be done. Physical proximity to such a fragment is quite dangerous, and results in a slow disintegration of the victim's body.

The Seed is believed to have beneficial effects as well. It is said to have a catabolic effect on certain servitors of the Other Gods. The fungi from Yuggoth and insects from Shaggai often make tools out of this material.

See Azathoth, Thyoph. ("Pickman's Student", Herber (C); *Spawn of Azathoth*, Herber (C); "In the Vaults Beneath", Herber.)

SELECTIONS DE LIVRE D'IVON. Commentary in French on the Latin *Book of Eibon* penned by Gaspard du Nord. It contains several protective charms to keep the user safe from the forces of evil, especially Nyarlathotep.

See *Book of Eibon*. ("New York", DiTillio and Willis (C).)

SERPENT PEOPLE. Race of bipedal reptiles which appeared during Earth's Permian period. With their great magic (and the aid of the fabled Cobra Crown) the serpent people conquered the empire of Valusia, an area which today forms part of both Europe and Africa. During this time the serpent people reared great stone cities, in which they built laboratories where they performed great works of science and magic as well as temples to Yig, Byatis, and

Tsathoggua. When the Triassic Age came, new conditions caused the race to go into decline for eons until they had a resurgence during the Pleistocene Era.

The coming of humanity proved to be the downfall of the serpent people's dominion over the world. This new race swept aside the old cities of the reptiles in order to build their new towns and fortresses. To escape this destruction, some of the reptiles crept into hidden burrows in the hills; others put themselves into deep hibernation; some used their magical abilities to disguise themselves, and concealed themselves among the invaders. Apart from one abortive attempt to capture the throne of Valusia, the serpents were never a serious threat to humanity thereafter.

Today the serpent people are small in numbers, and must do even more to keep their identities hidden. Despite this, many of this race are convinced that another resurgence of their race is imminent. For the most part the serpent people are so diffused and individualistic that any plans toward this end seem unlikely. If they did decide to eliminate humanity once and for all, their mastery of both scientific and magical techniques (as well as their advanced knowledge of poison manufacture) would make them formidable foes.

See Aklo, *Book of Skelos*, Byatis, gnoph-keh, Nameless City, Sss'haa, Valusia, voormis, Worms of the Earth. ("Where a God Shall Tread", Aniolowski (C); "Zoth-Ommog", Carter; *Conan the Buccaneer*, Carter and de Camp; "The Shadow Kingdom", Howard; "The Seven Geases", Smith.)

SEVEN CRYPTICAL BOOKS OF HSAN (also *SEVEN CRYPTICAL BOOKS OF EARTH*). Scrolls said to have been written in the 2nd century A.D. by Hsan the Greater. This book is said to have been smuggled out of China, and in 1940 Boston's Silver Key Press published an English translation made by Etienne-Laurent de Marigny. It is rumored that one of the seven original books has been lost. One copy of this book may be found at the Temple of the Elder Ones in Ulthar, and another is kept at Miskatonic University.

Little is known of these volumes. It is said that the fifth book contains the formula for creating the Eye of Light and Darkness, but the process is only contained in especially complete editions. In the "lost" book, information of how wisdom may be obtained from the dead is also kept.

See Barzai; de Marigny, Etienne-Laurent; Eye of Light and Darkness. ("Zoth-Ommog", Carter; "Shanghai", DiTillio and Willis (C); "Books of the Cthulhu Mythos", Herber and Ross (C); "The Dream-Quest of Unknown Kadath", Lovecraft; "The Strange High

House in the Mist", Lovecraft; "The Return of Zhosph", Myers;
"Typo", Winkle.)

SEVEN LOST SIGNS OF TERROR. Magical hand passes or sigils
that may protect a person from those from Outside.
("The Diary of Alonzo Typer", Lovecraft and Lumley, W.)

SEVEN THOUSAND APPELATIONS OF THE DAEMONS.
Work of which nothing is known, save that Yohk the Necromancer
consulted it.
("Yohk the Necromancer", Myers.)

SEVERNFORD. Town to the northwest of Brichester, on the
banks of the Severn River. Like many towns in the region, Severnford
is past its prime, with many of its buildings standing empty and
dilapidated. Near this town is the ruined castle in which the wizard Sir
Gilbert Morley resided, and an isle in the river nearby was once the site
of witches' sabbats.
See Camside. ("The Faces at Pine Dunes", Campbell; "The Plain
of Sound", Campbell; "The Room in the Castle", Campbell.)

SHABBITH. African tribe devoted to the worship of the Outer
God Shabbith-Ka. It is believed that the tribe was almost entirely
destroyed around the year 1300.
See Shabbith-Ka. ("What Goes Around, Comes Around",
Moeller, *TU08/9* (C).)

SHABBITH-KA. Mysterious entity which manifests as a cloud of
purple lightning. It was worshiped by a tribe known as the Shabbiths
long ago, and later by a cult called the Primal Song.
See Shabbith. ("What Goes Around, Comes Around",
Moeller, *TU08/9* (C).)

SHAGGAI. World of two emerald suns from which the shan, or
insects from Shaggai, first came. Shaggai was rocky, and covered with
black seas and tremendous jungles. In many places the shan had
reared huge cities of globular dwellings and conical or pyramidal
temples to Azathoth. From their home world the insects had colonized many of the nearby planets, but the majority of the shan
remained on Shaggai up until its destruction.

A strange celestial object destroyed this world more than eight hundred years ago. One day the insects spied a glowing red body in their sky, which slowly drew nearer to Shaggai. Three days later the object reached Shaggai, and the glowing object immolated the planet in a holocaust of light and flame. Only the shan who were in the teleporting temples of Azathoth or on the otherworldly colonies escaped the ruin of their home planet.

See Baoht Z'uqqa-Mogg, *Book of Eibon*, Glaaki, *Massa di Requiem per Shuggay*, shan, Xiclotl. ("The Insects from Shaggai", Campbell; "Shaggai", Carter; "The Haunter of the Dark", Lovecraft.)

SHAMBALLAH (or SHAMBHALA). City built fifty million years ago by Lemurians in the Great Eastern Desert, a reference usually taken to mean the Gobi. It still remains there, protected behind a screen of psychic force. Buddhists hold that when the entire world is engulfed in warfare, humanity's savior shall come forth from Shamballah. The wizard-priest Zanthu of Mu fled to the lands near this city when his home continent sank beneath the waves.

("The Thing in the Pit," Carter; "The Diary of Alonzo Typer," Lovecraft and Lumley, W.; "The Return of the Lloigor," C. Wilson.)

SHAN (also INSECTS FROM SHAGGAI). Race of insects about the size of a pigeon. They differ from earthly insects in that they have ten legs, three mouths, a set of feelers below their mouths, and tentacles sprouting from their legs. The shan are entirely photosynthetic, deriving their nourishment from the sun's rays; any prisoners taken are used either as slaves or for the insects' entertainment.

The shan were known as mighty wizards, who were mentioned in the ancient writings only with the greatest abhorrence. It is said that one of the greatest secrets of *Pnakotic Manuscripts* dealt with something these insects summoned and were forced to imprison within their world.

The shan originally came from the world of Shaggai, where they lived in gray, globular buildings and worshiped Azathoth in conical metal temples. After many years a huge red object, possibly identical with Ghroth the Harbinger, appeared in the skies of Shaggai, and shortly thereafter almost all of the shan were immolated and destroyed by the rays enamating from their visitor. Some of the shan did not perish, however. They had already colonized several nearby worlds, and the temples of Azathoth were able to teleport away from Shaggai. In this way, many escaped destruction.

The shan have spent hundreds of years looking for a new home. The activities of only one group are known, but if this hive's journeys are any indication, the insects have travelled extensively through space. This group travelled between many worlds, hopping from Shaggai to Xiclotl, then to Thuggon, next to L'gh'yx (a world known to humanity as Uranus), and finally to Earth. On their final stop, in the woods near the Severn River Valley, the shan became trapped, as the atmosphere contains some element which prevented their temples from teleporting.

It was then that these Earth-bound shan became involved with humanity. Since they were constructed of a different sort of matter than that of the native lifeforms, they found it possible to physically "enter" the brains of humans. By doing so, they built up a cult dedicated to Azathoth, using their mind control to induce feelings of elation in their hosts, as well as producing visions which revealed the history and discoveries of the insects to the worshipers. The famous witch hunter Matthew Hopkins destroyed this cult, and now the shan have no agents on Earth.

Even before they left Shaggai, the shan were extremely decadent. Their primary form of entertainment is the torture of their many slave races, making use of curious devices powered by psychic waves.

See Azathoth, Baoht Z'uqqa-Mogg, L'gy'hx, Lrogg, Seed of Azathoth, Shaggai, Thuggon, Xada-Hgla, Xiclotl. ("The Insects from Shaggai", Campbell.)

SHANTAK. Creature of the Dreamlands which appears to be a tremendous scaled bird with the head of a horse. Shantaks live in the mountains near to the Plateau of Leng, and have been known to aid the people of that place at times. Some say that these creatures also dwell on other planets in our own dimension, and that they constructed the huge stone towers found in Zimbabwe. The shantaks may serve Nyarlathotep, Gol-Goroth, or the Wendigo, having been connected with all these entities in various instances. A shantak may be used as a mount, but there is always a danger that the monster may ignore its rider's commands and attempt to bear its rider to the court of Azathoth.

See Fishers from Outside, Gol-Goroth, Quumyagga. ("The Fishers from Outside", Carter; "The Seal of R'lyeh", Derleth; "The Dream-Quest of Unknown Kadath", Lovecraft.)

SHARNOTH. World beyond the universe that holds the court of Nyarlathotep. A formula from Tartary that involves inscribing five concentric flaming circles about the wizard will allow the user to travel here, and though all things may there be learned, the cost is great.

("The Black Tome of Alsophocus", Lovecraft and Warnes.)

SHINING TRAPEZOHEDRON. Artifact used in the worship of Nyarlathotep's form of the Haunter of the Dark.

The Shining Trapezohedron antedates most earthly life. It was made in Yuggoth and brought to Earth by the mi-go, and then came into the possession of the Elder Things. It then travelled to Valusia, Lemuria, and Atlantis. A Minoan fisherman found the artifact and sold it to the pharaoh Nephren-Ka, who kept it in the labyrinths of Kish, where Nitocris later found and used it. There it remained until 1844, when Professor Enoch Bowen's archaeological dig of Kish unearthed it. The professor bore it back to his home in Providence, Rhode Island, where it became the sacred object of the Starry Wisdom cult. Following the cult's dissolution in 1877, the Trapezohedron remained in the deserted Starry Wisdom Church until 1934, when events connected with its disturbance prompted a local doctor to bear the artifact away and cast it into Narraganset Bay. It is believed that someday the Trapezohedron will be brought out of the waters and form the focus for a new Starry Wisdom cult.

The Trapezohedron may be used in many ways. It serves as a window in which one may gaze on all time and space. If someone gazes at the Trapezohedron for any length of time and then plunges the item into darkness, Nyarlathotep's Haunter of the Dark aspect will manifest itself nearby. The Trapezohedron's last power is to accelerate any bodily metamorphosis which may be taking place in its viewer (such as a deep one's transformation.)

See *Black Tome of Alsophocus*, Kish, Nephren-Ka, *Necronomicon* (Appendices), Nitocris, Nyarlathotep (Haunter of the Dark), Starry Wisdom Cult, Yuggoth. (*Strange Eons*, Bloch; "The Haunter of the Dark," Lovecraft; "The Mirror of Nitocris", Lumley.)

SHOGGOTH. Entity created as a servitor by the Elder Things billions of years ago. These beings were approximately 15' in diameter, and appeared as enormous black masses covered with whatever sensory organs and appendages their masters required. The shoggoths were strong and easily taught through hypnotic suggestion, and were used to build the great underwater stone cities of the Elder Things.

After millions of years serving the Elder Things, however, the shoggoths had become more intelligent and mocking of their task-makers. This discontent turned into open rebellion in the Permian period (150 million years ago). Though the shoggoths were initially successful, the Elder Things suppressed the rebellion; they then retrained the shoggoths and continued to use them, though more cautiously than before. During this time the shoggoths showed their ability to survive out of water, but such adaptation was discouraged by the Elder Things. When the Elder Things departed the cold Antarctic for their last underwater city, it is believed that their shoggoths were taken with them as well.

There have been some reports of shoggoth sightings in other places than in their normal Antarctic habitat, but thankfully these have been very rare. It is rumored that the deep ones make use of shoggoths in their schemes, and others of their kind protect the tomb of Cthulhu. Alhazred denied that shoggoths existed on Earth save in drug-induced hallucinations, which should impress upon the reader the foulness of these monsters.

See Elder Things, Ghooric Zone, mapulo, shoggoth-twsha, Ubbo-Sathla. ("At the Mountains of Madness", Lovecraft; "The Shadow Over Innsmouth", Lovecraft; "The Transition of Titus Crow", Lumley.)

SHOGGOTH-TWSHA. Deep one who has been charged with controlling those horrid beings known as shoggoths. A shoggoth-twsha, or priest, holds a mapulo in his hands, and gives commands to the shoggoth. The priest has no need of sleep, and this is fortunate, for he may take his attention away from the shoggoth for only a short length of time or it will rebel. Control is difficult, for it involves entering into telepathic rapport with the shoggoth, and there is always a chance the mapulo will eat the commander.

See mapulo, shoggoth. ("Shanghai", DiTillo and Willis (C).)

SHREWSBURY, LABAN (1864-1938?). Miskatonic University professor who at one time lived in Arkham, Massachusetts. Professor Shrewsbury made himself a controversial figure with the publication of his first book, *An Investigation into the Myth-Patterns of Latter-Day Primitives with Especial Reference to the* R'lyeh Text. In 1915, shortly after the release of his book, Shrewsbury disappeared while walking on a country lane near his hometown. He was given up for dead, and his collected notes on the latter 19th century were printed under the title *Cthulhu among the Victorians*.

Twenty years after he had vanished the Professor reappeared, giving no account as to where he had been. Having taken up residence

once again in Arkham, he began work on his next book, *Cthulhu in the*
Necronomicon. Sadly, the Professor never completed this volume. A
mysterious fire gutted Shrewsbury's house in 1938; the Professor is
presumed to have been killed in the blaze.

The first section of Shrewsbury's *Cthulhu in the* Necronomicon was
published posthumously. *Celaeno Fragments*, a manuscript transcribed
by Shrewsbury, still remains in the vaults of Miskatonic University.

See Celaeno, *Celaeno Fragments*; *Cthulhu among the Victorians*;
Cthulhu in the Necronomicon; *Investigation into the Myth-Patterns
of Latter-Day Primitives with Especial Reference to the* R'lyeh Text,
An; Nameless City; *Necronomicon* (Appendices). (*Cthulhu by Gaslight*, Barton (C); *The Trail of Cthulhu*, Derleth; *Keeper's Compendium*, Herber (C).)

SHUB-NIGGURATH (also THE BLACK GOAT OF THE
WOODS WITH A THOUSAND YOUNG). Outer God of fertility.
Little is known of this deity, as she is not often encountered. At the
rare times she shows herself to mortals, Shub-Niggurath appears as a
great noxious cloud from which hoofed feet and tendrils constantly
protrude and are reabsorbed.

The residence of Shub-Niggurath remains a mystery. One location that has been hypothesized is the planet Yaddith, beneath the
surface of which she resides with her dhole servitors. Others insist
that the Black Goat of the Woods came to Earth, building the city
Harag-Kolath in a cavern beneath southern Arabia where she
awaits the coming of her husband Hastur. It is also possible that
Shub-Niggurath remains at the court of Azathoth, or even in
another dimension entirely.

Shub-Niggurath is usually referred to as female, but has also been
known by the title "Ram with a Thousand Ewes", and one reference
in *Cthaat Aquadingen* says that the Outer God is both male and female.
It is likely that Shub-Niggurath signifies the cosmic principle of
fertility and childbearing, and attaching sex to any of the Outer Gods
is problematic at best.

Shub-Niggurath's cults may be the most widespread of any Mythos
entity. She is known to have been worshiped by the Tcho-Tchos,
Hyperboreans, Muvians, Greeks, Cretans, Egyptians, Druids, and the
people of Sarnath, as well as by the fungi from Yuggoth, the dholes,
and the Nug-Soth of Yaddith. Sicily was a stronghold of Shub-Niggurath's cult during the 9th century, and the secret rites performed to
her in her guise of Artemis of Ephesus are matters of legend. Others
worshiped her in the guise of the Norse Heid and the Greek Hecate,

and she may also have been propitiated in the guise of the Great Earth Mother around the world. Shub-Niggurath bestows bountiful harvests and many children to her worshipers, in return for blood sacrifices. Some references to Shub-Niggurath (including one from Ludvig Prinn) assert that there is some similarity between her bodily structure and our own, but the significance of this is uncertain.

References to Hastur the Unspeakable seem to indicate that Shub-Niggurath has mated or will mate with this Great Old One, producing the beings known as her Thousand Young. From this union, or possibly another with Yog-Sothoth, she has spawned the little-known entities Nug and Yeb.

See Ajar-Alazwat, Chthonioi, dark young of Shub-Niggurath, elemental theory, Ghatanothoa, Goatswood, gof'nn hupadgh Shub-Niggurath, Harag-Kolath, Hastur, hounds of Tindalos, K'n-yan, moon-lens, Nug and Yeb, Outer Gods, Ram with a Thousand Ewes, Ring of the Hyades, Sakkuth, *Sapientia Maglorum*, Sign of the Dark Mother, Tcho-Tcho, T'yog, Yaddith. ("No Pain, No Gain", Adams, Isinwyll, and Manui (C); "Dreams in the House of Weir", Carter; "Visions from Yaddith", Carter; *The Lurker at the Threshold*, Derleth and Lovecraft; "Further Notes on the *Necronomicon*", Hamblin (C); "Out of the Aeons", Heald and Lovecraft; "The Whisperer in Darkness", Lovecraft; *The Transition of Titus Crow*, Lumley; "Lovecraft's 'Artificial Mythology'", Price; *Heir to Darkness*, Rahman; "The Seed of the Star-God", Tierney.)

SHUDDE-M'ELL. Great Old One who is the leader of the cthonians, who appears as a huge member of that species. At one time a large number of Elder Signs imprisoned Shudde-M'ell beneath G'harne, but natural disasters and the theft of the warding stones by humans eventually freed him. His worship by the builders of the prehistoric megaliths of England and some particularly decadent shamans of America's Pacific coast is well documented, but today he is only known to be revered by the Jidhauas of Mongolia and possibly some African tribes near the site of G'harne.

See cthonian, Elder Sign, G'harne, Jidhaua. (*The Burrowers Beneath*, Lumley; "Cement Surroundings", Lumley; *The Transition of Titus Crow*, Lumley.)

SIGN OF BARZAI. Complex protective sigil possibly created by Barzai, the former high priest of the Temple of the Elder Gods in Ulthar. If touched to a human of normal willpower, it will render him helpless. The slightest mistake in its inscription, however, will render the Sign useless.

See Barzai. ("The Condemned", Herber (C).)

SIGN OF EIBON. Glyph resembling a three-legged swastika. It aids the user in remaining unnoticed by the minions of Nyarlathotep, but not by the Crawling Chaos himself.

See Eibon, Nyarlathotep. ("New York", DiTillio and Willis (C).)

SIGN OF KISH. Another name for the Elder Sign. Its name is derived from that of Kish, high priest of Sarnath, who used the Sign to escape his doomed city.

See Elder Sign, Kish. ("Zoth-Ommog", Carter; *The Trail of Cthulhu*, Derleth.)

SIGN OF KOTH. Sigil that is found both on the Tower of Koth in the City of the Gugs and at various physical gates from the waking world to the lands of dream; it possibly may be useful in sealing other gates as well. The Sign prevents certain nightmares from entering the waking world, and the Hyperborean wizard Eibon used it to project his spirit to faraway worlds. According to some sources, the Yellow Sign is a specialized representation of the Sign of Koth.

See Koth, Uoht, Yellow Sign. ("Shaggai", Carter; *The* Necronomicon: *The Book of Dead Names*, Hay, ed.; "The Case of Charles Dexter Ward", Lovecraft; "The Lurker in the Crypt", Miller (C); *House of the Toad*, Tierney.)

SIGN OF THE DARK MOTHER. Icon sacred to Shub-Niggurath. It bears some resemblance to a three-headed goat. This seems to imply some linkage between the Black Goat of the Woods and the Greek deities Hecate and Demeter, both of which were represented as three-headed fertility figures.

See Shub-Niggurath. ("Dawn Biozyme", Hike and Isinwyll (C).)

SILBERHUTTE, HANK. Texan telepath recruited by the Wilmarth Foundation in 1966. The Foundation valued Silberhutte for his ability to detect the mental patterns of alien creatures, a talent of which the Foundation made great use as part of their battle against the Cthulhu Mythos. When it came to telepathic links with humans, Silberhutte's powers failed him; the only exception was Juanita Alvarez, a native of Monterrey, with whom Silberhutte could initiate contact at will.

After the disappearance of his cousin, a government surveyor, in Canada some years ago, Silberhutte became obsessed with collecting native legends about Ithaqua, the Wendigo. Due to his erudition in this field, the Texan was made the head of the Wilmarth Foundation's efforts to track down this creature of the frozen north. It was during this endeavor that Silberhutte and the crew of his plane vanished on January 22, 1969. He maintained some sporadic telepathic contact through Ms. Alvarez, but in the end this was cut off, and the true fate of Silberhutte still remains a mystery.

(*In the Moons of Borea*, Lumley; *Spawn of the Winds*, Lumley.)

SILVER KEY. Artifact which resembles a 5" key of tarnished silver, carved with indecipherable hieroglyphics. The Silver Key is believed to have been forged in the land of Hyperborea many years ago. Most of its history has been forgotten, but the reputed wizard Edmund Carter of Salem, Massachusetts used it to great effect. The Carter family kept the key in the attic of their ancestral mansion, where it lay forgotten until the mystic Randolph Carter rediscovered it; he is believed to have taken it with him when he disappeared in 1928.

When certain words are spoken as the key is held up to the setting sun and rotated nine times, this device can physically transfer its user to any time desired. If the bearer is worthy, it may also be used to unlock the Ultimate Gate which 'Umr at-Tawil guards. Through the use of an enchantment also created in Hyperborea, the powers of the key can be greatly increased.

See Irem, 'Umr at-Tawil. ("The Silver Key", Lovecraft; "Through the Gates of the Silver Key", Lovecraft and Price.)

SIXTH SATHLATTA. Formula found in *Cthaat Aquadingen*, and reading as follows:

> *Ghe'phnglui, mglw'ngh ghee-yh, Yibb-Tstll,*
>
> *Fhtagn mglw y'tlette ngh'wgah, Yibb-Tstll,*
>
> *Ghe'phnglui mglw-ngh ahkobhg'shg, Yibb-Tstll;*
>
> *THABAITE! — YIBB-TSTLL, YIBB-TSTLL, YIBB-TSTLL!*

This incantation may be used in several ways. If inscribed upon a wafer of flour in its original Ptetholite characters and used in conjunction with the Hoy-Dhin Chant from *Necronomicon*, it may be used to call the Black upon one's enemies. Saying it once before sleep will allow the chanter to contact Yibb-Tstll in dreams. If thirteen say the formula on any "First Day" of a calendar year, Yibb-Tstll himself will be summoned. However, if at least seven of the callers are not "adepts," and unless the Barrier of Naach-Tith is used by the summoners, Yibb-Tstll may effect his horrible "reversals" upon his callers.

See Black, the; *Cthaat Aquadingen*; Ptetholite; Sathlattae; Yibb-Tstll. ("The Black Recalled", Lumley; "The Horror at Oakdeene", Lumley.)

SKAI. River of the Dreamlands. The river Skai springs from the slopes of Mount Lerion, passes by the towns of Hatheg, Nir, and Ulthar, and empties into the Southern Sea.

See Atal, Ulthar. ("The Dream-Quest of Unknown Kadath", Lovecraft.)

S'LGHUO, GULF OF. Alternate dimension mentioned in *Necronomicon*. In this place sounds created in our dimension form the matter, and matter as we know it manifests itself as an odor. The blue-skinned people of this region can only be harmed by certain sounds made in our own dimension, and are quite anxious to establish telepathic contact with those of our dimensions. Their motives are unknown, so anyone dealing with them should beware.

See Alala, Mao, *Reflections*, *Revelations of Glaaki*. ("The Plain of Sound", Campbell.)

SON OF YOG-SOTHOTH. Rank within the Masters of the Silver Twilight, just above Keeper of the Silver Gate.

See Masters of the Silver Twilight. ("The Hermetic Order of the Silver Twilight", Hutchinson (C).)

SONG OF YSTE. Mythos tome of great antiquity. *Song of Yste* is said to have been passed down to modern times by a family of magicians named Dirka, whose ancestry has been supposedly traced back to the earliest humans. These Dirkas are said to have translated this volume into the three languages of the dawn of humanity, then into Greek, Latin, Arabic, and Elizabethan English.

Among other things, *Song of Yste* discusses the mysterious entities known as the adumbrali.

See Adumbrali, Dirka. ("The Abyss", Lowndes.)

SOTHOTH. Outer God subservient to Azathoth. According to *The Sussex Manuscript*, this being created the Great Old Ones and is acknowledged by them as their master.

In Baron Frederic's *Manuscript*, Sothoth is said to have created Yog-Sothoth, so the two are not one and the same. It is possible that Sothoth may be Ubbo-Sathla; on the other hand, the entity Sothoth may only be a creation of the Baron's faulty translation.

("The Sussex Manuscript", Pelton.)

SOUL OF CHAOS, THE. First of four novels published at the expense of the author, Edgar Gordon.

See Gordon, Edgar Hengist. ("The Dark Demon", Bloch.)

SPACE-MEAD. Golden liquid used by those who will travel between the stars. The mead insulates the drinker from the detrimental effects of space travel, and leaves him in a dream-like state for the entire journey. It remains up to the person who drinks the mead to provide his own means of interstellar transportation.

According to some, those who drink space-mead do not actually leave this world. Rather, their physical bodies are left in some place on this planet, while their astral selves make the journey to the stars. This makes these expeditions no less dangerous, however.

See byakhee. (*The Trail of Cthulhu*, Derleth.)

SPHERES OF NATH. Device of the Elder Things mentioned in the notes of Professor Gordon Walmsley. According to this noted cryptographer, the Elder Things, knowing that their days of empire would soon come to an end, installed one of these devices in each of their cities and outposts. When initiated the device would destroy all traces of that particular location, including any artifacts borne away by outsiders, and tranport the entire complex to a site beneath the ocean. Whether there is any connection between this and the land of Nath is unknown.

See Elder Things, Nath. ("In the Vaults Beneath", Lumley.)

SSS'HAA. Leader of the Valusian serpent people, and high priest of Yig.

See serpent people, Yig. ("Zoth-Ommog", Carter.)

STANZAS OF DZYAN. See *Book of Dzyan.*

STAR-SPAWN OF CTHULHU. See Cthulhi.

STAR-STONE OF MNAR. Rock from the land of Mnar bearing the Elder Sign, possibly created by the Elder Gods themselves. Such stones are useful in protection against the minions of the Great Old Ones.

See Circles of Thaol, Elder Sign, Kish, Mnar. (*The Lurker at the Threshold*, Derleth and Lovecraft.)

STARKWEATHER-MOORE EXPEDITION. Scientific venture to Antarctica undertaken as a follow-up to Miskatonic's Pabodie Expedition. Professor William Dyer of Miskatonic University strongly protested against this new assault upon the polar continent, but his tales of a stone city built by an alien race only served to encourage these new explorers.

The Starkweather-Moore expedition, led by Professor Eustace Blake, left Bremen on December 20, 1931 with the highest hopes. If the backers of the venture were hoping for great scientific revelations, they were sadly disappointed. When the team arrived at the site given by Dyer, they found that any alien ruins which might have existed had collapsed into an underground network of caverns. The expedition had to return with no evidence of prehuman intelligences.

See Elder Things, Pabodie Expedition. (*Alone Against the Dark*, Costello (C); "At the Mountains of Madness", Lovecraft; "In the Vaults Beneath", Lumley.)

STARRY WISDOM CULT. Group of devotees of Nyarlathotep who met in Providence, Rhode Island, between 1844 and 1877. Professor Enoch Bowen, a well-known expert on the occult and archaeology, founded the cult after his return from an expedition in Egypt. The congregation, which met in the old Free-Will Church, swelled as time went on; in 1863, the Starry Wisdom Church had over two hundred members, and a branch church opened for a brief while in Townshend, Vermont.

The nature of the cult's worship was kept a secret, but several rumors began to be circulated. According to some sources, the cult owned a sacred artifact known only as the Shining Trapezohedron, which Professor Bowen had brought with him from Egypt. By gazing upon this sacred object, the members could call up a being known as the Haunter of the Dark, who shared dread secrets with the faithful. This being could only be summoned in absolute darkness, and if it were exposed to light for any period of time the brightness would banish it.

In 1877 the town leaders finally took action against the cult, due to evidence of the cult's involvement in the kidnapings of several individuals. The precise nature of this action is unknown, but 181 of the former cultists left the city before the end of the year. The Starry Wisdom cult had been disbanded, and its sacred books and relics remained within their crumbling old church until the town demolished the structure sometime in the mid-1930's. It is rumored that the sect continued its meetings in Providence in secret under the leadership of Asenath Bowen, a relative of Enoch.

Various cults giving themselves the Starry Wisdom name have come and gone over the years, including one in Yorkshire in the latter 19th century and another in San Francisco. Though it is possible that these groups had connections with the first church in Providence, it is impossible to be sure.

See ankh, *Necronomicon* (Appendices), Nyarlathotep (Haunter of the Dark), Shining Trapezohedron. ("The Yorkshire Horror", Barton (C); "The Shadow from the Steeple", Bloch; *Strange Eons*, Bloch; "The Horror from the Middle Span", Derleth and Lovecraft; "The Haunter of the Dark", Lovecraft; "Documents in the Case of Elizabeth Akeley", Lupoff.)

STREGOICAVAR. Village located in Hungary, west of the city of Budapest. Stregoicavar may be translated as "Witch Town", a title given to it due to a cult whose members once lived on the site (then known as Xuthltan) until its members were killed by Muslim forces in 1526. Although none of the original worshipers remain, the town's name has remained as a reminder of its past. Stregoicavar's most famous landmark is the Black Stone, a monument where the disbanded cult worshiped hundreds of years ago.

See Black Stone, Xuthltan. ("The Black Stone", Howard.)

STUDY OF THE BOOK OF DZYAN, *A*. Book published around 1930 by Joachim Feery which deals with Madame Blavatsky's famous text.

See *Book of Dzyan*; Feery, Joachim. (*Keeper's Compendium*, Herber (C).)

SUMMANUS. Great Old One who manifests himself as a mouthless man with pale tentacles beneath his garb.

The cult of Summanus was most popular in Roman times; he was the lord of the night sky and thieves. Hardly any details of the god's rites were revealed to outsiders, but the learned men of the time believed

Summanus to be the lord of Hell. Summanus may still be worshiped today, but if this is true, his cult is even more secretive than before. The proper ceremonies used in the propitiation of Summanus may be found in the book *Tuscan Rituals*.

See *Tuscan Rituals*. ("The Fairground Horror", Lumley; "What Dark God?", Lumley.)

SUNG, PLATEAU OF. Land often considered to be an extension of Leng. Within Sung lies the city of Alaozar, beneath which Lloigor and Zhar are imprisoned.

See Alaozar, Lloigor, Twin Obscenities, Zhar. ("The Lair of the Star-Spawn", Derleth and Schorer.)

SUSSEX MANUSCRIPT, THE. See *Cultus Maleficarum*, *Necronomicon* (Appendices).

SYNARCHOBIBLARON. Volume which originates somewhere in Earth's Dreamlands. When an attempt to read this book is made, *Synarchobiblaron* appears to be in the reader's native tongue (though this does not guarantee that the reader will comprehend the information in the book). If another person tries to peruse the volume, the language may change again, since the book is in fact a magical construct which transforms itself to match the mind of its reader.

The book is never the same for any two readers, as the contents shift as each person reads *Synarchobiblaron*. One item that does remain constant, however, is a potent exorcism contained in the fourth and final part of the book.

("With Malice Afterthought", Anderson and Lehmann (C).)

T

TABLETS OF NHING. Set of inscriptions kept on the planet Yaddith. It is unknown just what is contained within them, for no copy has been seen by humans for millions of years.

See Yaddith. ("Through the Gate of the Silver Key", Lovecraft and Price.)

TALE OF PRIEST KWAN. Chinese book that tells the tale of Kwan, a devotee of the Bloated Woman aspect of Nyarlathotep. With the aid of his goddess and the Great Faceless Lion (another aspect of the Beast avatar of Nyarlathotep), he overcame the might of Hun Tao, a powerful member of the Chinese nobility.

See Nyarlathotep (Bloated Woman). ("Shanghai", DiTillio and Willis (C).)

TANARIAN HILLS. Purple rises of the Dreamlands which hold many gateways to the waking world and other realms of dream. Beyond these hills lie the valley of Ooth-Narghai and the city of Celephais.

See Celephais. ("Celephais", Lovecraft; "The Dream-Quest of Unknown Kadath", Lovecraft.)

TCHORTCHA. Red-clothed, short-statured people who came from China, known for their horsemanship. It is possible that they are identical with the Tcho-Tchos.

(The Slayer of Souls, Chambers.)

TCHO-TCHO. Group of people encountered in such far-flung places as Burma, the Andaman Islands, Malaysia, and Tibet, but usually connected with the mysterious Plateau of Leng.

The Tcho-Tchos were said to have been created by interbreeding between men and monsters. At the beginning of time, their god Chaugnar Faugn created a race of dwarves known as the Miri Nigri from the flesh of prehistoric reptiles. The mating of the Miri with Chaugnar's human worshipers gave rise to the Tcho-Tcho. This strange race of dwarves then migrated to the east from their former home in the Pyrenees, carrying Chaugnar to his new dwelling place.

Though the Tcho-Tchos were once widespread throughout eastern Asia, more recently they have dwindled to only a few isolated populations. All nearby tribes despise their Tcho-Tcho neighbors and most anthropologists believed until recently that all of them had been exterminated by the Japanese. A few years ago, however, certain congressmen passed measures allowing for forty thousand Tcho-Tchos to take up residence in the United States. These immigrants seem determined to keep their native traditions alive in this new land.

Besides Chaugnar, Tcho-Tchos have also been known to worship Shub-Niggurath, Hastur, and Atlach-Nacha. They also engage in cannibalism, as well as other unpleasant rites which, nonetheless, allow their agricultural methods to yield abundant crops.

See Alaozar; Chaugnar Faugn; Leng; Miri Nigri; Nyarlathotep (Shugoron); Shub-Niggurath; Tchortcha; Tsang, Plateau of; *Unaussprechlichen Kulten*. ("The Curse of Chaugnar Faugn", Barton (C); "Lair of the Star-Spawn", Derleth and Schorer; "The Andaman Islands", Herber (C); "Dawn Biozyme", Hike and Isinwyll (C); "Black Man With a Horn", Klein.)

TEH ATHT OF KLUHN. Second-greatest wizard of the primal land of Theem'hdra, said to have been descended from the mighty Mylakhrion. The manuscript entitled *Legends of the Olden Runes*, discovered in a curious golden box after the creation of Surtsey, is attributed to him.

See Broken Columns of Geph, Exior K'mool, *Legends of the Olden Runes*, Theem'hdra. (*Elysia*, Lumley; "Introduction" to *The House of Cthulhu and Other Tales of the Primal Land*, Lumley; "Mylakhrion the Immortal", Lumley.)

TEMPHILL. Town located in the Cotswolds, east of Brichester. The town's original name was "Temple Hill", due to the rites conducted on a hill near the town's center in ancient times.

The founders of Temphill were a group of ex-Templars who, after King Edward II dissolved their order in 1307, travelled to this area bearing with them certain documents which their Order had discovered in Palestine. When these former knights attempted to assimilate themselves into the regular religious community, they were not entirely successful, and witch-burning and accusations of heresy were commonplace for hundreds of years thereafter.

In the early 19th century some sort of necromantic cult existed among the people of Temphill. According to legend, the worshipers convened in huge caverns beneath the graveyard on the hill, where they disinterred and reanimated the dead for the purpose of mating with them and having children with supernatural powers. The cult collapsed after a while, but it is rumored that most of Temphill's population still visits the church on the hill on Hallowe'en and Christmas Eve.

See Goatswood. ("The Church in High Street", Campbell; "The Horror from the Bridge", Campbell; "The Curate of Temphill", Cannon and Price.)

TEMPLE OF THE TOAD. Fane located somewhere within the jungles of Honduras. An Indian civilization that had decayed centuries before the Spaniards arrived were the builders of this edifice. Within the Temple's crumbled columns there is a throne, upon which sits the mummified remains of the temple's former high priest. A necklace bearing a gem carved into the shape of his god still encircles the mummy's neck. According to von Junzt's *Unaussprechlichen Kulten*, this gem is the key to the temple's treasure.

Only three explorers have ever visited the Temple of the Toad: Juan Gonzalles, a Spanish explorer who visited the temple in 1793; Friedrich von Junzt, author of *Unaussprechlichen Kulten*; and Tussmann, an archaeologist of some note. Tussmann brought something back with him, but he died shortly thereafter, and no trace of any such items were found.

("The Thing on the Roof", Howard.)

TESTAMENT OF CARNAMAGOS. Book penned by a Cimmerian oracle named Carnamagos, and originally discovered in a Greco-Bactrian tomb over a thousand years ago. A monk translated the book into Greek and penned two copies in the blood of a half-demon monstrosity. The fate of the original is unknown, and one of the two copies is thought to have been destroyed during the 13th century by the Inquisition.

A person who owns *Testament* should beware of the curious temporal effects which come with its reading. As a person reads the book, he and his surroundings age at a highly accelerated rate.

Although this is not necessarily fatal, it can be dangerous and very unpleasant. In addition, those who have desired death should also avoid reading the invocation of Quachil Uttaus, for this being sometimes comes unbidden to such people.

Testament contains many records of events in both the past and future. It deals in some detail with the entity known as Quachil Uttaus, gives information about Yamil Zacra, and contains an incantation to disintegrate a dead body.

See Quachil Uttaus. ("The Condemned", Herber (C); "The Infernal Star" (fragment), Smith; "The Treader of the Dust", Smith; "Xeethra", Smith.)

T'GAORL. Lost city on the Gold Coast of Africa. T'gaorl was a major center for trade in the area, and its sorceries are legendary. The people of this city were once enslaved by fire vampires due to a magician's ill-fated attempt to summon Cthugha.

See Gn'icht' Tyaacht. ("The Horror of the Glen", Tamlyn (C).)

THALE. 1) Character in the play *The King in Yellow*. 2) According to Hali, the second king to emblazon the Yellow Sign upon his cloak.

See King in Yellow. ("The Repairer of Reputations", Chambers; "Tell Me, Have You Seen the Yellow Sign?", Ross (C); *House of the Toad*, Tierney.)

THAMUTH-DJIG. Great Old One of whom only the name is known. (*The Clock of Dreams*, Lumley.)

THASAIDON (possibly also TISAIDA). God of Zothique who represents the principle of evil. Taking the form of a warrior in full armor, he attempts to seduce mortals to his own purposes. The power and prestige of his victims does not matter to Thasaidon; all of them will regret their decision in the end.

It is possible that Thasaidon is another form of Nyarlathotep; though there is no explicit link, their portfolios and *modus operandi* seem similar.

("The Dark Eidolon", Smith; "The Infernal Star" (fragment), Smith; "Xeethra", Smith.)

THAUMATURGICAL PRODIGIES IN THE NEW-ENGLISH CANAAN. Book by Reverend Ward Phillips of Second Church in Arkham, Massachusetts. Two editions were published, the first in 1794, and an expurgated version in Boston in 1801. Several years after the second edition became available, Reverend Phillips became involved in a dispute with Alijah Billington, who lived just outside Arkham. The reasons behind this feud are unclear, but seem to have dealt with accusations made in *Prodigies* against his ancestor Robert Billington. Shortly thereafter the Reverend tried to buy up all the copies of his book and burn them. A few years later, he passed away.

This book deals with the strange happenings and supposed sorcerers of New England, with especial focus upon the Arkham and Salem areas. What separates this from other works such as Cotton Mather's *Wonders of the Invisible World* is that Phillips' tales have an air of authenticity the other volumes lack.

See Billington, Alijah. ("The Winfield Inheritance", Carter; "The Lurker at the Threshold", Derleth and Lovecraft; "The Auction", McCall (C).)

THEEM'HDRA. Continent which existed before the Age of Dinosaurs. Home to many powerful wizards, including Mylakhrion, Exior K'mool, and Teh Atht.

See Broken Columns of Geph, Exior K'mool, Gleeth, Khrissa, *Legends of the Olden Runes*, Mnomquah, Mylakhrion, Sathlattae, Teh Atht of Kluhn. ("Name and Number", Lumley.)

THING THAT SHOULD NOT BE. See Nyogtha.

THIRTY-FIVE ABOMINABLE ADULATIONS OF THE BLOATED ONE. Rituals to the Great Old One Y'golonac.

See Y'golonac. ("Love's Lonely Children", Watts (C).)

THOG AND THOK. Twin moons of the planet Yuggoth.

See Ghooric Zone. (*Fungi from Yuggoth*, Lovecraft; "Discovery of the Ghooric Zone", Lupoff.)

THUGGON. Seemingly uninhabited world where the insects from Shaggai dwelt for a short time. Their slaves steadily disappeared, however, and upon searching for them, they found a black tower within a marsh, with the mutilated bodies of their servants nearby. The shan did not remain on Thuggon long thereafter.

See shan. ("The Insects from Shaggai", Campbell.)

THUUM'HA (also THUNN-HA). Amphibian creatures which came down from outer space to build the cities of Ib and Lh-Yib. They were mostly human in shape, but had flabby lips, bulging eyes, and a slimy hide, and were mute, qualities which did not endear them to the men of Sarnath. All of Ib's inhabitants were destroyed by the men of Sarnath, but some members of this race may still survive in Ib's sister city Lh-Yib.

See Bokrug, Ib, Lh-yib. ("Something in the Moonlight", Carter; "The Doom that Came to Sarnath", Lovecraft; *Beneath the Moors*, Lumley.)

THYOPH. Planet which, according to *G'harne Fragments*, a "nuclear chaos" (most likely a Seed of Azathoth) broke apart to create the asteroid belt.

(*Spawn of Azathoth*, Herber (C); "In the Vaults Beneath", Lumley.)

TIKKOUN ELIXIR. Another name for holy water. This substance is said to be proof against the Great Old One Nyogtha, and provides limited protection from the cthonians and other earth spirits.

See cthonian, Nyogtha. ("The Salem Horror", Kuttner; *The Burrowers Beneath*, Lumley.)

TIME-CLOCK. Alien artifact resembling an ornately carved, coffin-shaped grandfather clock with four hands which moved around its dial in seemingly random patterns. The clock seemed to operate without any outside power source whatsoever, and only rumors relate what those who opened the clock found within. It is believed that this was merely one device out of many similar styles, but it was the only one of its kind to have been encountered on Earth.

The Yogi Hiamaldi supposedly brought back the time-clock (as it was later called) from the alien city of Yian-Ho. He presented the clock as a gift to Etienne-Laurent de Marigny, the famous French mystic, who kept the object at his New Orleans retreat. It was here that the clock played an important role in the disappearance of Swami Chandraputra, an elderly Indian who had come to provide evidence to Randolph Carter's heirs that the dreamer survived. After de Marigny's death, a wealthy Frenchman purchased the clock; this individual later vanished. For a while, nothing was known of the clock's whereabouts until Titus Crow purchased it at an English antique auction. The clock remained in Crow's possession for years, until it vanished along with him and his friend Henri-Laurent de Marigny during a freak windstorm in 1969.

According to notes discovered in Crow's demolished manor, the clock operated as a gateway and a vehicle to other places, times, and dimensions. The user opened the clock, stepped inside, and was immediately able to utilize the device's powers of transportation. The clock was supposedly a tool created by the Elder Gods, however, and the time-clock's powers could be quite dangerous if misused.

("Through the Gates of the Silver Key", Lovecraft and Price; *The Burrowers Beneath*, Lumley; *The Clock of Dreams*, Lumley; "De Marigny's Clock", Lumley; *The Transition of Titus Crow*, Lumley.)

TINDALOS. World which may exist on Earth far in the past, on a faraway world near a black hole, or even floating throughout the temporal dimension. Its cities' corkscrew towers are the homes of the beings known as the Hounds of Tindalos.

See Hounds of Tindalos. (*The Transition of Titus Crow*, Lumley.)

TIND'LOSI HOUNDS. See Hounds of Tindalos.

TITANS POTENS. Phrase from the Middle Ages used to describe certain wooden or stone idols carved by various cultures at many times. It is said that such idols crave the life blood of humans and, when fed with a great deal of this, can come to life. Such statues then embark on a wholesale rampage of killing and destruction. Many of the largest statues of the Great Old Ones have this ability, though some may come alive when the god is invoked instead, with the statue holding the Old One's essence. Fortunately, most of the cults that worshiped these statues have died out, and today these statues may be approached safely.

("The Hills Rise Wild", Isinwyll and Morrison (C).)

TOK'L. Metal used on Tond and Yuggoth for the user to gain a sort of immortality. Every thirty-five years the creature's brain must be transferred from one body to another. During this transition the brain must be kept in a container made of tok'l metal. The nearest source of this mineral is the planet Yuggoth.

See Tond, Yuggoth. ("The Mine on Yuggoth", Campbell.)

TOMB-HERD. Beings mentioned in *Necronomicon* who feed upon the occupants of tombs. They are said to come from another dimension, and must possess other beings to enter our own space-time continuum and feast upon the dead. The tomb-herd has the limited ability to warp space; for example, a chosen victim might find herself unable to escape from an area where the tomb-herd waits, as every road circles back on itself and returns her to the dwellings of the herd.

Outside assistance may be of some help in eluding the tomb-herd, but they often catch their victims in the end despite all precautions.

The tomb-herd may be allied to some degree with the Great Old One Glaaki, and are said to serve Yog-Sothoth. Some cults focussing around the tomb-herd have been known to exist; the worshipers allow the herd to possess them, in return for certain benefits. These beings are probably not connected with ghouls, who are not allied with Yog-Sothoth, and who seem to have material bodies in this dimension.

("The Church in High Street", Campbell; "The Inhabitant of the Lake", Campbell; "Through the Gate of the Silver Key", Lovecraft and Price.)

TOND. Planet that circles the stars Baalbo and Yifne, and is mentioned in works such as *Necronomicon* and *Revelations of Glaaki*. On this planet live the yarkdao, who have built curious cities of black stone and bluish metal. It has been said that Glaaki spent some time upon this world on his way to Earth. The only way a human can behold Tond is through the use of the Crystallizer of Dreams.

See Baalbo, Chig, Crystallizer of Dreams, Daoloth, Glaaki, puslt, tok'l, yarkdao, Yifne. ("The Inhabitant of the Lake", Campbell.)

TORCH OF NUG. Alien device which will emerge from the Arctic ice before the Great Old Ones' return, which will clear off the Earth for its masters.

("To Clear the Earth", Murray.)

TORMANTIUS. Planet mentioned in the Voynich Manuscript, said to be the home world of certain powerful entities.

("The Return of the Lloigor", C. Wilson.)

TREADER OF THE DUST. See Quachil Uttaus.

TRONE TABLES. Set of highly abstruse mathematical equations used in the Great Northern Expedition.

See Great Northern Expedition. (*The Great White Space*, Copper.)

TRUE MAGIK (or *TRUE MAGICK*). Book written by a sorcerer named Theophilus Wenn (most likely a pseudonym), of whom little is known save that he was an erudite scholar of the occult. One copy, published in 1872 by Oakley Press, may be found at the Miskatonic University Library, and other manuscript copies have also been circulated.

In addition to the usual references to demons, vampires, and the like, the book also contains seven incantations of great power. Three of these are for the creation of various charms, and another three may be used against the wizard's enemies. The seventh, which summons a hideous demon, is especially perilous, as it requires a blood sacrifice made at an altar to the Great Old Ones, but it will also bestow upon its user great wealth.

("The Seventh Incantation", Brennan; *Devil's Children*, Conyers, Godley, and Witteveen (C).)

TRU'NEMBRA. Outer God also known as the Angel of Music, which manifests itself as a series of unearthly melodies. Tru'nembra only comes to Earth when a master musician has knowingly or unknowingly been brought to the god's attention. The musician hears music which cannot be perceived by anyone else, and becomes more and more captivated by these melodies. Eventually, Tru'nembra manifests itself to bear the musician's spirit back to the court of Azathoth, to play there for all eternity.

(*Ye Booke of Monstres*, Aniolowski (C); "The Music of Erich Zann", Lovecraft.)

TSAN-CHAN. Oriental empire which will come into being three thousand years in the future. I am uncertain what connection this has with Cthulhu and his kindred, but it may be that by this time the return of the Great Old Ones will have occurred, and that this empire will be ruled by non-human masters.

("Beyond the Wall of Sleep", Lovecraft; "The Shadow Out of Time", Lovecraft.)

TSANG, PLATEAU OF. Region in Asia said to be inhabited by the Tcho-Tcho people. Some maintain that this place is identical to the Plateau of Leng; perhaps Tsang is a point where Leng intersects our own dimension. In a cavern somewhere on Tsang rests Chaugnar Faugn, the Tcho-Tcho's god. Here he awaits the time when he shall journey west and devour the world.

The mountains beyond Tsang, according to Harold Copeland, were at one time the home of a group of refugees who fled the destruction of Mu. These survivors were led by the great wizard Zanthu, whose followers buried him in an ancient graveyard somewhere in this region.

See Chaugnar Faugn; Copeland, Harold Hadley; Miri Nigri; Tcho-Tcho; Zanthu Tablets. ("The Curse of Chaugnar Faugn", Barton (C); "The Dweller in the Tomb", Carter; *The Horror from the Hills*, Long.)

TSATH. Capital city of the subterranean land of K'n-yan. The people of this land named their capital in honor of the Great Old One Tsathoggua, before they banned his worship.

See K'n-yan, Tsathoggua. ("The Mound", Heald and Lovecraft.)

TSATH-YO. Primal language used in the land of Hyperborea millions of years ago.

("Through the Gates of the Silver Key", Lovecraft and Price.)

TSATHOGGUA (also SADOGUI, SAINT TOAD, or ZHOTHAQQUAH). Great Old One whose amorphous body usually takes the form of a furry toadlike being.

Shortly after our world's creation, Tsathoggua came to Earth from Saturn, taking up residence in the black caverns of N'Kai. The serpent men of the red-lit cavern of Yoth were the first to worship him, and from Yoth his worship spread to K'n-Yan, and thence to the Arctic land of Lomar and the outer world. First the voormis and later the human invaders who replaced them revered the toad god. He is believed to have taken up residence beneath Mount Voormithadreth for a brief while, but retreated to his former home when his worship declined and the ice whelmed Hyperborea. It is not certain whether any cults of Tsathoggua survive today.

The beasts of the wood held a special reverence for Tsathoggua. In addition, he is served by formless black entities known as his spawn, though the exact degree of relationship to him is unknown. We know only of the following fragmentary ritual regarding him:

N'ggah-kthn-y'hhu! Cthua t'lh gup r'lhob-g'th'gg lgh thok! G'llh-ya, Tsathoggua! Y'kn'nh, Tsathoggua!

It hath come!

Homage, Lord Tsathoggua, Father of Night!

Glory, Elder One, First-Born of Outer Entity!

Hail, Thou Who wast Ancient beyond Memory

Ere the Stars Spawned Great Cthulhu!

Power, Hoary Crawler in Mu's fungoid places!

Ia! Ia! G'noth-ykagga-ha!

Ia, Ia, Tsathoggua!

See Atlach-Nacha; *Book of Eibon*; Commoriom; *Cthaat Aquadingen*; Cxaxukluth; Cykranosh; Eibon; elemental theory; Fishers from Outside; Ghisguth; Great Old Ones; Hyperborea; Hziulquoigmnzhah;

K'n-yan; Kythamil; N'kai; Nug and Yeb; Ossadagowah; *Parchments of Pnom*; Saint Toad; serpent people; voormis; Voormithadreth, Mount; Yhoundeh; Yoth; Yuggoth. ("The Mound", Bishop and Lovecraft; "Observations on the Carter Glossary", Cockcroft; "The Door to Saturn", Smith; "The Seven Geases", Smith; "The Tale of Satampra Zeiros", Smith.)

TSATHOGGUANS. Beings who infest the minds of every person, according to some. Although the name suggests the Mythos, they are totally unconnected with Tsathoggua or any other Great Old One.
(*The Mind Parasites*, C. Wilson.)

TULZSCHA. Being who appears to be a pillar of green flame, and is said to be one of the dancers at Azathoth's court, from whence it may be called to Earth. It is worshiped in the West Indies, France, Italy, and possibly the Middle East. A cult based in Kingsport, Massachusetts disbanded approximately two hundred and fifty years ago.

Rites of Tulzscha are always performed at equinoxes, solstices, or other astronomically significant times. It is said that the most faithful of Tulzscha's worshipers survive after death, dwelling in their own rotting corpses.

See Outer Gods, Outer Ones. ("The Kingsport Cult", Ross (C).)

TUNNELER BELOW, THE. Book of poems by Georg Reuter Fischer, a young man from Vulture's Roost, California. Much as other writers, Fischer received the inspiration for this volume of poems from his dreams; in addition, he acknowledged the influence of Derby's *Azathoth and Other Horrors* upon his work. Unfortunately, a year after the publication of this small volume by Hollywood's Ptolemy Press in 1936, Fischer perished in an earthquake which destroyed his home. Copies of this book are held both at UCLA and Miskatonic University.

The poems in *The Tunneler Below* contain veiled references to "Cutlu", "Rulay", and "Nath", though the author explains little about what these terms mean.

See *Azathoth and Other Horrors*. ("The Terror from the Depths", Leiber.)

TURNER CODEX. Book of thin copper plates discovered in the late 18th century in Guatemalan ruins by Maplethorpe Turner, a rich and well-travelled man. Turner spent eleven years deciphering the hieroglyphics painstakingly hammered into the metal, and then published his findings in 1902 in a thousand-copy limited edition. The archaeological establishment of his day, however, did not accept the book, since its translator refused to reveal his collaborators, possibly to keep all the credit for himself. The metal originals were destroyed in a fire in 1919, and Turner never received any recognition for his work. Despite the attitudes of the scholars who disparaged the book, copies may still be found in the libraries of Miskatonic, Harvard, and Duke Universities, among others.

Turner Codex is a series of prayers and libations to the Unspeakable One, Hastur. Included in this volume are rites that will return Hastur to this planet, as well as the creation of the Chime of Tezchaptl.

See Chime of Tezchaptl, Hastur. ("The Evil Stars", Herber (C).)

TUSCAN RITUALS. Volume which, according to the Roman historian Pliny, contains information on the rites of Summanus. This book originated in the Tuscany province of Italy, and a copy of *Tuscan Rituals* is held by the British Museum.

See Summanus. ("What Dark God?", Lumley.)

TWIN OBSCENITIES. Title given to the Great Old Ones Zhar and Lloigor, who lie imprisoned together beneath the Plateau of Sung.

See Lloigor, Zhar. ("The Lair of the Star-Spawn", Derleth and Schorer.)

T'YOG. High priest of Shub-Niggurath in the country of K'naa on Mu. He made a special scroll to protect him during his confrontation with Ghatanothoa, but Ghatanothoa's priests substituted another scroll for his. As a result of this, T'yog did not make it through the confrontation unscathed.

See Ghatanothoa, Shub-Niggurath. ("Out of the Aeons", Heald and Lovecraft.)

U

UBAR. See Irem.

UBB. Being known as "The Father of Worms." Ubb is the leader of the mysterious race known as the yuggya.

See yuggya. ("Out of the Aeons", Carter.)

UBBO-SATHLA. Great protoplasmic being said to have been manufactured by the Elder Things in order to produce their shoggoths. Ubbo-Sathla did this and more; it spawned all manner of creatures, becoming the progenitor of all earthly life. It is said that as all life came from this being, thus in the end all shall return to Ubbo-Sathla.

Some say that Ubbo-Sathla is the parent of all of the Great Old Ones who opposed the Elder Gods, but considering the extraterrestrial origins of most of the Great Old Ones, this is probably inaccurate. Rather, it is likely that Ubbo-Sathla entered into an alliance with the Great Old Ones when they came down from the stars and aided them in their designs. A few of the Great Old Ones, such as Nyogtha, Yig, and Zuchequon, seem to have originated upon this planet, and these may be the spawn of Ubbo-Sathla to which these passages refer.

It has been said that eons ago, when our world was in an alternate universe, the Elder Gods created both Azathoth and Ubbo-Sathla to be their slaves. Ubbo-Sathla rebelled against its makers, using knowledge stolen from them to send itself and Earth into this dimension. During the battle which ensued, the Elder Gods captured Ubbo-Sathla and made it mindless, as they were purported to have done with Azathoth as well.

Ubbo-Sathla dwells beneath the ground in grey-lit Y'qaa, guarding a set of stone tablets said to bear the knowledge of the Elder Gods themselves. Many wizards have attempted to gain these tablets, but not one has ever succeeded.

See Elder Things, Sothoth, Y'qaa, Zon Mezzamalech. ("Zoth-Ommog", Carter; "The Lurker at the Threshold", Derleth and Lovecraft; *The Burrowers Beneath*, Lumley; "Ubbo-Sathla", Smith.)

UBBOTH. Black lake beneath the surface of the moon in which Mnomquah dwells.

See Mnomquah. (*Mad Moon of Dreams*, Lumley.)

ULTHAR. 1) A town of the Dreamlands, near the river Skai. Ulthar is a small village of medieval cottages and cobblestoned streets. In Ulthar the killing of a cat is strictly forbidden, due to a mysterious event which took place two hundred years ago. As a consequence, this city is a great favorite for felines. On Ulthar's highest hill stands the Temple of the Elder Ones, where the high priest Atal may be found. See Atal, Barrier of Naach-Tith, Barzai, *Fourth Book of D'harsis*, *Pnakotic Manuscripts*, *Seven Cryptical Books of Hsan*, Skai. ("The Cats of Ulthar", Lovecraft; "The Dream-Quest of Unknown Kadath", Lovecraft.)

2) One of the Elder Gods mentioned in *The Sussex Manuscript*. See B'kal, N'gah-Kthun, Ultharathotep. (*The Sussex Manuscript*, Pelton.)

ULTHARATHOTEP. Avatar of the Elder God Ulthar, whom the assembled high priests summoned once every thousand years to the city of N'gah-Kthun.

See Ulthar. (*The Sussex Manuscript*, Pelton.)

'UMR AT-TAWIL (more properly TAWIL AT-'UMR). God whose Arabic name literally translates as "The Prolonged of Life." Tawil at-'Umr appears as a figure draped in gray fabric, holding in its hand a sphere of iridescent metal. This being is the head of the Ancient Ones, as well as the guardian of the final gateway opened by the owner of the Silver Key. According to both *Necronomicon* and *Book of Thoth*, dealing with this entity is fraught with peril, and none whom he accepts ever return.

Tawil at-'Umr is thought to be connected with the Outer God Yog-Sothoth.

See Ancient Ones, *Book of Thoth*, Klarkash-Ton, Silver Key, Yog-Sothoth. ("Through the Gate of the Silver Key", Lovecraft and Price.)

UNAUSSPRECHLICHEN KULTEN (also the *BLACK BOOK* or *NAMELESS CULTS*). Volume written by Friedrich Wilheim von Junzt, an occultist and explorer of some note. He travelled to Hungary and Central America as well as other locations, and collected information on various cults, which he then recorded in his book. (It is also rumored that von Junzt was one of the few to peruse the *Necronomicon*'s Greek translation, and that he was the only known human to read *Ghorl Nigral*.) A Dusseldorf publisher put out *Unaussprechlichen Kulten* in 1839. Many who owned the book, however, destroyed it later, after they learned of its author's horrible death in 1840.

In 1845, Bridewall published the first English edition of *Nameless Cults*. This edition was riddled with mistakes and misspellings, illustrated with cheap woodcuts, and served only to further discredit the original.

Golden Goblin Press of New York took its own translation of the German book to the presses in 1909, with color plates executed by Diego Velasquez. Though more accurately translated than the Bridewall edition, the translators expurgated over a quarter of the original volume, and the cost of the book was so high as to be prohibitive to the general public.

Copies of *Unaussprechlichen Kulten* are kept at the Miskatonic University Library, the Sanbourne Institute in California, and the Huntington Library.

Within his book von Junzt discusses his many findings regarding worship patterns across the world. At certain points, though, his rational presentation of these cults breaks down into disjointed ramblings. Part of this volume deals with commonly known secret societies, such as the Indian thuggees and the African leopard societies. The main part of the work, which is prefaced by a lengthy essay entitled "Narrative of the Elder World", deals with the worship of Cthulhu and his ilk, including the Tcho-Tcho cults of Leng, the people of the Black Stone, and the worldwide sects of Ghatanothoa.

See Bran Mak Morn; Ghatanothoa; Kn'aa; Naacal; "Papyrus of the Dark Wisdom"; Temple of the Toad; von Junzt, Friedrich; Yog-Sothoth. ("Zoth-Ommog", Carter; "Out of the Aeons", Heald and Lovecraft; "The Black Stone", Howard; "The Children of the Night", Howard; "The Thing on the Roof", Howard.)

UNSPEAKABLE ONE. See Hastur.

UNTER ZEE KULTEN. German volume dealing with aquatic horrors, written by Graf Gauberg. Many believed that all copies of this book were destroyed in the 17th century, but it is now clear that some escaped this destruction.

This book tells much about the deep ones and their ways of life, including a description of a strange mollusk used for food and building. The unknown author of *Cthaat Aquadingen* quotes this volume at least once.

("The Aquarium", Jacobi; "Return of the Deep Ones", Lumley; "Fischbuchs", Ross, *TUO2* (C).)

UOHT. 1) Royal contender for the throne of Yhtill in the play *The King in Yellow*. 2) In the writings of Hali, the first king of Carcosa to emblazon the Sign of Koth in yellow upon his cloak.

See King in Yellow. ("The Repairer of Reputations", Chambers; *House of the Toad*, Tierney.)

URALTE SCHRECKEN. Monograph written by Graf von Konnenberg in the 19th century. In his book von Konnenberg asserted that he had traced the myth patterns of all cultures back to their origins as projections of something he called Mlandoth. Who, what, or where Mlandoth is, von Konnenberg did not explain; this likely explains the book's cool reception among the public and reputable scholars alike. Aside from Mlandoth, this volume also mentions such entities as Ngyr-Khorath, 'Ymnar, and Yidhra.

See Mlandoth, Ngyr-Khorath, 'Ymnar. ("Where Yidhra Walks", DeBill.)

UZULDAROUM. Capital city of Hyperborea. When the people of the former capital city of Commoriom fled their homes, due either to the prophecy of the White Sybil of Polarion or to other less pleasant causes, they established Uzuldaroum a day's journey from the deserted metropolis.

See Commoriom, Hyperborea. ("The Tale of Satampra Zeiros", Smith; "The Testament of Athammaus", Smith.)

V

VACH-VIRAJ INCANTATION. Chant used to ward off the Great Old One Nyogtha, and which is efficacious to a lesser degree against Cyaegha and the cthonians. This is one version of the Vach-Viraj chant:

> *Ya na kadishtu nilgh'ri stell-bsna Nyogtha;*
>
> *K'yarnak phlegethor l'ebumna syha'h n'ghft.*
>
> *Ya hai kadishtu ep r'luh-eeh Nyogtha eeh,*
>
> *S'uhn-ngh athg li'hee orr'e syha'h.*

It is believed that the Vach-Viraj, when spoken in reverse, may release the same earth elementals it is meant to disperse.

See cthonian, *Necronomicon* (Appendices), Nyogtha. ("Darkness, My Name Is", Bertin; "The Salem Horror", Kuttner; *The Burrowers Beneath*, Lumley.)

VAEYEN. Guardian spirits associated with the cult of Cyaegha. They are held in five statues placed around the worship area: the Black Light, the White Fire, the White Dark, the Winged Woman, and the Green Moon. These spirits are said to protect Cyaegha in some way, and are also used in the ceremonies of Cyaegha to ensure that the Great Old One does not break free due to the rituals supposedly performed in his honor.

See Cyaegha. ("Darkness, My Name Is", Bertin.)

VALE OF PNATH. See Pnath, Vale of.

VALUSIA. Ancient land of the serpent people. It consists of what is now southern Europe and northern Africa.

See serpent people. ("The Shadow Kingdom", Howard.)

VATICAN CODEX. Mayan document found several years ago in the Vatican Library. It is in the form of a piece of bark paper 8" wide and 7' long, painted with various colors. This is the only known copy of this work, and is also one of the few Mayan books to have survived the ecclesiastical zeal of the Spanish priests. Why the religious authorities spared this book from destruction and sent it back to Rome is unknown.

In most respects this document parallels the Mayan creation myths as detailed in the Popol Vuh. At one point, however, the story varies from the more common version. A being known as both Ghatanothoa and Yig comes down to Earth from the star Arcturus. Seeing the goddess of the dawn bathing, he attempts to force himself upon her, but she escapes. Yig's semen falls into the sea, eventually giving rise to the various animals which populate the Earth. The Ancient Ones (as the benevolent gods are called in this document) attack Yig and imprison him within the ground. Having done so, they take some of his seed and use it to create humanity. Then a Golden Age begins, which is ended when Yig calls down disaster upon humanity.

(*The Philosopher's Stone*, C. Wilson.)

VAULTS OF ZIN. See Zin, Vaults of.

VHOORL. Planet located within the twenty-third nebula, wherever that might be. It was Kathulhn, a student of mathematics on Vhoorl, who first broke through the barriers between this dimension and the others where the Great Old Ones once lived. The lords of Yaddith are also known to have visited this world.

Some have connected the "Kathulhn" who once dwelt on Vhoorl with the Great Old One Cthulhu. If this linkage is valid, Vhoorl may be the place from whence Cthulhu first came that Akeley hinted of in his discourse with Wilmarth.

See Cthulhu. ("The Guardian of the Book", Hasse; "The Whisperer in Darkness", Lovecraft.)

VISIONS FROM YADDITH. Volume of poetry written by Ariel Prescott (most likely a pseudonym), who was confined and later died within Oakdeene Sanitarium. Charnel House Publishers of London published the volume in a limited edition in 1927, and it became fashionable for a brief while among certain elements of Cambridge

University's student body. Ariel Prescott's family, however, managed to purchase and destroy almost all copies of the book.

The poems of this book, which were inspired by the author's nightly visions, tell the story of the last days of Yaddith, its inhabitants' attempts to save their dying world, and their final flight throughout the cosmos.

("Dreams in the House of Weir", Carter; "Visions from Yaddith", Carter.)

VON DENEN VERTDAMMTEN ("Of the Damned"). Volume originally written by Kazaj Heinz Vogel, a German who immigrated to America over two centuries ago. He returned to his native Germany, and there completed his untitled book. After its publication the authorities seized the volumes and all but two copies were destroyed. Vogel himself vanished shortly thereafter.

The two remaining copies of this volume remained in the restricted collections of German libraries. In 1907 a young woman named Edith Brendall gained access to one of the volumes. Using her photographic memory, she memorized the entire book and later rewrote it, added notes gathered from her own research, and entitled it *Von denen Vertdammten*. Ms. Brendall then had the book published at her own expense. As soon as the publishers released the book, most of the copies were bought hastily or stolen by persons unknown. Ms. Brendall believed someone was following her, and moved from city to city in an attempt to elude her pursuers. She disappeared from Bonn on March 27, 1910, and her body was discovered in the Rhine on April 4 of the same year.

This book is subtitled "A Treaty about the Hideous Cults of Old", and is known to hold information on the worship of a being known as the Waiting Dark.

("Darkness, My Name Is", Bertin.)

VON JUNZT, FRIEDRICH WILHEIM (1795-1840). Noted explorer and author of *Unaussprechlichen Kulten*. Von Juntz was born in Cologne in 1795, and taught for a time at the University of Wurttemberg. He had a great love of the uncanny, and he travelled throughout the world, investigating and joining as many secret societies as he could discover. Von Juntz compiled the results of his research in his *Unaussprechlichen Kulten*, also known as the *Black Book*, published in Dusseldorf in 1839.

It is known that von Juntz was one of the few people to see the *Necronomicon*'s Greek translation, though the location of this book has never been stated. Rumor has it that the German scholar in fact made a German translation of the book entitled *Das Verichteraraberbuch*, published posthumously in 1848. It is less widely known that von Junzt also perused the *Ghorl Nigral* said to be kept in the city of Yian-ho, providing his friend Gottfried Mulder with the material later collected in *The Secret Mysteries of Asia, with a Commentary on the* Ghorl Nigral.

Following his last trip, an expedition to Mongolia, von Junzt secluded himself in a locked and barred room in Dusseldorf, writing a manuscript whose exact nature remains a mystery. Six months later, he was found strangled in his lodgings with the marks of talons on his throat, the chamber's locks still intact, and his notes torn and scattered about him. Alexis Ladeau, a Frenchman who had been von Juntz's best friend in life, took the mutilated pages of the manuscript and put them together. After having read them, he burnt the manuscript and cut his own throat with a razor. Following these events, many copies of the *Black Book* were burnt by their frantic owners.

See Abbith; Black Stone; Bran Mak Morn; Ghatanothoa; *Ghorl Nigral*; Kn'aa; *Necronomicon* (Appendices); Pnakotus; *Secret Mysteries of Asia, with a Commentary on the* Ghorl Nigral; Temple of the Toad; *Unaussprechlichen Kulten*; Yog-Sothoth. ("Zoth-Ommog", Carter; "The Black Stone", Howard; "The Children of the Night", Howard; "The Thing on the Roof", Howard; *Schrodinger's Cat Trilogy*, R. Wilson.)

VOOLA RITUAL. Incantation which will bring the aid of a creature living beneath a rock somewhere within the Severn River Valley. Several people must perform the ritual if it is to be effective.

("The Mine on Yuggoth", Campbell; "The White People", Machen.)

VOOR. Kingdom beyond the edge of the world where, according to the *Green Book*, the light goes away when it is put out and the water leaves when the sun disappears. This may be the land from which the Voorish Sign originated.

See Deep Dendo, *Green Book*, *Voorish Rituals*, Voorish Sign. ("The White People", Machen.)

VOORISH RITUALS. Book written by Schiavoni and Malamocco whose contents are unknown. From its title, it is likely that this book deals both with the land of Voor and the Voorish Sign.

See Voor, Voorish Sign. ("The Star Pools", Attansio.)

VOORISH SIGN. Hand passes or glyph that may aid in making the invisible visible.

See Voor. ("The Dunwich Horror", Lovecraft.)

VOORMIS. Race of subhuman entities who lived in the land of Hyperborea (present-day Greenland) before the coming of humans. All voormis traced their ancestry back to Voorm, a being allegedly the product of the mating of Shathak, a minor deity, and Tsathoggua. Originally, the voormis were bred during the Pleistocene as a race of slaves by the Valusian serpent men. With the decline of their masters, the voormis broke free of their enslavement and went to live on the continent of Hyperborea. There they beat back the horrible gnoph-keh into the polar wasteland and laid the groundwork for a new civilization.

The worship of Tsathoggua, the founder of their race, was especially important to the voormis, many of whom dwelt underground so as to be closer to their lord. At one point in their history, however, the voormis became involved in a rebellion in which the worshipers of the new god Ithaqua struck out against the followers of Tsathoggua. In the end Ithaqua's followers were soundly beaten and exiled from the lands of the more orthodox voormis.

Between this great civil war and the coming cold, the voormis' civilization had been exhausted by the time the first humans arrived in Hyperborea. At first the voormis aided these newcomers in finding food and shelter, and later instructed them in the scientific and magical arts. As the number of humans increased, the voormis slowly dwindled, until the few remaining left their cities to hide in the mountains, with their largest colony at Mount Voormithadreth. The humans quickly forgot about their one-time benefactors and proclaimed themselves lords of Hyperborea, often hunting the voormis for sport.

Many years later, when the cold came once again to Hyperborea, the voormis, who had sunk to almost bestial levels, made raids on human villages for food. The Hyperboreans retaliated, crushing most of the remaining voormis, and staging periodic hunting expeditions to exterminate the rest. Little has been heard of this once-great race following the fall of Hyperborea, but it is rumored that the mysterious ape-men, such as the yeti and Bigfoot, sighted in various parts of the world are the last surviving remnants of the voormis.

See gnoph-keh; Hyperborea; Tsathoggua; Voormithadreth, Mount. ("The Scroll of Morloc", Carter and Smith; "The Curse of Tsathoggua", Herber (C); *The Trail of Tsathoggua*, Herber (C); "The Seven Geases", Smith.)

VOORMITHADRETH, MOUNT. Highest peak of the Eiglophian Mountains, located in Hyperborea. This mountain was volcanic in origin (though the wizard Eibon declared it was artificial), and was named in honor of the voormis who inhabited the tunnels which honeycombed it.

The toad god Tsathoggua lurked in deep caverns beneath this peak, and because of this the Hyperborean cultists of Tsathoggua turned toward Mount Voormithadreth during their worship of the Great Old One. There were darker rumors that even more hideous beings dwelt under Voormithadreth.

See Abhoth, Atlach-Nacha, Eibon, Haon-Dor, Tsathoggua, voor-mis. ("Shaggai", Carter; "The Seven Geases", Smith.)

VORVADOSS. Entity known as the Flaming One or the Troubler of the Sands, and sometimes referred to as Vorvadoss of the Gray Gulf of Yarnak (or Bel Yarnak). The people of Mu revered Vorvadoss at the peak of the mountain Nergu-K'nyan, and many considered him to be the mightiest of Earth's gods. In one invocation of Vorvadoss the being seemed to be beneficent toward humanity, though in such matters it is difficult to be certain.

("The Invaders", Kuttner.)

VULTHOOM. Being said to be one of Yog-Sothoth's sons. Vulthoom resembles a many-rooted plant with a gigantic bole, with a monstrous blossom at the top holding the semblance of a tiny elfin creature. Vulthoom dwells in the cavern of Ravormos on Mars.

Millions of years ago Vulthoom fled to Mars in its ether-ship from a conflict with vastly more powerful entities. Upon its arrival on the red planet, it subjugated the natives of that world using its vast knowledge of science and technology. After a while Vulthoom tired of its worshipers, and retired beneath the ground into the caverns of Ravormos. Over several centuries the people forgot the true nature of the visitor and eventually believed that Vulthoom was the devil and his home in Ravormos was the underworld. Soon the majority of the Aihai people had dismissed Vulthoom as a legend.

A cult dedicated to Vulthoom managed to survive among the lower classes. According to this group, Vulthoom still lives; though the creature is not immortal, its lifespan is immeasurable. The monster dwells within the caverns of Ravormos, where it undergoes a cycle of a thousand years of activity, followed by a thousand years of rest. Those who are especially faithful may be blessed by Vulthoom with the same longevity, falling asleep when Vulthoom does so and awakening at the same time as their master. When awake, these servants make plots to expand the worship of their master across Mars and to other worlds.

According to *Revelations of Glaaki*, Vulthoom is the merest child of the race upon which the legends of vampires are based.

See Yog-Sothoth. ("The Inhabitant of the Lake", Campbell; "Zoth-Ommog", Carter; "Vulthoom", Smith.)

W

WAITE, ASENATH. Daughter of Ephraim Waite and an unknown mother. Asenath Waite grew up in the Innsmouth home of her father, but following his madness and death, she became a ward of the principal of Kingsport's Hall School, and later went on to Miskatonic University.

It was at Miskatonic that Asenath met Edward Derby, poet and author of *Azathoth and Other Horrors*. The two became attracted to one another and married shortly thereafter. During their marriage Asenath became Derby's tutor in the magical arts; although on the surface their union was happy, those close to Derby noticed a shocking change in his personality during this period. About three years after the marriage, Asenath disappeared; Derby insisted that his wife had gone on an extended vacation, and no one thought anything amiss. Later, after her husband had been confined to an asylum, her body turned up just outside the house of Daniel Upton, Derby's close friend, presumably having been left there by persons unknown.

See Derby, Edward Pickman; Waite, Ephraim. ("The Thing on the Doorstep", Lovecraft.)

WAITE, EPHRAIM. Resident of Innsmouth, Massachusetts, who many considered to be a wizard of some power. Ephraim, who came from one of Innsmouth's oldest families, had the power of weather control, and he often travelled to Miskatonic University to consult that institution's occult holdings. He also participated in certain rites within the forests of Maine.

In his later years Waite took a wife whose face no one ever saw and who disappeared shortly after she bore his daughter Asenath.

When his daughter was in her early teens, Ephraim lost his mind, and Asenath confined him in the attic of their Innsmouth residence. Ephraim died not long following his imprisonment; some suspected poison, but most of Innsmouth's residents had no misgivings about Asenath, and no one ever charged her with his death.

See Derby, Edward Pickman; Waite, Asenath. ("The Thing on the Doorstep", Lovecraft.)

WALL OF NAACH-TITH. See Barrier of Naach-Tith.

WALMSLEY, GORDON (OF GOOLE). One-time Professor-Curator of the Wharby Museum in Yorkshire, and author of the celebrated book *Notes on Deciphering Codes, Cryptograms, and Ancient Inscriptions*. At various times, his aid in deciphering such inscriptions as the Phitmar Stone and the Geph Columns characters proved invaluable. This famous expert on cryptography was murdered in his rooms near the museum, a crime which remains unsolved. Walmsley is best remembered for his work at translating *G'harne Fragments*, an effort which was at first considered spurious but has aided later scholars immeasurably.

See Brick Cylinders of Kadatheron, Broken Columns of Geph, *Geph Transcriptions*, *G'harne Fragments*, Spheres of Nath. ("The Fairground Horror", Lumley; "In the Vaults Beneath", Lumley; "Rising with Surtsey", Lumley; *The Transition of Titus Crow*, Lumley.)

WARDER OF KNOWLEDGE. Being mentioned on the nineteenth Eltdown shard. The translation is somewhat garbled at this point, but seems to contain a ritual for summoning this entity. Unfortunately, it seems that the proper procedure for returning the Warder to its home spheres is missing from the shards, so caution is advised.

See *Eltdown Shards*. ("The Warder of Knowledge", Searight.)

WARREN, HARLEY. Carolina occultist and friend of Randolph Carter. He first came to distinction in the years 1916-18, when he was a member of a Boston society dedicated to the investigation of psychic matters. Following World War I Warren took up occult studies of a more personal nature, accompanied by Carter. In December of 1919 Warren vanished while on an expedition of unknown intent in the Big Cypress Swamp of Florida; the police held Carter, who had accompanied him at the time, but allowed him to go free when no definite evidence linking him to Warren's disappearance could be found.

See Carter, Randolph; Hiamaldi, Yogi. ("The Statement of Randolph Carter", Lovecraft; "Through the Gates of the Silver Key", Lovecraft and Price; *The Transition of Titus Crow*, Lumley.)

WATCHERS ON THE OTHER SIDE. Novel by Nayland Colum, a relatively unknown young author. Colum's book met with some success on the popular market, and the author was writing a sequel when he vanished, most likely sometime during the '40's.

What exactly this novel contained is unknown, but it seems that Colum had some sort of "dream-link" with the Great Old Ones which added certain unusual concepts to his writings.

(*The Trail of Cthulhu*, Derleth.)

WE PASS FROM VIEW. Volume published by True Light Press in 1964. Its author and publisher, Roland Franklyn, was the leader of a small cult based in Brichester, England. Rumor has it that most copies of the book disappeared from Franklyn's house before they could be distributed. In the years following the author's death in 1967, many of the remaining copies have also disappeared.

In his book Franklyn set forth the assertion followed by his sect. One of his rather peculiar doctrines was that the soul could be incarnated in more than one body at the same time. To get in touch with these other incarnations, the author instructs the initiate to use hallucinogenic drugs and chants to such beings as Daoloth and Eihort. Furthermore, for the soul to be reincarnated after death, a person's body must be cremated, lest the burrowers of the graveyards drag the corpse below to the feast of Eihort.

See Brichester; Eihort; Franklyn, Roland. ("The Franklyn Paragraphs", Campbell.)

WENDIGO. 1) Cannibalistic demon feared by the Native Americans of the northern U.S. and Canada. In the Mythos, this being is identical with the Great Old One Ithaqua, although in one reference the Wendigo is referred to as Ithaqua's cousin. ("The Windigo", Blackwood; "The Thing that Walked on the Wind", Derleth; "The Seal of R'lyeh", Derleth.)

2) Hypothetical species of which Ithaqua is a member. It is believed that by mating with humans, a wendigo can beget others of its own kind. Two wendigos were once sighted together, but the creatures engaged in a tremendous battle which ended only when one of the combatants perished. ("Born of the Winds", Lumley.)

3) Transformed servitor race created by Ithaqua out of those he captures. These appear much as Ithaqua himself, but are of lesser size

and power. ("The Windigo", Blackwood; *Alone against the Wendigo*, Rahman (C).)

See Ithaqua.

WENDY-SMITH, SIR AMERY (?-1933). Noted archaeologist, author of *On Ancient Civilizations* and inventor of the Wendy-Smith test for the dating of artifacts, who became a knight in 1901. Wendy-Smith's earlier accomplishments, however, have been greatly over-shadowed by his eccentric behavior later in life.

Near the end of his career, this great scientist worked to translate *G'harne Fragments*, a set of writings taken from the jungles of Africa by the explorer Windrop. His research in this direction culminated with a journey to the lost city of G'harne, during which the other members of the expedition were killed in an earthquake and only Wendy-Smith escaped to civilization. It is believed that this tragedy affected Sir Amery's mind, and his condition forced him to retire after his return. Wendy-Smith died in 1933 when his cottage on the Yorkshire moors collapsed.

See A'byy, G'harne, *G'harne Fragments*. (*Keeper's Compendium*, Herber (C); *Beneath the Moors*, Lumley; *The Burrowers Beneath*, Lumley; "In the Vaults Beneath", Lumley.)

WHITE ACOLYTE. Important figure in the worship of the Great Old One Chaugnar Faugn. It is said that this white man from the west will come to take Chaugnar Faugn away with him to his own land, and will nurse the god until it becomes so powerful that it no longer needs him. At this time Chaugnar will devour the entire universe, and every-thing will come to an end.

See Chaugnar Faugn. (*The Horror from the Hills*, Long.)

WILMARTH, ALBERT N. (?-1937). Noted folklorist and Assistant Professor of English at Miskatonic University. Wilmarth is noted for becoming involved in the debate over the inhuman bodies seen after the Vermont floods of 1927. This man strongly asserted that the creatures sighted in the waters did not exist, and after a spirited defense of his viewpoints dropped out of the debate entirely. Later he visited a corre-spondent in Vermont, but after Wilmarth's first night there his friend disappeared. The subsequent investigation turned up little evidence, and Wilmarth returned to Arkham baffled.

Following these events Wilmarth confided in his colleagues Henry Armitage and Nathaniel Peaslee about his discoveries. These men began a campaign to discover the sources behind the legends which were the groundwork of their own experiences. Wilmarth made many long trips in order to visit sites and talk to his network of informants. In the end this proved to be his undoing. Overwrought by his experiences and horrified by the results of a trip to visit the West Coast poet Georg Fischer, Wilmarth became ill in 1937 and died shortly thereafter.

See Magellanic Clouds, Vhoorl. ("The Terror from the Depths", Leiber; "The Whisperer in Darkness", Lovecraft; *The Burrowers Beneath*, Lumley.)

WILMARTH FOUNDATION. Organization based at Miskatonic University, the purpose of which is to continue the pioneering work of Albert Wilmarth. The founders established this organization just before Wilmarth's death, and although its basic premises were thought absurd by many, the organization grew by leaps and bounds, gaining much support from highly placed individuals in various governments and corporations. Since then the Wilmarth Foundation has mounted expeditions to many countries, including England, France, and Turkey, in search of their foes. Despite a major setback in 1980, when a storm and flood destroyed Miskatonic University, the institute has continued in its work, with a high degree of success.

An operation coordinated by the Wilmarth Foundation is usually organized in much the same way. First, telepaths capable of detecting Mythos entities are sent on a surveying mission to pinpoint the locations of any targets. Next, Foundation members bearing Elder Sign pendants arrive in the area, and use their influence on local authorities to keep their actions secret from the public. Finally, the threat is dealt with using the creature's natural weakness, or, barring knowledge of that, through the use of a carefully chosen amount of explosives. It is by using this basic plan that the Wilmarth Foundation dealt with the American and British cthonian threat during the 1970's.

The Wilmarth Foundation is governed by a board of directors made up of senior professors at Miskatonic, headed by a president. During the 1970's, Wingate Peaslee held this post. Following his death in the events following the bombing of Devil's Reef in 1980, the post has been taken up by Arthur Meyer.

See Crow, Titus; de Marigny, Henri-Laurent; *G'harne Fragments*; Peaslee, Wingate; Silberhutte, Hank. (*The Burrowers Beneath*, Lumley; *The Transition of Titus Crow*, Lumley.)

WIND-WALKER. See Ithaqua.

WINGED ONES. Entities who, according to some ancient traditions, came from the stars to Earth to instruct humanity in the Elder Lore. These creatures might have been the mi-go, but the Elder Things and the Fishers from Outside are also possible candidates.

("Through the Gate of the Silver Key", Lovecraft and Price.)

WONDROUS INTELLIGENCES. Book written in the 17th century by James Woodville, a Suffolk gentleman of Cromwell's time. This book contains much self-praise and descriptions of the author's perverse sexual practices, but between these passages information on the Great Race of Yith and its history may be found.

See Great Race of Yith. ("City in the Sands", DiTillio and Willis (C); "The Shadow out of Time", Lovecraft.)

WOOD OF N'GAI. See Ngai, Wood of.

WORMIUS, OLAUS. Scholar who translated Necronomicon from Greek into Latin in the year 1228. This Olaus Wormius, who is not to be confused with the later doctor of the same name, was born in Jutland, and later went on to perform other translations in both Latin and Greek.

See Necronomicon (Appendices). ("Zoth-Ommog", Carter; "History of the Necronomicon", Lovecraft.)

WORMS OF THE EARTH. Creatures that share the traits of both humans and reptiles. It is likely that the Worms of the Earth were cross-breeds between normal snakes and the serpent people of Valusia, who withdrew into Britain during the serpent men's decline. The Worms were the first people of that island, but were driven from their surface homes by the Picts. They withdrew into their burrows and caverns, from which they emerged only in the greatest need.

Over the years the Worms of the Earth became less and less human in form, but their magical power grew as it never had before. As memory of the battles between the Picts and their foes faded, the Worms became the bogeymen of the newcomers, who blamed them for the abduction of infants from their cradles and other nefarious deeds.

Several scholars have advanced the belief that the "little people" of legend were actually the aboriginal inhabitants of Britain, who fled into the wilds when other groups began to colonize their former lands and who carried out acts of guerrilla warfare against their foes. Traditionally, the Little Folk were believed to possess many supernatural powers, such as being able to curdle milk, destroy crops, and steal away people who came too near the hills in which they lived. It would seem that the Worms are the source behind these myths, as well as the Norse tales of the dvergar. It is unknown whether any of the Worms of the Earth still survive, or whether they have become extinct in the centuries since their exodus to their burrows.

The title "Worms of the Earth" has also been given to the yuggya, but it is unlikely that any connection between these and the cave-dwellers of Britain exists.

See Bran Mak Morn, serpent people. ("The Winfield Inheritance", Carter; "People of the Dark", Howard; "The Worms of the Earth", Howard; *Heir to Darkness*, Rahman.)

X

XADA-HGLA. Azathoth's only known avatar. It resembles a shell much like that of a clam, from which many long pseudopods protrude and containing a hairy, green-eyed face. It was this form which Azathoth possessed before the Elder Gods took away his reason, and images of Xada-Hgla may still be found in the shan's teleporting temples.

See Azathoth, shan. (*Ye Booke of Monstres*, Aniolowski (C); "The Insects from Shaggai", Campbell.)

XICLOTL. World in the same system as Shaggai. The insects from that planet had colonized this world, enslaving the large, semi-intelligent carnivorous monsters which were native to the planet. After the destruction of Shaggai, the shan came together on this world and made it their home for a time. The insects finally left this world when they discovered the truths behind the Xiclotlians' singular religious practices.

See shan. ("The Insects from Shaggai", Campbell.)

XOTH (or possibly ZOTH). Green binary star from which Cthulhu came to Earth, and home of the being Idh-yaa, upon whom Cthulhu is said to have spawned four children. This system may be found within the constellation Taurus in a cluster with the stars Abbith, Zaoth, and Ymar, but cannot be viewed with a conventional telescope.

See Abbith, Cthulhu, Cthylla, Ghatanothoa, Idh-yaa, Zstylzhemghi. ("The Thing in the Pit", Carter; "Zoth-Ommog", Carter; "Some Observations on the Carter Glossary", Cockcroft; *The Transition of Titus Crow*, Lumley.)

XUTHLTAN. 1) Former name of the town of Stregoicavar, Hungary. Xuthltan was the home to a cult which sacrificed victims kidnapped from neighboring communities at a monument known as the Black Stone. When the Muslim army came to this region in 1526, they destroyed Xuthltan and massacred all its people. See Black Stone, *People of the Monolith*, Stregoicavar. ("The Black Stone", Howard.)

2) Magician of ancient Arabia. In ages past he travelled to a dark cavern in a distant land, stealing a magical gem known as the Fire of Asshurbanipal from a sleeping demon. While residing in the city of Kara-Shehr, the king imprisoned and tortured him to gain the gem. Xuthltan died, and with his last breath he brought a curse down upon the king and his people. The city of Kara-Shehr still lies beneath the desert sands, holding the Fire of Asshurbanipal. See Kara-Shehr. ("The Fire of Asshurbanipal", Howard.)

Y

YAD-THADDAG. The Elder God who is the equivalent to the evil Yog-Sothoth, according to some sources.

See Elder Gods. (*Elysia*, Lumley.)

YADDITH. Planet circling five suns millions of light years from Earth, in the same section of the sky where Deneb can be seen from Earth. Eons in the past the Nug-Soth, tapir-snouted beings who shared both reptilian and mammalian characteristics, inhabited this world. From what little we know of them, they seem to have been a race of scholars ruled by the Arch-Ancient Buo. These people explored the universe, not only in their "light-wave envelopes" which could take them to twenty-eight nearby galaxies, but also by the use of dream control and time travel.

Despite all their magical and scientific knowledge, the Nug-Soth found themselves unable to stop the dholes which dwelt in their burrows deep beneath Yaddith's surface. For thousands of years the sages of Yaddith conferred with each other and plumbed the universe for any means to put an end to this menace. All their efforts failed. Eventually the dholes which dwelt within Yaddith overwhelmed it, and the cities of Yaddith were destroyed. Most of its inhabitants escaped the destruction of their home, but according to some, even then they were hunted in their dreams by the dholes.

Some say that Yaddith was once the home of Shub-Niggurath, who dwelt beneath the planet's surface with her dhole servitors. Whether this is true or not, both the dholes and the Nug-Soth were the servitors of Shub-Niggurath, though this did nothing to abate their conflict.

See dhole, *Ghorl Nigral*, Harag-Kolath, Mthura, Nug-Soth, Shub-Niggurath, Tablets of Nhing, Vhoorl, *Visions from Yaddith*, Zkauba. ("Visions from Yaddith", Carter; "Dreams in the House of Weir", Carter; "Zoth-Ommog", Carter; "Through the Gate of the Silver Key", Lovecraft and Price.)

YADDITH-GHO. Mountain in the kingdom of Kn'aa on Mu. Before the advent of humanity, beings from Yuggoth had built a fortress here to hold in the Great Old One Ghatanothoa. This site became of prime religious significance when humans dwelt on Mu, and remained the holiest place in that land until it sank into the ocean. It is said that Yaddith-Gho shall rise once again when the Old Ones finally return.

See Ghatanothoa. ("Out of the Aeons", Heald and Lovecraft.)

YAKSH. Another name for the planet Neptune. It is especially noted for its curious fungoid inhabitants.

See Hziulquoigmnzhah. ("Some Observations on the Carter Glossary", Cockcroft.)

YAKTHOOB. Tutor and master of the young sorcerer's apprentice Abdul Alhazred. The tale of this man and his eventual end may be found in *Necronomicon*.

See Abdul Alhazred, *Necronomicon* (Appendices), *Yhe Rituals*. ("The Doom of Yakthoob", Carter.)

YAMIL ZACRA. Star located somewhere between Algol and Polaris. Yamil Zacra is circled by its dark companion Yuzh, as well as by the ill-famed world of Pnidleethon. The people of Hyperborea believed it to be the source of all the universe's evil. According to their legends, this star throws off tiny "fires" throughout all space, which have become imbedded in every living being. Those who own a great concentration of these bodies may become great necromancers, and some may even leave their home world to dwell with the masters of Pnidleethon.

See Pnidleethon, *Testament of Carnamagos*, Yuzh. ("The Infernal Star" (fragment), Smith.)

YARKDAO. According to *Revelations of Glaaki*, a race of humanoid beings with retractable ears which rule the world of Tond. These may be the "incubi of Tond" mentioned in *Necronomicon*.

See Tond. ("The Inhabitant of the Lake", Campbell; "The Mine on Yuggoth", Campbell.)

YATTA-UC. Ruined city of the deep ones hidden beneath Lake Titicaca. This outpost had its heyday nearly five hundred million years ago, and even today lesser amphibians congregate at this spot.

("The Return of the Deep Ones", Lumley.)

YEB. Being given the title "Yeb of the Whispering Mists." Sometimes Yeb is called the servitor of Abhoth, but usually it is connected with Nug.

See Black Rituals of Nug and Yeb, Furnace of Yeb, K'n-yan, Nug and Yeb, Shub-Niggurath. ("The Thing in the Pit", Carter; "The Descent into the Abyss", Carter and Smith; "Out of the Aeons", Heald and Lovecraft.)

YEGG-HA. Minor Mythos being who took the form of a 10' bipedal monster with tiny wings and a featureless face. It is believed that this creature entered our dimension thousands of years ago through a gateway somewhere near Hadrian's Wall. Various tribes in pre-Roman Britain worshiped this faceless being. According to Lollius Urbicus' *Frontier Garrison*, a company of Roman soldiers killed Yegg-ha, but not until the enemy had slain over fifty of their number. The Romans, fearing that the tribesmen would discover the creature's remains and return it to life, secretly buried its remains somewhere near Hadrian's Wall.

It has been said that Yegg-ha is the ruler of the nightgaunts, and in return serves Nyarlathotep. Aside from the physical similarity, however, there is no evidence to support this theory.

See *Frontier Garrison*, nightgaunt. ("The Winfield Inheritance", Carter; "An Item of Supporting Evidence", Lumley; *The Transition of Titus Crow*, Lumley.)

YEKUB. World located in a far-off galaxy, populated by a race of centipede-like beings ruled by Juk-Shabb, a spherical being of untold might. According to *Eltdown Shards*, these beings became capable of space travel, and exterminated all other intelligent lifeforms in their galaxy. Yet, their desire for conquest was unabated.

The Yekubians began to construct cubes of a quartz-like material which, when placed in light, had a hypnotic effect upon their viewers. They then sent these cubes out from their home galaxy. When one of these items came upon a solid body's gravitational field, it would shed its protective covering and land there. If an intelligent being found this cube, the Yekubians would exchange its mind with that of one of their explorers. While the Yekubians interrogated the alien's mind for information about its home world, the Yekkubian would explore this new world, and report back its findings to its fellows.

Usually, after this had taken place, the two minds would be returned to their proper bodies. On the other hand, if the scientists of Yekub found a planet whose inhabitants were capable of space travel, they would employ the cube to capture their minds and destroy that world's people, or would send more of their number to subjugate them entirely. If the latter occurred, the Yekubians would destroy the captive alien minds and create a rough duplicate of their former civilization upon this new planet.

In the entire history of the planet Earth, only one of these cubes has ever landed upon our world. This was during the era when the Great Race held sway over the planet. After a few Yithians were taken over by the Yekubians, the Great Race discovered the danger and destroyed these scouts, even though this stranded their captive minds upon Yekub. They did not want to destroy the cube, as it might prove useful later, so they kept it from all light and heat and guarded it vigilantly. During a war millions of years later, however, the artifact was lost, and it is unknown whether the cube has survived to this day.

See *Eltdown Shards*, Juk-Shabb. (*Ye Booke of Monstres*, Aniolowski (C); "The Challenge from Beyond", Lovecraft *et al.*)

YELLOW SIGN. Symbol that is a focus for the power of Hastur, the Unspeakable One. This sign is usually useless until the arrival of the King in Yellow into our world. Then it would warp the dreams of the people who saw it, and would give them visions of the city of Carcosa on the Lake of Hali. This sign is the major symbol of the cult of Hastur.

See Brothers of the Yellow Sign, Great Race of Yith, Hastur, Keeper of the Yellow Sign, King in Yellow, Sign of Koth, Thale. ("The Yellow Sign", Chambers; "Tell Me, Have You Seen the Yellow Sign?", Ross (C).)

Y'GOLONAC. Great Old One who takes the form of a flabby headless human with mouths on the palms of his hands. Usually Y'golonac manifests himself in order that he may choose new priests for his earthly cult. These acolytes are normally chosen from among those who have suppressed unnatural desires, which Y'golonac allows them to experience in return for servitude. Fortunately, Y'golonac is not widely worshiped, and he can only call upon or affect those who have read a page from *Revelations of Glaaki*.

See *Reveleations of Glaaki*, Thirty-five Abominable Adulations of the Bloated One. ("Cold Print", Campbell; "Love's Lonely Children", Watts (C).)

Y'HA-NTHLEI. City of the deep ones located off of Innsmouth, Massachusetts, near the outcropping known as Devil's Reef. A submarine's torpedoes damaged this city during the government raid on Innsmouth in 1928 and it was totally destroyed in underwater explosions set by the Wilmarth Foundation in 1974, but the deep ones have returned to the site to rebuild one of their greatest metropoli.

See Ahu-Y'hloa, deep one, Innsmouth. ("The Shadow over Innsmouth", Lovecraft; *The Transition of Titus Crow*, Lumley.)

YHE. Province of the land of Mu, now sunken beneath the Pacific Ocean. This place lies far to the south of Cthulhu's tomb at R'lyeh, and it is mentioned in certain prayers sacred to Dagon. In addition, the mysterious being Ythogtha is said to be imprisoned there.

See *Yhe Rituals*, Ythogtha, Zanthu. ("Out of the Aeons", Carter; "Zoth-Ommog", Carter; *The Trail of Cthulhu*, Derleth.)

YHE RITUALS. Text penned by Niggoum-Zhog, a prehuman prophet. The cult of Ythogtha preserved these writings, which they passed down from each high priest to his successor. Ythogtha's last high priest, Zanthu, was said to have destroyed them as Mu sank beneath the waves. Many centuries later in Poseidonis, scribes found a copy of *Yhe Rituals* in the library of Malygris following that powerful wizard's death. Yakthoob, the sorcerer to whom Alhazred was apprenticed in his youth, also owned a copy, and, more recently, a copy turned up in an Egyptian tomb in 1903.

This book holds thirty-one secret rituals used in the worship of Ythogtha. The thirty-first, "The Key That Openeth The Door To Yhe", will summon forth Ythogtha if performed, and Niggoum-Zhog warns that this should only be used if a worshiper is in direst peril.

See Yhe, Ythogtha. ("The Thing in the Pit", Carter.)

YHOUNDEH. Goddess whose worship became prevalent in the later years of the Hyperborean civilization. The priests of Yhoundeh began an inquisition which targeted many different heresies, but especially the worship of Tsathoggua. This inquisition culminated with an assault upon the tower of the great sorcerer Eibon, who dealt with Tsathoggua regularly in return for magical knowledge. During this attack Eibon escaped, and High Priest Morghi, the head of the raiding party, disappeared soon thereafter. Due to this humiliating defeat, the worship of Tsathoggua superseded that of Yhoundeh during Hyperborea's final years.

See Cykranosh, Eibon, Hyperborea. ("The Door to Saturn", Smith.)

YHTILL. 1) According to one source, the name of the capital city in which the play *The King in Yellow* is set. See Aldones, Naotalba, Uoht. ("Tell Me, Have You Seen the Yellow Sign?", Ross (C).)

2) The word "yhtill" means "stranger" in the language of the city of Alar. It is this word that the Pallid Mask gives as his name when he enters the city of Hastur. See Aldones, King in Yellow, Pallid Mask. ("More Light", Blish.)

YIAN. City located in the depths of China, "across the seven oceans and the river which is longer than from the earth to the moon." In Yian it is always summer, a great river winds under a thousand bridges, and the air is filled with the music of silver bells. Only a few foreigners have ever come to this city. The city serves as the headquarters of the Kuen-Yuin, so it may possibly be the center of the Chinese Cthulhu cult.

See Kuen-Yuin. ("The Maker of Moons", Chambers; *The Slayer of Souls*, Chambers; "The Whisperer in Darkness", Lovecraft.)

YIAN-HO. Deserted metropolis beneath the ground of upstate New York or possibly Asia, and said to be the legacy of the Plateau of Leng. All humans are said to hold ancestral memories of this great city. Yian-Ho is guarded by a monster whose exact nature is unknown, and which only a mighty sorcerer who has the proper knowledge may pass. The Yogi Hiamaldi brought the mysterious four-handed clock, which both Etienne-Laurent de Marigny and Titus Crow later owned, from Yian-Ho. It may also be the only place on Earth where a complete copy of *Ghorl Nigral* is kept.

See *Book of Hidden Things*; *Ghorl Nigral*; Hiamaldi, Yogi; time-clock; von Junzt, Friedrich Wilheim. ("Zoth-Ommog", Carter; "The Diary of Alonzo Typer", Lovecraft and Lumley, W.; "Through the Gate of the Silver Key", Lovecraft and Price; *The Transition of Titus Crow*, Lumley.)

YIBB-TSTLL. Alien god who may be found in chaotic realms outside of this universe, which can be reached from behind the Palace of the Sacred Fount in the Dreamlands' Jungle of Kled. He may also be encountered by being contacted (through the dreams of those who use the Sixth Sathlatta) or summoned (by thirteen people saying the Sixth Sathlatta three times).

This deity is omniscient, and may be asked questions about anything by those brave enough to approach him. If the god is not pleased, Yibb-Tstll might reach out and touch the petitioner, beginning the dreaded reversal. Usually this process turns the subject inside out or leaves him dead or permanently insane, though it occasionally gives the victim some benefit.

Yibb-Tstll's body is covered with a green cloak, beneath which may be seen many breasts, upon which Yibb-Tstll's servant night-gaunts feed. Yibb-Tstll's flaky black blood is called the Black, and may itself be summoned by wizards to attack their foes.

See Barrier of Naach-Tith; Black, the; *Cthaat Aquadingen*; Kant, Ernst; *Legends of the Olden Runes*; nightgaunt; *Pnakotic Manuscripts*; Priests of the Ivory Blade; Sixth Sathlatta. ("Ulthar and Beyond", Herber (C); "The Caller of the Black", Lumley; "The Horror at Oakdeene", Lumley.)

YIDHRA. Creature which came into being at the same time life came into being on this planet. Yidhra was a protoplasmic entity which could take on the appearances of any organism she devoured. Thus, over billions of years, Yidhra learned to adapt to the changing world and expand her power. Without other forms of life to feed upon, Yidhra could not have survived.

Today Yidhra still exists, though she now has split herself into several different entities. At various times in history these fragments have established religions with the purpose of adding to Yidhra's might; these cults have sprung up in such widely separated places as Chad, Laos, Burma, Sumeria, Texas, and New Mexico. In each of these places Yidhra has taken a different yet attractive form in which she visits her followers. Though these forms are not perfect, she is able to conceal her true nature from her congregation.

Those who serve Yidhra are guaranteed good crops, no matter what disasters may befall them, and some may even gain eternal life. On the other hand, however, just as Yidhra becomes more like her worshipers with close contact, so they become more like her. As a consequence, many of the members of her cults' inner circles, who are able to see Yidhra in her true form, gradually develop bestial traits.

See *Black Sutra, Chronicles of Thrang, Cthonic Revelations, Uralte Schrecken*. ("Where Yidhra Walks," DeBill.)

YIFNE. Green sun about which the world of Tond revolves.
See Tond. ("The Inhabitant of the Lake", Campbell.)

YIG. Great Old One who takes the form of a great serpent man. Unlike most of his fellow Great Old Ones, he is rather benevolent toward humanity. In the autumn, however, it is necessary to propitiate him through drum-beating, offerings of corn, and various rituals, lest he visit his wrath upon those who harm the serpents, who are his spawn. Yig's wrath takes the form of madness and visits by his "children", snakes with a crescent moon-shaped patch on their heads. Those who especially displease the god may themselves be transformed into snakes.

The worship of Yig is thought to have begun in the underground land of K'n-yan. From there it spread throughout western North America, and south into Mexico (where he possibly inspired the myths of Quetzalcouatl and Kulkulcan), and also to Mu and Valusia. He may also be linked with a few fringe voodoo cults. A few Native American tribes of the Great Plains still worship him today.

See Byatis, Fang of Yig, Han, K'n-yan, serpent people, Sss'haa, Ubbo-Sathla, *Vatican Codex*. ("Where a God Shall Tread", Aniolowski; "The Curse of Yig", Bishop and Lovecraft; "The Mound", Heald and Lovecraft; "Out of the Aeons", Heald and Lovecraft.)

YIKILTH. Tremendous iceberg upon which the palace of Rlim Shaikorth rested.

See Rlim Shaikorth. ("The Coming of the White Worm", Smith.)

YLIDHEEM ("Cold Ones"). Title given to those who serve Rlim Shaikorth, and who have been protected from the intense cold which his home radiates.

See Rlim Shaikorth. ("The Fishers from Outside", Carter.)

Y'M-BHI. Reanimated bodies of dead slaves who form an important part of the work force in the underground land of K'n-yan.

See K'n-yan. ("The Mound", Heald and Lovecraft.)

'YMNAR. Avatar of Ngyr-Khorath, according to the book *Uralte Schrecken*. 'Ymnar cloaked itself with an earthly form and was sent to our world by its master so that it might lead humanity toward its ultimate destruction. 'Ymnar seems much like Nyarlathotep, but the connection is disputable.

See *Uralte Schrecken*. ("Where Yidhra Walks", DeBill.)

YOG-SOTHOTH (also IOG-SOTOT). Outer God also known by the title Lurker at the Threshold. According to von Junzt's *Unaussprechlichen Kulten*, Yog-Sothoth is the father of Cthulhu, Hastur, and Vulthoom. In the Mythos, Yog-Sothoth seems to share the rulership of the universe with Azathoth, and may be opposed to some degree by Nodens, Lord of the Great Abyss.

Yog-Sothoth is known as "the key to the gate, whereby the spheres meet", and is said to exist everywhere in time and space. Paradoxically, the Lurker at the Threshold appears to be shut out from our own dimension, and may only come to this world when summoned. Perhaps Yog-Sothoth dwells in a parallel dimension which intersects with our own only at certain points, or else he is omnipresent but can fully manifest itself only with the aid of certain ceremonies.

In the guise of the Beyond-One, Yog-Sothoth is worshiped by the mi-go, and he is also known to certain minds made of vapor as a mysterious Sign. On our own world, certain sorcerers worship Yog-Sothoth in exchange for limited command of both time and space. Using these abilities, the worshiper can do anything from warping space to hold a chosen victim, to stepping outside of time itself to return to Earth after hundreds or thousands of years have passed. Yog-Sothoth eventually takes all of these misguided souls to himself, a fate from which not even physical destruction can save them.

To summon Yog-Sothoth, a tall stone tower or circle of standing stones is usually used. Upon speaking the words of the summoning, an intelligent being must be sacrificed to the god. The proximity of the chosen sacrifice is unimportant. Only after these conditions are met may Yog-Sothoth manifest itself.

Yog-Sothoth's usual form is a congerie of iridescent spheres, but it is said that the Outer God has many more forms. One of these, the Lurker at the Threshold, appears as a black amorphous horror, and another, Ramasekva, takes the form of a many-limbed human much like a Hindu deity. Others say that Tawil at'Umr is in actuality Yog-Sothoth disguised, and certain manifestations of UFO's have been attributed to appearances of Yog-Sothoth.

Two interesting theories about Yog-Sothoth deserve mention here. The first is that Yog-Sothoth is diametrically opposed to Nodens, the Lord of the Great Abyss, whom he shall pursue until the end of time. Another holds that Yog-Sothoth lay beneath an Elder Sign at Mount Sinai until freed by Moses, and that Yahweh is in fact a manifestation of the Outer God. Considering what little is known about the Lurker at the Threshold, I cannot say whether either of these is correct or not.

See Bugg-Shash, Cthulhu, Gog and Magog, Great Old Ones, Klarkash-Ton, *Liber Damnatus Damnationum*, Mlandoth, *Necronomicon* (Appendices), Nodens, Nug and Yeb, Othuum, Outer Gods, Ramasekva, *Reflections*, Shub-Niggurath, Son of Yog-Sothoth, Sothoth, tomb-herd, 'Umr at-Tawil, Vulthoom, Yad-Thaddag. ("Glimpses", Attansio; "The Church on the High Street", Campbell; "Zoth-Ommog", Carter; "The Lurker at the Threshold", Derleth and Lovecraft; "The Horror in the Museum", Heald and Lovecraft; "The

Dunwich Horror", Lovecraft; "Through the Gates of the Silver Key", Lovecraft and Price; *The Transition of Titus Crow*, Lumley; "The Holiness of Azedarac", Smith; *The Winds of Zarr*, Tierney.)

YOTH. Red-lit caverns found beneath the underground realm of K'n-Yan. In these caverns lie several deserted cities built by the serpent people, who fled to Yoth following the destruction of their homeland Valusia. These reptilian creatures manufactured many types of beasts for their pleasure, as well as creating new bodies for themselves. The decline of the colony came when the serpent people turned from their worship of Yig to embrace the new god Tsathoggua, whose images they had found in black N'kai. Yig brought down his curse upon them, and the few who remained loyal to the snake god fled to the caverns beneath Mount Voormithadreth. This place is still visited occasionally.

See emanation from Yoth, gyaa-yothn, N'kai, Tsathoggua, Zin. ("The Mound", Bishop and Lovecraft; "The Descent into the Abyss", Carter and Smith.)

YOTHIC MANUSCRIPTS. Written lore detailing the customs of the people of Yoth. They were found in the Vaults of Zin, beneath Yoth's greatest city.

See Zin, Vaults of. ("The Mound", Bishop and Lovecraft.)

Y'QAA. Gray-lit cavern in which Ubbo-Sathla dwells. This place is said to be multidimensional, and the seeker may find gates to it in many places and times.

See Ubbo-Sathla. ("Zoth-Ommog", Carter.)

YR-NHHNGR. Set of formulae that may be used both to bring beings to this dimension and to send them back, though the complete version of all of these formulae is difficult to obtain. Yr and Nhhngr may also be other dimensions which lie on the far side of Kadath in the Cold Waste.

See Kadath in the Cold Waste. ("The Lurker at the Threshold", Derleth and Lovecraft; "The Dunwich Horror", Lovecraft.)

YTHOGTHA. One of Great Cthulhu's supposed "sons", along with Ghatanothoa and Zoth-Ommog. He is currently imprisoned beneath an Elder Sign within the Abyss of Yhe, located in the sunken land of Mu far to the south of R'lyeh. He is served by the worm-like yuggya.

Ythogtha's cult was powerful in Mu for many years, but gradually lost power as Ghatanothoa's worship gained ascendancy. The last

Muvian priest of Ythogtha, Zanthu, conceived of a daring plan to raise his god up from his chasm and regain his religion's former power. Ythogtha's ascent, however, set a series of catastrophic events in motion which destroyed the land of Mu.

From time to time statues of Ythogtha have come into the possession of humans. Through these idols Ythogtha can manifest himself through the dreams of the owner. Madness is the most common result of this contact.

See Cthulhu, Ghatanothoa, Idh-yaa, Yhe, *Yhe Rituals*, yuggya, Zanthu, Zanthu Tablets. ("Out of the Ages", Carter; "Perchance to Dream", Carter; "The Thing in the Pit", Carter; *The Transition of Titus Crow*, Lumley.)

YUGGOTH. Trans-Neptunian planet usually said to be identical with Pluto, but which is sometimes described as a huge world beyond the nine known planets which rotates perpendicular to our solar system's orbital plane.

This world serves as a base for the mi-go, or fungi from Yuggoth. From those humans who have, by one means or another, travelled to or viewed Yuggoth, we hear that it is a planet of cities filled with black, windowless towers beneath warm seas, great mines of tok'l and other strange minerals, and rivers of pitch crossed by cyclopean bridges. Glaaki stopped for a time on this world on his way to Earth, and it is here that the mi-go constructed the Shining Trapezohedron. Yuggoth served as a home for Rhan-Tegoth before he came to Earth, and Tsathoggua's grandfather Cxaxukluth may still dwell beneath its surface.

The mi-go were not the first creatures to live on Yuggoth. A city of green pyramids rests on a ledge in a cleft near one of the fungi's metropoli, and the mi-go take care to desert that particular town at certain times of the year. Aside from this precaution, though, the mi-go are the undisputed masters of Yuggoth.

See Cxaxukluth, Daoloth, Fly-the-Light, Ghatanothoa, Ghisguth, Ghooric Zone, Glaaki, Hziulquoigmnzhah, Nithon, Nyarlathotep (Haunter of the Dark), Rhan-Tegoth, Shining Trapezohedron, Thog and Thok, tok'l, Yaddith-Gho, Zaman, Zone of the Thirteen Faveolate Colossi. ("The Mine on Yuggoth", Campbell; "Some Observations on the Carter Glossary", Cockcroft; "The Horror in the Museum", Heald and Lovecraft; "Out of the Aeons", Heald and Lovecraft; "The Haunter of the Dark", Lovecraft; "The Whisperer in Darkness", Lovecraft; "The Discovery of the Ghooric Zone", Lupoff; "Documents in the Case of Elizabeth Akeley", Lupoff.)

YUGGYA. Servitors of Ythogtha and Zoth-Ommog who resemble huge, slimy white worms. These monsters dwell beneath the Pacific Ocean and the Earth's crust, where, under the direction of their leader Ubb, they seek to free their imprisoned masters. In exchange for continued human sacrifice, they will bestow great wealth upon a bargainer. A formula for summoning one of these beings may be found in the Zanthu Tablets.

See Ubb, Worms of the Earth, Ythogtha, *Yuggya Chants*, Zoth-Ommog. ("Out of the Ages", Carter; "The Winfield Inheritance", Carter.)

YUGGYA CHANTS. Volume only known to scholars by rumor. It is said that the eccentric anthropologist Harold Hadley Copeland purchased a copy of this manuscript from a sailor in San Francisco shortly before his demise, though no such manuscript turned up in a search of his library.

See yuggya. ("Out of the Ages", Carter.)

YUZH. Dark companion body to the star Yamil Zacra.

See Yamil Zacra. ("The Infernal Star" (fragment), Smith.)

Z

ZAK. City in the Mongolian desert. This Moorish-styled city is home to almost ten thousand people. The Mir of Zak's palace is made of a white brick, has six courtyards, and is walled with pinkish granite. This is also the name of a city in the Dreamlands, though that is probably a coincidence.

See Nylstrom. (*The Great White Space*, Copper.)

ZAMAN. According to some sources, one of Yuggoth's moons.

(*Fungi from Yuggoth*, Lovecraft; "Discovery of the Ghooric Zone", Lupoff.)

ZANN, ERICH. Mute German violinist who dwelt in the rue d'Auseil in Paris during the 1920's. Little is known of Zann's early life, except that at one time he lived in Stuttgart, married, and had at least one child. One day, however, he unaccountably left his family and journeyed to Paris.

In Paris Zann joined an orchestra at a cheap theater to provide himself with income. He became known to the tenants of his apartment because of the strange unearthly violin music which he played at night. He is believed to have vanished while performing one of his "experimental pieces" in his garret apartment one night. The police were baffled by the lack of clues, and soon afterward called a halt to their search.

("The Music of Erich Zann", Lovecraft; "The Silence of Erika Zann", Wade.)

ZANTHU. Last high priest of Ythogtha on the continent of Mu. By the time Zanthu took this office, the priests of Ghatanothoa had been consolidating their power for the previous ten thousand years. Just after Zanthu had accepted the priesthood, the priests of Ghatanothoa banned the worship of all gods except their own throughout the lands of Mu.

Zanthu could not accept this affront. Searching through the annals of his predecessors, he discovered a formula which would call forth Ythogtha from his home in the Abyss of Yhe. When he and the other priests of Ythogtha used this formula, however, something went wrong, and a cataclysm took place that in the end was to destroy the entire continent. Zanthu and his fellow priests escaped in their sky-chariots to the Plateau of Tsang in central Asia, where Zanthu carved the ten stone plaques known to modern scholars as the Zanthu Tablets. Zanthu died on the Plateau, and his followers buried him with his tablets in a stone mausoleum.

See Copeland, Harold Hadley; Ghatanothoa; *Ponape Scripture*; Shamballah; Tsang, Plateau of; Ythogtha. ("The Dweller in the Tomb", Carter; "The Thing in the Pit", Carter.)

ZANTHU TABLETS. Ten black pieces of jade inscribed in the hieratic Naacal tongue by a high priest of Mu named Zanthu. This Zanthu, who according to some brought down the wrath of the gods upon Mu and caused its destruction, fled to the Plateau of Tsang in central Asia, where he later died.

In 1913, the controversial anthropologist Harold Copeland, following the instructions given in *Ponape Scripture*, mounted an Asian expedition to discover the tomb of Zanthu and reclaim the tablets. Three months after he set out Copeland walked into an outpost in Mongolia, raving of the things he had seen and having no idea of the other members' fates. Following his recovery from this ordeal, Copeland worked on his translation of the tablets, and published his findings in 1916 in a privately published pamphlet, *The Zanthu Tablets: A Conjectural Translation*. Both the public and the scientific community denounced this work, and two years after its publication, Copeland was committed to an asylum.

The original tablets are still held at the Sanbourne Institute in California, and copies of Copeland's pamphlet may still be found in various collections. The Tablets contain the writings of Zanthu, including how the great wizard destroyed the continent of Mu through his summoning of Ythogtha.

See Copeland, Harold Hadley; Naacal; yuggya. ("The Thing in the Pit", Carter; "The Dweller in the Tomb", Carter; "Out of the Ages", Carter.)

ZARR. Alien creatures who had subjugated much of their own galaxy before being contacted by the Great Old One Zathog. Zathog, who had taken up residence on a planet near that galaxy's core, asked the Zarr to aid him in freeing the other Great Old Ones, in exchange for providing them with a universe to conquer. The Zarr agreed, and were given the power to travel through space and time by the grateful Zathog.

When the Zarr come to a world which they desire to conquer, they usually rain down destruction upon its civilizations through the use of nuclear weapons and their powers of weather control. Then the Zarr take on board certain members of that planet's civilization, so that they may use them as tools in destroying the rest of the population. Sometimes, one of these representatives has been known to halt the Zarr and keep them from destroying all of the intelligent life on the world, but even then the aliens may return at another time period to attack once again. Wherever they go, the Zarr search for the tombs of the Great Old Ones, and strive to free them from their sleep.

See Othuyeg, Zathog. (*The Winds of Zarr*, Tierney.)

ZATHOG. Great Old One who dwells on a world at the center of a nearby galaxy. Upon his arrival on this planet following the war with the Elder Gods, Zathog made contact with the Zarr, a race which had ruthlessly conquered most of their home galaxy. Knowing that he had found the perfect tool for his revenge, Zathog promised the Zarr an entire universe to conquer if they would help him free his imprisoned brothers. The Zarr acquiesced, and Zathog bestowed upon them the ability to travel through time and space on their raids. Zathog remains on the world to which he originally came, awaiting the time when all the Great Old Ones shall be freed.

See Othuyeg, Zarr. (*The Winds of Zarr*, Tierney.)

ZHAR. Great Old One who came to Earth from Arcturus, and now lives beneath the city of Alaozar, on the Plateau of Sung in Burma (or possibly in Tibet). It is worshiped by the Tcho-Tcho, with whom it communicates telepathically sporadically, and is physically connected to the being Lloigor.

See elemental theory; Lloigor; Sung, Plateau of; Twin Obscenities. ("The Sandwin Compact", Derleth; "The Lair of the Star-Spawn", Derleth and Schorer.)

ZHOTHAQQUAH. See Tsathoggua.

ZIN, VAULTS OF. Tunnel complex that lies both beneath Yoth and in the Dreamlands' Underworld. The vaults lie beneath the ruins of Yoth's largest city. The men of K'n-yan found the Yothian manuscripts within these vaults.

In the Dreamlands, the outer portions of the vaults seem to have been carved into the shape of some titanic building. The entrance to the vaults there is quite near the huge city built by the gugs. Ghasts, a race of white-skinned, partially human monstrosities, live within the vaults, and feed upon lone gugs and each other. Though they may serve as a connection between the lands of dream and the waking world, the Vaults of Zin are best avoided.

See ghast, gug, gyaa-yothn, Yothic Manuscripts. ("The Mound", Heald and Lovecraft; "The Dream-Quest of Unknown Kadath", Lovecraft.)

ZKAUBA. Wizard of Yaddith who is remembered for bearing the Ghorl Nigral from the burrows of the dholes beneath his world's surface, and aiding his fellows' attempt to find the rituals to save their world from the worm-like beings. Unaccountably, during this effort Zkauba disappeared on a trip to a nearby star in his light-wave envelope, leaving his Yaddithian brothers to their fate.

See *Ghorl Nigral*. ("Dreams in the House of Weir", Carter; "Zoth-Ommog", Carter; "Through the Gates of the Silver Key", Lovecraft and Price.)

ZOBNA. Land from which the people of Lomar fled the cold, destroying the cannibalistic gnoph-keh to build a new empire. Little is known of it, but the Lomarians still put great faith in the wisdom of their ancestors in Lomar at the time of that land's destruction.

See gnoph-keh, Lomar. ("Polaris", Lovecraft.)

ZON MEZZAMALECH. Wizard of Mhu Thulan who is mentioned in *Book of Eibon*. According to Eibon, Zon Mezzamalech possessed a crystal that enabled him to see through time and space whenever he desired. He reputedly disappeared while attempting to use this crystal to gaze upon the wisdom of the Elder Gods kept by Ubbo-Sathla.

See Hyperborea, Mhu Thulan. ("Ubbo-Sathla", Smith.)

ZONE OF THE THIRTEEN FAVEOLATE COLOSSI. Region beyond which Yuggoth lies.

("The Mine on Yuggoth", Campbell.)

ZOOG. Rodent-like creature native to the Dreamlands' Enchanted Wood. In appearance, a zoog resembles a mouse about the size of a cat, but with a row of tentacles between its nose and mouth.

Zoogs dwell in the Enchanted Wood, the forest in which those who enter the Dreamlands first find themselves. These woodland dwellers have a taste for flesh, and have been known to attack travellers in or near the forest around nighttime. If a dreamer avoids the wood at night and stays on the path within the forest in the day, the zoogs should give him no trouble. For those lucky enough to learn the fluting speech of the zoogs, great opportunity for friendship with these shy creatures exists.

The zoogs in the Enchanted Wood are ruled by a council of sages, which makes decisions for the zoogs as a whole. These wise old zoogs are quite well informed, as their kind have many agents throughout the nearer realms of dream. Those who deal with the zoogs may learn much interesting information, but they should be careful afterward, since the zoogs often send spies after their "friends" to keep track of their whereabouts.

In the two places where the Enchanted Wood intersects with the waking world, zoogs may enter our world and have been responsible for many disappearances. Fortunately, no human knows where these two locations are.

See Dreamlands, Enchanted Wood. ("The Dream-Quest of Unknown Kadath", Lovecraft; *Hero of Dreams*, Lumley; "To Sleep, Perchance to Dream", Okamoto (C).)

ZOTH-OMMOG. Great Old One which has a conical body topped with four starfish-like tentacles and a serpent-bearded lizard head. Zoth-Ommog is said to be the son of Cthulhu, and is believed to sleep in the section of R'lyeh which is just off the coast of Ponape.

This Great Old One is able to call out to humans through his dreams, much as his master Cthulhu. Zoth-Ommog's ability, however, is able to manifest itself only through his statues. When a person keeps one of these artifacts, he is visited in dreams with visions of the glory of Zoth-Ommog. Through these means Zoth-Ommog is able to gain new devotees and spread his cult.

The primary center of Zoth-Ommog's worship is Ponape, but other cults revering him may be found as far away as New Zealand and South Indochina. In his tomb, Zoth-Ommog is also served by the mysterious yuggya.

See Cthulhu, elemental theory, Gloon, Idh-yaa, Ythogtha, yug-gya. ("Out of the Ages", Carter; "Zoth-Ommog", Carter; *The Transition of Titus Crow*, Lumley.)

ZOTHIQUE. The last continent upon which humans will live eons in the future, according to certain legends. Zothique will rise when all other continents have sunk beneath the waves.

In Zothique humans will rediscover many of the gods revered in past civilizations and worship them once more. Also, some of the world's most powerful wizards will live during this age. The magical energies present in this entire continent will cause fluxes to form in the space-time continuum, leading to the formation of interdimensional gateways in which the unwary might become caught.

At least one portal between our time and that of Zothique has been discovered, and others may exist.

See Thasaidon. ("Slow Boat", Jeffrey and Morrison (C); "The Dark Eidolon", Smith; *Strange Shadows*, Smith.)

ZSTYLZHEMGHI. Mother of Tsathoggua. She was spawned by the fission of a being from the dark star Xoth.

("Some Observations on the Carter Glossary", Cockcroft.)

ZUCHEQUON (also ZULCHEQUON or ZUSHAKON). Entity which seems to have originated on Earth, described as being the last scion of old Night. This could be one of those "black spirits of earth" referred to by Castro. Zuchequon may be summoned forth by chants or certain deep-toned sounds, and may also manifest itself in earthquakes. When it comes, Zuchequon brings darkness and cold. The people of K'n-yan and Mu worshiped Zuchequon with the ringing of bells and chanting; the west coast Native American tribes once knew how to summon it, but such information has probably been lost. Zuchequon is served by the "Hidden Ones", whose leader is Tsunth.

See Ubbo-Sathla. ("The Descent into the Abyss", Carter and Smith; "Bells of Horror", Kuttner.)

APPENDIX A: CHRONOLOGY OF THE HISTORY OF THE *NECRONOMICON*

c. 730 A.D. — Abdul Alhazred writes *Kitab Al-Azif*. ("History of the *Necronomicon*", Lovecraft.) [1]

738 — According to Ibn Khallikan, the famous Arabian biographer, Abdul Alhazred is torn apart by an invisible beast in the streets of Damascus. ("History of the *Necronomicon*", Lovecraft.) [2]

950 — Theodorus Philetas, a scholar of Constantinople, translates *Kitab Al-Azif* from Arabic into Greek, renaming the volume *Necronomicon*. ("History of the *Necronomicon*", Lovecraft.)

1050 — Patriarch Michael, having heard rumors of the experiments attempted with this book, burns many copies of *Necronomicon*. Olaus Wormius' introduction to the Latin edition states that all Arabic editions were destroyed at this time. (*The Trail of Cthulhu*, Derleth; "History of the *Necronomicon*", Lovecraft.) [3]

1228 — Olaus Wormius translates the Greek version of *Necronomicon* into Latin. ("History of the *Necronomicon*", Lovecraft.) [4]

1232 — Both the Greek and Latin editions of *Necronomicon* are placed on the Index Expurgatorius by Pope Gregory IX. (*Selected Letters, Vol. 2*; Lovecraft.) [5]

15th century — German(?) printing in black-letter of the Latin translation of Olaus Wormius. ("History of the *Necronomicon*", Lovecraft.)

1472 — An Olaus Wormius translation is published in Lyons, France. (*The Illuminatus! Trilogy*, Shea and R. Wilson.) [6]

1501 — Italian printing of the Greek text. Aldus Manutius, founder of the Aldine Press, is a likely candidate for this edition's publisher. ("History of the *Necronomicon*", Lovecraft.)

1583 — John Dee and Edward Kelley supposedly discover a copy of *Necronomicon* in Prague while visiting Emperor Rudolph II. (*The* Necronomicon: *The Book of Dead Names*, Hay, ed.; "History of the *Necronomicon*", Lovecraft.)

1586 — According to another source, it is in this year that John Dee translates *Necronomicon* into English. It is said that this translation contains material from the Latin edition of Olaus Wormius, a Greek manuscript found in the possession of a Transylvanian noble, and Dee's own comments on certain subjects. ("Castle Dark", Herber (C); "Eyes for the Blind", Hallett and Isinwyll (C); "The Space-Eaters", Long; "History of the *Necronomicon*", Lovecraft.) [7]

1598 — Baron Frederick I of Sussex, England publishes his own English translation of the Latin *Necronomicon* of Wormius, entitling it *Cultus Maleficarum*. This edition, more widely known as *The Sussex Manuscript*, is very confused and is not considered reliable. (*The Sussex Manuscript*, Pelton.)

1622 — Wormius' translation printed once again, this time in Spain. ("The Shadow from the Steeple", Lovecraft; "The History of the *Necronomicon*", Lovecraft.)

1641 — *My Understanding of the Great Booke* by Joachim Kindler published in the city of Buda. Within this volume Kindler speaks of a volume of *Necronomicon* written in Gothic, a tongue spoken by an ancient Germanic tribe. According to the author, this translation "offers proofs logickal and glorious" of the "stellar numbers, potentiated objecks, signs and passes, probatories, phylacteries, and craftsmanly artes" required for the rituals elucidated therein — in other words, a *Necronomicon* with all the allegory and obscurity banished. Fortunately for the sake of humanity, Kindler is the only person in history to describe this volume, so he might have invented this new edition (or possibly the Gothic *Necronomicon* no longer exists). ("The Lurker from the Crypt", Miller.)

1722 — Breakup of the infamous cult of Kingsport, Massachusetts. *Necronomicon* played an important role in the rituals of this group, though whether the raiders found a copy is uncertain. ("The Festival", Lovecraft; "The Kingsport Cult", Ross.)

1771 — A raid is made upon a farm outside Providence, Rhode Island which is owned by Joseph Curwen, a reputed sorcerer who owned a Latin copy of *Necronomicon*. Curwen is supposedly killed, but little is damaged during the raid. ("The Case of Charles Dexter Ward", Lovecraft.) [8]

1811 — A mysterious foreigner leaves a Latin copy of *Necronomicon* at the Bibliothèque Nationale. He is found the next day in a squalid apartment, having been poisoned by persons unknown. ("The *Necronomicon*", Herber.)

1848 — Von Junzt's German translation of *Necronomicon, Das Verichteraraberbuch*, published at Ingolstadt, Bavaria, eight years after the translator's death. (*Schrodinger's Cat Trilogy*, R. Wilson.) [9]

1895-1900 — Henry Armitage, recently appointed to the post of head librarian at Miskatonic University, purchases a copy of *Necronomicon* from Providence businessman Whipple Phillips, the grandfather of H. P. Lovecraft. ("The *Necronomicon*", Herber.) [10]

1912 — Wilfred Voynich, an American bookseller, discovers an enciphered medieval manuscript in an Italian castle. Along with this document, which comes to be known as the Voynich Manuscript, Voynich finds a letter which asserts that the book is the work of the famous scientist Roger Bacon. ("The Return of the Lloigor", C. Wilson.) [11]

1912 — American millionaire Harry Widener adds a copy of *Necronomicon* to his collection shortly before his fatal trip aboard the Titanic. After his death, his books are donated to Harvard University. ("The *Necronomicon*", Herber.)

1921 — Professor W. Romaine Newbold declares that he has deciphered the Voynich Manuscript. In his account Newbold claimed the document was a scientific treatise proving that Roger Bacon had developed the microscope centuries before Leeuwenhoek. Unfortunately, Newbold dies in 1926 before he can finish deciphering the manuscript. ("The Return of the Lloigor", C. Wilson.)

1922 — H. P. Lovecraft makes the first mention of *Necronomicon* in his story "The Hound." ("The Hound", Lovecraft.)

1929 — Benjamino Evangelista is found murdered, along with the rest of his family, in his home in Detroit. The investigation into his death finds that Evangelista was a priest in some sort of cult, and had written a divinely-inspired book called *The Oldest History of the World*. This book is notable because it contains references to a volume of magic called "Necremicon," "Necromicon," and "Necronemicon", which is also titled "Al Azif." These passages were supposedly written before Lovecraft ever used *Necronomicon* in his stories. (*The Philosopher's Stone*, C. Wilson.)

1931 — A Professor Manly, looking over Newbold's notes on the decipherment of the Voynich Manuscript, deduces that Newbold's supposed "cipher" is in fact the result of fading of the manuscript's ink. Newbold's results are discredited by the scientific community. ("The Return of the Lloigor", C. Wilson.)

1934 — Death of Joachim Feery. Before his death, this man had written the book *Notes on the* Necronomicon, which he published in both complete and expurgated editions. The authenticity of this volume is highly suspect, especially since Feery claimed to have inserted his own dream-messages into the passages from the dreaded book. ("Aunt Hester", Lumley; "Name and Number", Lumley.)

1938 — The house of Professor Laban Shrewsbury of Arkham, Massachusetts is burned to the ground shortly after that noted scholar sent the first volume of his work *Cthulhu in the* Necronomicon to the printers. Although no trace of Shrewsbury was found in the ruins, it is believed that he perished in the fire. (*The Trail of Cthulhu*, Derleth.)

1939 — *Cthulhu in the* Necronomicon by Professor Laban Shrewsbury published(?). ("Books of the Cthulhu Mythos", Herber and Ross (C).)

c. 1950? — Henrietta Montague completes her task of translating the British Museum's *Necronomicon* into English at the request of that institution's directors. This expurgated translation is later published in an edition intended for scholarly use only. Sadly, Montague succumbed to a wasting disease shortly after the project's completion. (*The Burrowers Beneath*, Lumley.)

1967 — Professor Lang of the University of Virginia takes up his study of the Voynich Manuscript, discovering that it is written in Greek and Latin using Arabic letters. His work, which is continued by other scholars after his disappearance in 1969, proves that the Voynich Manuscript is actually a commentary on certain passages of *Necronomicon* written by a monk named Martin Gardener. (*The Philosopher's Stone*, C. Wilson; "The Return of the Lloigor", C. Wilson.)

1973 — Owl Wick's Press of Philadelphia publishes the edition of *Al-Azif* currently located in the Brown University library. However, this copy is in Duraic, not Arabic, and the manuscript appears to be the same eight pages copied over and over.

1977 — "Simon" publishes his own version of *Necronomicon*, which soon thereafter is released as a paperback. The "translator" claimed to have derived the volume from a Greek manuscript, of which only parts were included in his book. [12]

1978 — *The* Necronomicon: *The Book of Dead Names* published by Neville Spearman Press. According to Colin Wilson, the original manuscript existed in cipher among John Dee's papers at the British Museum, and constitutes part of the Arabic scholar Alkindi's *Book of the Essence of the Soul*. By use of computer analysis, the authors translated the volume and published it soon thereafter. (*The* Necronomicon: *The Book of Dead Names*, Hay, ed.)

1979 — During a visit to a Cairo bookseller, Professor Phileus Sadowsky of the University of Sofia discovers a page bearing Alhazred's famous couplet in Arabic. Unfortunately, this page disappears on its way through Customs. ("Notes on a Fragment of the *Necronomicon*", Hamblin.)

1988 — Death of noted fantasy/science fiction author Lin Carter. One of his unfinished works was a manuscript of *Necronomicon*. (Note: To my knowledge, this copy has never been published.)

Notes on the Chronology

[1] — There has been some confusion as to the exact origins of the name "Abdul Alhazred." One school of thought holds that this is a corruption of this scribe's true name, Abd al-Azrad (Abd=servant, zarada=to strangle or devour, thus "servant of the great strangler or devourer"). Others say that the name has no connection with Arabic at all; rather, it actually means "one-who-sees-what-shouldn't-be-seen" in Yemenite. ("The Freshman", Farmer; "Notes on a Fragment of the *Necronomicon*", Hamblin.)

[2] — I have found no biography of Abdul Alhazred, or any of the commonly accepted variants on that name, in Ibn Khallikan's biography. It is possible that Alhazred is still included under another name, or that later scribes expunged this particular entry from the work.

[3] — "Patriarch Michael" is probably Michael Cerularius, Patriarch of Constantinople from 1043-58. By way of his actions against Rome, Patriarch Michael was largely responsible for the eventual break between the Roman Catholic and Greek Orthodox churches. He was deposed and exiled in 1058 for inflammatory remarks against the emperor; he died shortly thereafter.

[4] — This Olaus Wormius is sometimes confused with a famous Danish physician of the same name, who lived almost four hundred years later. The earlier Olaus Wormius was born in Jutland, and went on to make many other Greek and Latin translations of ancient books.

Wormius indicates in his prefatory note to his translation that the Arabic edition of *Necronomicon* no longer existed. Possibly the ecclesiastics destroyed only the copy which Wormius had seen, and the translator believed that this had been the last copy of that book in Arabic. Most of the rumors of the Arabic *Necronomicon* since have been unsubstantiated, however. (*The Trail of Cthulhu*, Derleth; "History of the *Necronomicon*", Lovecraft.)

[5] — A year before his decision to censor *Necronomicon* on the Index Expurgatorius, Pope Gregory IX had instituted the papal Inquisition to combat the rise of heresy within the church. Thus, it seems certain that he would have had *Necronomicon* banned.

A mistake has been made by previous scholars, however. At this time, the Index Expurgatorius did not exist, so Pope Gregory could not have placed *Necronomicon* within it. Other such lists did exist at this time, and it is likely the authorities included *Necronomicon* in one of these.

[6] — This may indeed be the edition commonly considered to be German, not only because both versions are said to have been printed at much the same time, but also since these two editions are considered to be muddled and confusing in comparison to the 17th century printing. ("Out of the Ages", Carter.)

[7] — No mention is made in Dee's diaries of a trip to present-day Romania to see the noble's copy of *Necronomicon*. He lived in a castle in southern Bohemia at the time, however; would he have had time to make an unrecorded trip to the Baron's home? Or did the Baron come to him?

[8] — It is likely that one of the raiders kept Curwen's copy of *Necronomicon*, or possibly that a thief bore it away from the abandoned farm. In any event, this particular copy, distinguished by its cover bearing the false title "Qanoon-e-Islam", disappears for almost a century.

[9] — One other edition of *Necronomicon* mostly in an ancient form of German has been discovered. This one, however, was hand-written, and probably is not identical with the von Junzt edition. ("The Fairground Horror", Lumley.)

[10] The span of five years that I have used is merely speculative. It is possible that Lovecraft did not have personal experience early in life with *Necronomicon*, and that he gained his knowledge of that tome from the stories of his grandfather, or possibly from another source entirely.

It is noteworthy that the copy owned by Phillips was that taken from Curwen's farm after the raid of 1771. It may have been passed down in the family by one of the raiders, or other circumstances may have been at work.

As to why Armitage became so interested in obtaining a copy of *Necronomicon*, some speculate that it had something to do with a mysterious meteor which had fallen in 1882 near Arkham, the nature of which had disturbed Armitage enough to prompt further research in that direction. ("The Terror from the Depths", Leiber.)

[11] The Voynich Manuscript is in fact a real document, which is preserved at Yale University.

[12] — Though the author/translator claims that this is the true work, the version given leaves out so many of the commonly accepted quotations that it is difficult to proclaim its veracity or fraudulence. Many of the same arguments could also be made against the Hay manuscript.

Appendix B:
Locations of the *Necronomicon*

(This list is by no means complete. It is likely that others exist elsewhere, unknown to scholars and investigators alike.)

Alhazred, Abdul — Some have said that a copy of Alhazred's *Al-Azif* may still be found in the tomb of its author, the location of which is unknown. If this is true, Professor Laban Shrewsbury bore it away from its hiding place on his expedition to Alhazred's resting place. (*The Trail of Cthulhu*, Derleth.)

Bibliothèque Nationale — Holds the Olaus Wormius edition of 1622. ("The Dunwich Horror", Lovecraft.)

British Museum — Holds one of the few 15th century Latin printings in existence, as well as Henrietta Montague's English scholarly translation. Access to both volumes is severely limited, however. Though some thought at one time that a copy of *Al-Azif* existed among the uncatalogued documents, this rumor has been proven false. (*Cthulhu by Gaslight*, Barton (C); "History of the *Necronomicon*", Herber; "The Dunwich Horror", Lovecraft; "The *Necronomicon*", Lovecraft; "Billy's Oak", Lumley; *The Burrowers Beneath*, Lumley.)

Cairo — The Egyptian Museum here is reputed to own a copy of the *Al-Azif*. ("The Lurker at the Threshold", Derleth and Lovecraft; "Cairo", DiTillio and Willis (C).)

Curwen, Joseph — This reputed sorcerer vanished following a raid on his home in 1771. He owned a copy of the Latin *Necronomicon* bound in a cover bearing the title "Qanoon-e-Islam." If this is true, this volume passed through the hands of the Phillips family of Providence, R.I., and now rests in the vaults of Miskatonic University. ("The Case of Charles Dexter Ward", Lovecraft.)

Dee, John — This scholar and mystic is rumored to have owned a 15th century Latin printing of *Necronomicon*. Those who catalogued his library, however, did not find this copy after his death. ("Eyes for the Blind", Hallett and Isinwyll (C).)

Dexter, Ambrose — A medical doctor and noted nuclear physicist from Providence, Dexter bore away the 17th century Latin printing of *Necronomicon* from the Starry Wisdom Church before the city levelled that structure. Whether he is alive or not is unknown; if he still survives, he would be well into his nineties. ("The Shadow from the Steeple", Bloch; "The Haunter of the Dark", Lovecraft.)

Field Museum, Chicago, Illinois — A copy of unknown language and edition is preserved in the library of this institution. ("The Horror from the Depths", Derleth and Schorer.)

Harvard University — It has been said that Widener Library keeps a 17th century Latin edition. Some evidence, however, suggests that someone stole or destroyed this book sometime in the middle of this century. ("To Arkham and the Stars", Leiber; "The Dunwich Horror", Lovecraft; "History of the *Necronomicon*", Lovecraft.)

Hauptman, Baron — Doctor Dee saw a copy of the Greek *Necronomicon* which this Romanian nobleman owned. A priest stole this book from its owner in 1627, and nothing more has been heard of it. ("Castle Dark", Herber (C).)

Kester Library — Holds one of the few surviving copies of the 15th century printing of Olaus Wormius. ("The Salem Horror", Kuttner.)

Magyar Tudomanyos Akademia Orientalisztikai Kozlemenyei — This Hungarian collection at one time owned a copy of Alhazred's *Al-Azif*, but this document burned in a fire at the home of Professor Sadowsky of the University of Sofia. ("Further Notes on the *Necronomicon*", Hamblin.)

Miskatonic University Library — The library at this institution holds the most complete 17th century Latin printing in this hemisphere, purchased from the library of Providence businessman Whipple Phillips. In 1924 Miskatonic obtained a partial English manuscript entitled *Al-Azif* from the estate of Ambrose Dewart, and the library obtained Wilbur Whateley's holdings, including a fragmentary copy of Dee's translation, in 1928. (*The Lurker at the Threshold*, Derleth and Lovecraft; "The Dunwich Horror", Lovecraft.)

Pickman family — This family of Salem, Massachusetts owned a Greek copy, which disappeared with the artist Richard Upton Pickman. Since Pickman vanished, it has been rumored that he has taken up residence in the Dreamlands. This may be a line of research to be pursued by an enterprising dreamer. ("The Dream-Quest of Unknown Kadath", Lovecraft; "The *Necronomicon*", Lovecraft; "Pickman's Model", Lovecraft.)

San Marcos of Lima — A Greek translation printed in Italy is kept at this Peruvian university. ("Out of the Ages", Carter; "The Lurker at the Threshold", Derleth and Lovecraft.)

Shrewsbury, Laban — This investigator of the links between mythologies across the world and the Cthulhu Mythos is said to have taken an incomplete Arabic edition from the tomb of Abdul Alhazred himself sometime around 1940. It is rumored that he may be found at the Great Library of Celaeno. (*The Trail of Cthulhu*, Derleth.)

Starry Wisdom Church of Providence, Rhode Island — The cult held a 17th century Olaus Wormius edition here, but Doctor Ambrose Dexter removed it in 1935, at the same time he removed the Shining Trapezohedron. ("The Shadow from the Steeple", Bloch; "The Haunter of the Dark", Lovecraft.)

Szolyhaza, Hungary — A copy is held in a private collection in this small town, but the exact edition is unknown. ("The Second Wish", Lumley.)

University of Buenos Aires — This institution holds a 17th century printing of Olaus Wormius's translation. ("The Dunwich Horror", Lovecraft.)

Vatican — It is rumored that a copy of *Necronomicon* rests within the Papal Archives, but details are lacking. ("The Lurker at the Threshold", Derleth and Lovecraft.)

Zebulon Pharr Collection — Pharr was a famous West Coast occultist and anthropologist of the late 19th century. His library is rumored to contain a Latin copy of *Necronomicon*, but even the most reputable institutions have been denied access to this collection. ("Statue of the Sorcerer", Edwards and Elliott (C).)

Appendix C:
Some Contents of the
Necronomicon

— the famous couplet:

That is not dead which can eternal lie,

And with strange eons even death may die.

A literal translation from the Arabic would be:

That thing is not dead which has the capacity to continue to exist eternally,

And if the abnormal (bizarre, strange) ones (things, times) come, then death may cease to be.

("Notes on a Fragment of the *Necronomicon*", Hamblin; "The Nameless City", Lovecraft.)

— A formula for calling Yog-Sothoth can be found on page 751. ("The Dunwich Horror", Lovecraft.)

— On page 224 is the Hoy-Dhin Chant, which is necessary to call the Black. Unfortunately, the rest of this procedure is in *Cthaat Aquadingen*. ("The Horror at Oakdeene", Lumley.)

— a copy of the Elder Sign. ("Castle Dark", Herber (C).)

— the Vach-Viraj Incantation, which is used against Nyogtha. ("The Salem Horror", Kuttner.)

— a formula for calling Nyogtha himself. ("The Salem Horror," Kuttner.)

— the tale of the death of Yakthoob, Alhazred's former teacher. ("The Doom of Yakthoob", Carter.)

— the story of how Kish and his followers escaped Sarnath before that city's destruction. ("Zoth-Ommog", Carter.)

— an exorcism in which a hundred names of ghosts and demons are named (this formula did not appear in the Wormius translation, though). ("The Return of the Sorcerer", Smith.)

— a spell allowing the caster to switch minds with a victim. ("The Thing on the Doorstep", Lovecraft.)

— a way to create a gate in the place of the Sphinx beneath the pyramids of Giza, which will send a person directly to Nyarlathotep. ("Cairo", DiTillio and Willis (C).)

— the Voorish Sign. ("The Dunwich Horror", Lovecraft.)

— the Mao rite. ("The Plain of Sound", Campbell.)

— the Zoan ritual, which protects its user against Mnomquah. ("Something in the Moonlight", Carter.)

— a chart showing the positions of various celestial objects (which is partial and outdated). ("The Horror from the Bridge", Campbell.)

— a spell that may be used to dispel Bugg-Shash when he comes to this dimension. ("The Kiss of Bugg-Shash", Lumley.)

— and possibly the key to telepathy. ("I Know What You Need", King.)

Bibliography

Books and Short Stories

Aniolowski, Scott D. "An Early Frost" (1994).

Attansio, Albert A. "Glimpses" (1975), "The Star-Pools" (1980).

Bertin, Eddy. "Darkness, My Name Is" (1976).

Bierce, Ambrose. "The Death of Halpin Frayser" (1893), "Haita the Shepherd" (1893), "An Inhabitant of Carcosa" (1891).

Blackwood, Algernon. "The Windigo" (1910).

Blish, James. "More Light" (1970).

Bloch, Robert. "The Brood of Bubastis" (1937), "The Dark Demon" (1936), "The Faceless God" (1936), "Fane of the Black Pharaoh" (1937), "The Grinning Ghoul" (1936), "The Mannikin" (1936), "Notebook Found in a Deserted House" (1951), "The Secret of Sebek" (1937), "The Shadow from the Steeple" (1950), "The Shambler from the Stars" (1935), *Strange Eons* (1979), "The Suicide in the Study" (1935).

Breach, Arthur W. "The Return of the White Ship" (1994).

Brennan, Josef Payne. "The Feaster from Afar" (1976), "The Keeper of the Dust" (1962), "The Seventh Incantation" (1973).

Burnham, Crispin. "The Seven Cities of Gold" (1994).

Campbell, Ramsey. "Before the Storm" (1980), "The Church in High Street" (1962), "Cold Print" (1969), "The Faces at Pine Dunes" (1980), "The Franklyn Paragraphs" (1973), "The Horror from the Bridge" (1964), "The Inhabitant of the Lake" (1964), "The Insects from Shaggai" (1964), "The Mine on Yuggoth" (1964), "The Moon-Lens" (1964), "The Plain of Sound" (1964), "The Render of the Veils" (1964), "The Return of the Witch" (1964), "The Room in the Castle" (1964), "The Tower from Yuggoth" (1986), "A Word from the Author" (1964).

Carter, Lin. "The Books" (1956), "Carcosa Story about Hali" (1993), Dreams from R'lyeh (1975), "Dreams in the House of Weir" (1980), "The Dweller in the Tomb" (1971), "The Gods" (1956), "In the Vale of Pnath" (1975), "Litany to Hastur" (1971), "Out of the Ages" (1975), "Shaggai" (1971), "Something in the Moonlight" (1981), "The Thing in the Pit" (1980), "The Vengeance of Yig" (1983), *Visions from Yaddith* (1988), "The Winfield Inheritance" (1981), "Zoth-Ommog" (1976).

— and L. Sprague deCamp. *Conan the Buccaneer* (1971).

— and Clark Ashton Smith. "The Descent into the Abyss" (1981), "The Light from the Pole" (1980), "The Scroll of Morloc" (1975), "The Stairs in the Crypt" (1976).

Chambers, Robert W. "The Maker of Moons" (1895), "The Repairer of Reputations" (1895), *The Slayer of Souls* (1920), "The Yellow Sign" (1895).

Chappell, Fred. *Dagon* (1968).

Cockcroft, T. G. L. "Some Observations on the Carter Glossary" (1959).

Copper, Basil. *The Great White Space* (1974).

DeBill, Walter C. "In 'Ygiroth" (1975), "K'n-yan" (1971), "Where Yidhra Walks" (1976).

Derleth, August. "Beyond the Threshold" (1941), "Black Island" (1952), "The Dweller in Darkness" (1944), "The House on Curwin Street" (1944), "Ithaqua" (1941), "The Keeper of the Key" (1951), "The Passing of Eric Holm" (1939), "The Return of Hastur" (1939), "The Sandwin Compact" (1940), "The Seal of R'lyeh" (1957), "Something from Out There" (1951), "The Testament of Claiborne Boyd" (1949), "The Thing that Walked on the Wind" (1933).

— and H. P. Lovecraft. "The Fisherman of Falcon Point" (1959), "The Gable Window" (1957), "The Horror from the Middle Span" (1967), "The Lamp of Alhazred" (1957), *The Lurker at the Threshold* (1945), "The Shuttered Room" (1959), "The Survivor" (1954).

— and Mark Schorer. "The Horror from the Depths" (1940), "Lair of the Star-Spawn" (1932), "Spawn of the Maelstrom" (1939).

Drake, David. "Than Curse the Darkness" (1980).

Dunsany, Edward Plunkett. "Bethmoora" (1910), "The Hashish-Man" (1910).

Farmer, Philip Jose. "The Freshman" (1979).

Glasby, John S. "The Ring of the Hyades" (1989).

Hasse, Henry. "The Guardian of the Book" (1937).

Hay, George, ed. *The* Necronomicon: *The Book of Dead Names* (1978).

Hjort, James W. "Andalous and the Chimera" (1980).

Hodgson, William H. "The Whistling Room" (1911).

Howard, Robert E. "The Black Stone" (1931), "The Children of the Night" (1931), "The Dark Man" (1931), "Dig Me No Grave" (1937), "The Fire of Asshurbanipal" (1936), "The Gods of Bal-Sagoth" (1931), "The Hyborian Age" (1936), "The Shadow Kingdom" (1929), "Skull-Face" (1929), "The Thing on the Roof" (1932), "Worms of the Earth" (1932).

Jacobi, Carl. "The Aquarium" (original) (1992).

King, Stephen. "I Know What You Need" (1976), "Jerusalem's Lot" (1978).

Klein, T. E. D. "Black Man with a Horn" (1984), *The Ceremonies* (1984).

Kuttner, Henry. "Bells of Horror" (1939), "The Hunt" (1939), "The Invaders" (1939), "The Salem Horror" (1937).

Leiber, Fritz. "The Terror from the Depths" (1976), "To Arkham and the Stars" (1966).

Ligotti, Thomas. "The Prodigy of Dreams" (1994), "Vastarien" (1988).

Long, Frank B. "The Horror from the Hills" (1931), "The Hounds of Tindalos" (1931), "When Chaugnar Wakes" (1932).

Lovecraft, H. P. "At the Mountains of Madness" (1936), "Beyond the Wall of Sleep" (1919), "The Call of Cthulhu" (1928), "The Case of Charles Dexter Ward" (1941), "The Cats of Ulthar" (1920), "Celephais" (1934), "Dagon" (1919), "The Doom that Came to Sarnath" (1920), "The Dream-Quest of Unknown Kadath" (1948), *Dreams and Fancies* (1962), "The Dreams in the Witch House" (1933), "The Dunwich Horror" (1929), "The Festival" (1925), "Fungi from Yuggoth" (1941), "Herbert West — Reanimator" (1922), "The Haunter of the Dark" (1936), "History of the *Necronomicon*" (1936), "The Hound" (1924), "Hypnos" (1923), "The Music of Erich Zann" (1922), "Nameless City" (1921), "Nyarlathotep" (1920), "The Other Gods" (1933), "The Outpost" (1934), "Pickman's Model" (1927), "Polaris" (1920), "The Rats in the Walls" (1924), *Selected Letters II* (1968), *Selected Letters III* (1971), *Selected Letters V* (1976), "The Shadow over Innsmouth" (1936), "The Silver Key" (1929), "The Statement of Randolph Carter" (1919), "The Shadow Out of Time" (1936), "The Strange High House in the Mist" (1931), "The Temple" (1925), "The Terrible Old Man" (1921), "The Thing on the Doorstep" (1937), "The Unnamable" (1925), "The Whisperer in Darkness" (1931), "The White Ship" (1919).

— and Zealia Bishop. "The Curse of Yig" (1929), "The Mound" (1940).

— and Adolphe de Castro. "The Last Test" (1928).

— and Sonia Greene. "The Horror at Martin's Beach" (1923).

— and Hazel Heald. "The Horror in the Museum" (1933), "The Man of Stone" (1932), "Out of the Aeons" (1935), "Winged Death" (1933).

— and Harry Houdini. "Under the Pyramids" (1924).

— and William Lumley. "The Diary of Alonzo Typer" (1938).

— and E. Hoffman Price. "Through the Gates of the Silver Key" (1934).

— and Duane W. Rimel. "The Tree on the Hill" (1940).

Lowndes, Robert A. "The Abyss" (1965).

Lumley, Brian. "A-Mazed in Oriab" (1991), "Aunt Hester" (1977), *Beneath the Moors* (1974), "Billy's Oak" (1970), "The Black Recalled" (1987), "Born of the Winds" (1977), *The Burrowers Beneath* (1974), "The Caller of the Black" (1971), "Cement Surroundings" (1969), *The Clock of Dreams* (1978), "Cryptically Yours" (1979), "De Marigny's Clock" (1971), "Dylath-Leen" (1971), Elysia (1989), "The Fairground Horror" (1976), *Hero of Dreams* (1986), "The Horror at Oakdeene" (1977), "The House of Cthulhu" (1973), *In the Moons of Borea* (1979), "In the Vaults Beneath" (1971), "Inception" (1987), "Introduction" to *The House of Cthulhu* (1984), "Isles of the Suhm-Yi" (1984), "An Item of Supporting Evidence" (1970), "The Kiss of Bugg-Shash" (1978), "The Last Rite" (1974), "Lord of the Worms" (1987), *Mad Moon of Dreams* (1987), "The Mirror of Nitocris" (1971), "Mylakhrion the Immortal" (1977), "Name and Number" (1987), "The Return of the Deep Ones" (1984), "Rising with Surtsey" (1971), "The Running Man" (1987), "The Second Wish" (1980), "The Sorcerer's Book" (1984), "The Sorcerer's Dream" (1979), *Spawn of the Winds* (1978), *The Transition of Titus Crow* (1975), "What Dark God?" (1975).

Lupoff, Richard A. "The Discovery of the Ghooric Zone — March 15, 2337" (1977), "Documents in the Case of Elizabeth Akeley" (1982).

Machen, Arthur. "The Novel of the Black Seal" (1948), "The White People" (1948).

Merritt, A. *et al.* "The Challenge from Beyond" (1935).

Milan, Victor. "Mr. Skin" (1994).

Murray, Will. "To Clear the Earth" (1994).

Myers, Gary. "The House of the Worm" (1970), "The Passing of a Dreamer" (1971), "The Return of Zhosph" (1975), "The Three Enchantments" (1975), "Xiurhn" (1975), "Yokh the Necromancer" (1971).

Pelton, Fred L. "The Sussex Manuscript" (1989).

Price, Robert M. "Behold, I Stand at the Door and Knock" (1994).

— and Peter Cannon. "The Curate of Temphill" (1994).

Rahman, Glenn. *Heir to Darkness* (1989).

Rimel, Duane W. "Music of the Stars" (c. 1930).

Russell, Bertram. "The Spawn of B'moth" (1929).

Shea, Robert and Robert Anton Wilson. *The Illuminatus! Trilogy* (1984).

Smith, Clark Ashton. "The Beast of Averoigne" (1933), "The Colossus of Ylourgne" (1933), "The Coming of the White Worm" (1941), "The Dark Eidolon" (1935), "The Death of Malygris" (1934), "The Door to Saturn" (1932), "The End of the Story" (1930), "The Ice-Demon" (1933), "The Infernal Star" (1989), "The Plutonian Drug" (1934), "A Rendezvous in Averoigne" (1931), "The Return of the Sorcerer" (1931), "The Seven Geases" (1934), *Strange Shadows* (1989), "The Tale of Satampra Zeiros" (1931), "The Testament of Athammaus" (1932), "The Treader of the Dust" (1935), "Ubbo-Sathla" (1933), "Vulthoom" (1935), "Xeethra" (1934).

Tierney, Robert. "The Cthulhu Mythos in Mesoamerican Religion" (1983), *The House of the Toad* (1993), "Prayer to Zathog" (1981), "The Seed of the Star-God" (1984), *The Winds of Zarr* (1971).

Wade, James. "The Deep Ones" (1969), "The Silence of Erika Zann" (1976).

Wagner, Karl Edward. "Sticks" (1974).

Wandrei, Donald. "The Fire Vampires" (1933).

Warnes, Martin and H. P. Lovecraft. "The Black Tome of Alsophocus" (1980).

Wilson, Colin. *The Mind Parasites* (1967), *The Philosopher's Stone* (1971), "The Return of the Lloigor" (1969).

Wilson, F. Paul. *The Keep* (1982).

Wilson, Robert A. *Schrodinger's Cat Trilogy* (1988).

Winkle, Michael D. "Typo" (1994).

Zelazny, Roger. *A Night in the Lonesome October* (1993).

Chaosium Products

Aniolowski, Scott. "Eyes of a Stranger" (1993), "Fade to Grey" (1991), "The Marsh Mansion" (1992), *Ye Booke of Monstres* (1994).

— and L. N. Isinwyll and Herbert Hike. "Where a God Shall Tread" (1990).

— and Michael Szymanski. "The Temple of the Moon" (1986).

Barton, William. *Cthulhu by Gaslight* (1986), "The Curse of Chaugnar Faugn" (1990), "The Yorkshire Horrors" (1988).

Behrendt, Fred. "Mansion of Madness" (1990), "Sacraments of Evil" (1993).

Bishop, Andre. "This Fire Shall Kill" (1992).

Conyers, David and David Godley and David Witteveen. *Devil's Children* (1993).

Costello, Matthew. *Alone Against the Dark* (1985).

Detwiler, Denis and L. N. Isinwyll. "The Songs of Fantari" (1990).

DeWolfe, Michael. "Mister Corbitt" (1990).

DiTillio, Larry and Lynn Willis. "City Beneath the Sands" (1987), *Masks of Nyarlathotep* (1984).

Elliott, Chris and Richard Edwards. "The Statue of the Sorcerer" (1986).

Gillan, Geoff. "By the Skin of the Teeth" (1990), "Regiment of Dread" (1991).

Hallett, David with L. N. Isinwyll. "Eyes for the Blind" (1991).

Hamblin, William. "Further Notes on the *Necronomicon*" (1983), "Notes on the *Necronomicon*" (???), "Thoth's Dagger" (1984).

Hargrave, David. "Black Devil Mountain" (1983), "Dark Carnival" (1984).

Harmon, Mark. "The Madman" (1983).

Herber, Keith. "The Condemned" (1990), "Dead of Night" (1990), "The Evil Stars" (1987), *Fungi from Yuggoth* (1984), *Keeper's Compendium* (1993), "Pickman's Student" (1988), *Return to Dunwich* (1991), *Spawn of Azathoth* (1986), *Trail of Tsathogghua* (1984).

— and Kevin Ross. "Books of the Cthulhu Mythos" (1992).

Herber, Keith *et al*. *Arkham Unveiled* (1990).

Hutchinson, Marc. "The Hermetic Order of the Silver Twilight" (1982).

Isinwyll, L. N. with Herbert Hike. "Dawn Biozyme" (1990).

Jeffrey, Peter and Mark Morrison. "Slow Boat" (1992).

Launius, Richard. "Season of the Witch" (1988).

Leman, Andrew and Jamie Anderson. "With Malice Aforethought" (1993).

Louis, Mike and Simon Price. "The Vanishing Conjuror" (1986).

Lyons, Doug. "The Pits of Bendal-Dolum" (1986).

— and L. N. Isinwyll. "One in Darkness" (1989).

McCall, Randy. "The Asylum" (1983), "The Auction" (1983).

McConnell, Paul and Neal Sutton. *The Thing at the Threshold* (1992).

Manui, Barbara and Chris Adams with L. N. Isinwyll. "No Pain, No Gain" (1990).

Miller, Kurt. "The Lurker in the Crypt" (1990).

Morrison, Mark with L. N. Isynwill. "The Hills Rise Wild" (1990).

Okamoto, Jeff. "To Sleep, Perchance to Dream" (1986).

Petersen, Sandy. "The Rise of R'lyeh" (1982).

— and John B. Monroe. "The Ten Commandments of Cthulhu Hunting" (1990).

— and Mark Pettigrew. "The Secret of Castronegro" (1983).

— and Lynn Willis. *Call of Cthulhu: Horror Roleplaying in the Worlds of H. P. Lovecraft* (1992), "Entering the Dreamlands" (1986), "Miskatonic University Graduation Kit" (1987).

Peterson, Sandy *et al*. *S. Petersen's Field Guide to Creatures of the Dreamlands* (1989), *S. Petersen's Field Guide to Cthulhu Monsters* (1988).

Rahman, Glenn. *Alone against the Wendigo* (1985).

Ross, Kevin. "The Pale God" (1989), "Plant y Daear" (1993), "Signs Writ in Scarlet" (1993), "Tell Me, Have You Seen the Yellow Sign?" (1989).

Ross, Kevin *et al*. *Escape from Innsmouth* (1992), *Kingsport* (1991).

Sumpter, Gary. "The Gates of Delirium" (1992), "The King of Chicago" (1994).

Szymanski, Michael. "Dreams Dark and Deadly" (1987), "Web of Memory" (1993).

Tamlyn, ???. "The Horror from the Glen" (1987).

Thomas, G. W. and Lynn Willis. "The City in the Sea" (1987).

Watts, Richard. "Love's Lonely Children" (1992).

— and Penelope Love. "Tatterdemalion" (1990).

The Unspeakable Oath articles

Aniolowski, Scott *et al*. "Mysterious Manuscripts" (*TUO*3, 1991).

Eastland, Kim. "The Last Dawn" (*TUO*7, 1992).

Moeller, Jeff. "What Goes Around, Comes Around" (*TUO*8/9, 1993).

Ross, Kevin. "Dark Harvest" (*TUO*8/9, 1993), "Fischbuchs" (*TUO*2, 1991).

Tynes, John. "Convergence" (*TUO*7, 1992).

Chaosium Inc.
SELECTED TITLES
SINCE 1974

PLAY THIS BOOK: VOLUME 1

Discover a twilight world in which secret societies wage unseen wars for control of the five magical fields and, ultimately, master y of the world.

NEPHILIM GAMEMASTERS' VEIL _____ $14.95
[#3001] The *Nephilim Gamemasters' Veil* provides the players with the tools that help make playing *Nephilim* easier.

CHRONICLE OF THE AWAKENINGS _____ $12.95
[#3102] Each Nephilim has experienced many lives in the past. With each incarnation, a Nephilim draws closer to enlightenment. This book expands upon the Past Lives chapter of the *Nephilim* rulesbook and presents a variety of historical era during which your character might have lived.

PLAY THIS BOOK

NEXUS _____ $19.95
[#6500] A complete live-action science-fiction game system which can be played over a weekend. Features 44 complete characters, many handouts, detailed instructions.

PENDRAGON

PENDRAGON _____ $26.95
[#2716] PENDRAGON is a roleplaying game based on the legends of King Arthur, Lance-

lot, Guenever, and the Knights of the Round Table. This is the basic rulesbook, and includes everything that you need to play, except dice.

SAVAGE MOUNTAINS _____ $18.95
[#2710] Four adventures set in the wild mountains of legendary Wales.

BLOOD & LUST _____ $18.95
[#2711] Four adventures set across Britain.

PERILOUS FOREST_ $18.95
[#2712] Extensive background for western Cumbria and the Perilous Forest.

PAGAN SHORE _____ $18.95
[#2713] Ireland during the time of King Arthur's reign in legendary Britain.

THE SPECTRE KING _____ $18.95
[#2714] Dead saxon king Hengist rises from the grave to avenge his dishonorable

death; and five other adventures.

ELRIC!

ELRIC! _____ $19.95
[#2900] ELRIC! is a new swords & sorcery game situated within the fantasy world of the Young Kingdoms. This is the basic rulesbook. Everything you need to play is here, except dice.

MELNIBONÉ _____ $20.95
[#2901] Melnibonéans are Dragon Lords and mighty sorcerers with ancient pacts with the Lords of Chaos.

ELRIC GAMEMASTER SCREEN
[#2902] 8.5x38" screen, reference cards, bookmark, prices summary, many new GM forms, new scenario, extensive weapons tables, and an evocative map.